Emerson's Ethics

Emerson's Ethics

Gustaaf Van Cromphout

University of Missouri Press
Columbia and London

Copyright © 1999 by
The Curators of the University of Missouri
University of Missouri Press, Columbia, Missouri 65201
Printed and bound in the United States of America
All rights reserved
5 4 3 2 1   03 02 01 00 99

Library of Congress Cataloging-in-Publication Data

Van Cromphout, Gustaaf.
  Emerson's ethics / Gustaaf Van Cromphout.
    p.   cm.
  Includes bibliographical references (p. 167) and index.
  ISBN 0-8262-1215-8 (alk. paper)
    1. Emerson, Ralph Waldo, 1803–1882—Ethics.   2. Ethics,
Modern—19th century.   3. Ethics, American.   I. Title.
PS1642.E8V36   1999
814'.3—dc21   98-50777
                                                    CIP

⊗™ This paper meets the requirements of the
American National Standard for Permanence of Paper
for Printed Library Materials, Z39.48, 1984.

Designer: Stephanie Foley
Typesetter: BOOKCOMP
Printer and binder: Thomson-Shore, Inc.
Typefaces: ITC Giovanni and Medici Script

This book has been published with the
generous assistance of the Graduate School
and the College of Liberal Arts and Sciences
of Northern Illinois University.

To Luz:
Feremi ne lo cor sempre tua luce,
come raggio in la stella,
poi che l'anima mia fu fatta ancella
de la tua podestà primeramente.

Contents

Acknowledgments

It is a pleasure to acknowledge the debts of gratitude I have incurred in the course of writing this book. I owe special thanks to Arra Garab for his careful reading and detailed criticism of my manuscript. I am very grateful also to three other colleagues and friends: James R. Giles, William C. Johnson, and James M. Mellard were invariably patient and helpful whenever I was searching, with near Flaubertian obsessiveness, for *le mot juste*. My book has also benefited from the thoughtful critiques of two anonymous readers for the University of Missouri Press.

Warm thanks for invaluable technical support and advice are due to Karen Blaser, Supervisor of Manuscript Services in our College of Liberal Arts and Sciences.

At the University of Missouri Press I want to thank especially Mr. Clair Willcox, Acquisitions Editor; Ms. Jane Lago, Managing Editor; and Mr. John Brenner, Manuscript Editor. Their courtesy, professionalism, and expertise made working with them a pleasant and rewarding experience.

Abbreviations

For references to Emerson's works, I use the following abbreviations:

CEC *The Correspondence of Emerson and Carlyle.* Edited by Joseph Slater. New York: Columbia University Press, 1964.

CHS "The Character of Socrates." In Edward Everett Hale, *Ralph Waldo Emerson: Together with Two Early Essays of Emerson.* Boston: American Unitarian Association, 1902. Pp. 57–93.

CS *The Complete Sermons of Ralph Waldo Emerson.* Edited by Albert J. von Frank et al. 4 vols. Columbia: University of Missouri Press, 1989–1992.

CW *The Collected Works of Ralph Waldo Emerson.* Edited by Alfred R. Ferguson et al. 5 vols. to date. Cambridge, Mass.: Harvard University Press, 1971–.

EL *The Early Lectures of Ralph Waldo Emerson.* Edited by Stephen E. Whicher, Robert E. Spiller, and Wallace E. Williams. 3 vols. Cambridge, Mass.: Harvard University Press, 1959–1972.

EP "The Present State of Ethical Philosophy." In Edward Everett Hale, *Ralph Waldo Emerson: Together with Two Early Essays of Emerson.* Boston: American Unitarian Association, 1902. Pp. 97–135.

JMN *The Journals and Miscellaneous Notebooks of Ralph Waldo Emerson.* Edited by William H. Gilman et al. 16 vols. Cambridge, Mass.: Harvard University Press, 1960–1982.

L   *The Letters of Ralph Waldo Emerson.* Edited by Ralph L. Rusk (vols. 1–6) and Eleanor M. Tilton (vols. 7–10). 10 vols. New York: Columbia University Press, 1939–1995.

W   *The Complete Works of Ralph Waldo Emerson.* Edited by Edward Waldo Emerson. 12 vols. Boston: Houghton Mifflin Co., 1903–1904.

Unless otherwise attributed, all translations in this book are my own.

Emerson's Ethics

Introduction

*A*mong the questions that confronted Emerson in the course of his long life, none was more important and insistent than "How shall I live?" Some of the writings that survive from his late teens already show, as Robert D. Richardson has pointed out, that the question that really concerned Emerson was not "What can I know?" but "How shall I live?" It was a question he would keep asking for the next fifty years. The old Emerson of the 1870s was still attempting to answer, in Robert E. Burkholder's words, "the question that had dogged him even in his earliest work—How shall I live?"[1]

How one should live is the fundamental question of ethics. It was the question of Socrates, whose attempts to answer it may be said to have begun Western speculation on ethics proper.[2] And scholars such as Bernard Williams and Martha C. Nussbaum maintain that Socrates' question is to this day the best starting point for ethical inquiry.[3] As these statements suggest, the term "ethics," like the term "history," has two basic meanings: it refers both to an inescapable human experience (also called "morality") and to the philosophical study of that experience (also called "moral philosophy"). Emerson devoted much of his intellectual energy to attempts to achieve a deeper philosophical understanding of the question of how he should live and to find philosophical grounds for his answers to it. Not surprisingly, he called ethics "the most important science" (*L* 1:348) and said that there

1. Robert D. Richardson Jr., *Emerson: The Mind on Fire. A Biography,* 16; Robert E. Burkholder, Review of *The Topical Notebooks of Ralph Waldo Emerson,* vol. 2, ed. Ronald A. Bosco, 117.
2. Plato, *Republic* 352D.
3. Bernard Williams, *Ethics and the Limits of Philosophy,* 4; Martha C. Nussbaum, *The Fragility of Goodness: Luck and Ethics in Greek Tragedy and Philosophy,* 428n12.

1

was "one study that [he] hope[d] to make proficiency in, Ethical Science" (*L* 4:145). My book examines Emerson's understanding of and contribution to "Ethical Science."

Ethics stands apart from the other branches of philosophical inquiry through its concern with the *ought*—the "resisted imperative," as Geoffrey Harpham aptly calls it.[4] Emerson's "How shall I live?" suggests the breadth of his conception of the *ought*. His reaching back to Socrates' question shows that he resisted the all too common reduction of morality to matters of right and wrong (or "moral"/"immoral") and embraced instead the more comprehensive Greek view, according to which everything of value to the human good and thus conducive to the good life falls under the rubric of ethics. The reach of ethics as conceived by Emerson may be inferred from his statement, in his first book, that "All things are moral" (*CW* 1:25).

In view of the preponderance of moral concerns in Emerson's writings, it is understandable that almost every extensive study of his thought has referred to or dealt with aspects of his ethics. Surprisingly, however, no book has examined his ethics as such. One reason for this lack is the perception that, strictly as a moralist, Emerson tends to be too general, vague, or obvious, and is thus not very interesting. Stephen Whicher says that most of his book on Emerson "is to be read under the invisible running title: 'All things are moral,' " but after having devoted a few pages to Emerson's moral thought, he remarks:

> I shall not have much more to say about Emerson as a moralist. His ethical teachings, though unquestionably edifying, and valuable in their aphoristic force, are on the whole neither original nor specific enough to command particular attention. What is interesting in his thought can usually be discussed without much reference to virtue and moral law; that fact is one reason why his thought is interesting.[5]

A related assumption is that although Emerson was an exciting, even at times a revolutionary thinker in matters religious, social, and literary, he remained traditional, and was thus again rather obvious and uninteresting, in his moral thought. As Joel Porte puts it,

    4. Geoffrey Galt Harpham, *Getting It Right: Language, Literature, and Ethics*, 2.
    5. Stephen E. Whicher, *Freedom and Fate: An Inner Life of Ralph Waldo Emerson*, 44.

Emerson nowhere shows greater affinity to the [British] eighteenth century than in his firm belief in the "moral sense," or "moral sentiment," or "Moral Law." And nothing more amazingly exhibits what small effect, at heart, a lifetime of reading his European contemporaries had on his ideas. In this sense at least, one might say that Emerson never developed at all.[6]

Over the years I have learned much from Whicher's and Porte's remarkable contributions to Emerson studies, and I am pleased to record my gratitude here. Their influence on me has sometimes, however, taken the form of provocation. I would not have written this book had I not disagreed profoundly with the statements just quoted. As I hope to show, Emerson was a fascinating thinker on the subject of ethics and an aware participant in the most advanced ethical arguments of his day.

Even scholars who have shown enthusiasm for Emerson's moral thought have tended to interweave his ethics with other, presumably more determinate or challenging concerns of his. A distinguished recent example is David M. Robinson's *Emerson and the Conduct of Life: Pragmatism and Ethical Purpose in the Later Work.* Robinson states that "although Emerson could arguably be labeled a moral philosopher throughout his career, that is emphatically true of his final productive decades," when he produced "texts indicat[ing] clearly that moral philosophy permeated all aspects of his thought." Robinson provides a subtle and nuanced examination of that "moral permeating" and its effect on Emerson's career and preoccupations. As Robinson himself says, his book

> traces Emerson's evolution from mystic to pragmatist, emphasizing his increasing concern with social relations, political issues, and questions of ethical conduct. . . . Emerson's social and ethical orientation, though submerged in the middle and late 1830s, begins to grow in response to his loss of ecstatic vision. . . . Emerson's turn to ethics as an answer to a fading mysticism was reinforced by his journey to England in the late 1840s, which immersed him in both social density and technological modernity, and by the highly charged American political atmosphere of the

6. Joel Porte, *Emerson and Thoreau: Transcendentalists in Conflict,* 68.

1850s, a scene that he entered with two addresses on the Fugitive
Slave Law, among his most rhetorically accomplished works.[7]

Robinson's book, in a word, is a masterful study of how Emerson's
ethical pragmatism became a powerful factor in his later development
and increasingly affected his perceptions of power, politics, society,
and culture.

Another recent and important example of this approach is Anders
Hallengren's *The Code of Concord: Emerson's Search for Universal Laws.*
Hallengren points out that "Emerson the Moralist has never been
studied in full," and that his "aim is to reconstruct Emerson's search
for moral absolutes." He also says, however, that his "purpose . . . is to
detect a pattern: the concordance of Ethics and Aesthetics, Poetics and
Politics in the most . . . representative American thinker of the Nineteenth century."[8] What Hallengren provides in his huge, immensely
learned, and unfocused book is a discussion of almost every aspect
of Emerson's thought and almost every possible influence upon it.
In sum, neither Robinson's nor Hallengren's nor, for that matter, any
other book on Emerson that I know of, is devoted primarily to an
examination of Emerson's ethics as such. My book is an attempt to fill
this important lacuna in Emerson studies.

One of the signal merits of Robert D. Richardson's biography,
Emerson: The Mind on Fire, consists in its having shown how deeply
implicated Emerson's ideas were in his personal and social life. To
Emerson, ideas were not purely theoretical constructs but lived and
experienced realities. The Emerson emerging from Richardson's pages
goes far toward proving the Fichtean claim that "the kind of philosophy one embraces depends on the kind of person one is." Or as
Goethe explained more amply, in reference to Kant, the philosopher,
like every other individual, has an innate "right to principles that do
not destroy his individuality." The philosopher, therefore, demands "a
philosophy that accords with his innate inclinations." Such inwardly

---

7. David M. Robinson, *Emerson and the Conduct of Life: Pragmatism and Ethical
Purpose in the Later Work,* 182; "Emerson, Thoreau, Fuller, and Transcendentalism,"
6–7.
   8. Anders Hallengren, *The Code of Concord: Emerson's Search for Universal Laws,* 9
and *n3.*

sanctioned philosophy entails that every true philosopher "must cope with the world in his own fashion."[9] Emerson's thought certainly bears the stamp not only of his distinct personality but also of his experience, which is but another name for *his* coping in his own fashion with "the world"—family, friendships, work, social life, politics, and tragedy.

This argument does not mean, however, that a thinker's life and personality can fully account for, let alone explain, his or her thought. Giving thought a *Sitz im Leben*—connecting it with personal or communal life and circumstances—may throw light on some of its features but does not clarify what it is intrinsically. Description of its antecedents, in other words, does not tell us what it is. Northrop Frye was right in warning us against "the fallacy of thinking that we have explained the nature of something by accounting for its origin in something else."[10] Thought, after all, never simply reflects experience but interprets, adjusts, sublates, or compensates for it in order to make it fit into its ideal structure. Ideas, moreover, often develop in ways unrelated to any experience: they connect, interact, combine, refine in accordance with "ideal" principles, with laws of thought itself. Thought frequently does its own thinking. As Nietzsche says, "a thought comes when 'it' wants to, not when 'I' want it to."[11] Ideas, as a result, often take us by surprise, appear in unexpected associations, or assume meanings we did not anticipate.

Although undoubtedly rooted in his personality and experience, Emerson's ethical thinking has ultimately, therefore, a content and form transcending them. Emerson's thought owes its significance in large measure to its escape from the confines of personality, time, and place. As he himself said in 1840,

> The great man, even whilst he relates a private fact personal to him, is really leading us away from him to an universal experience. . . . The great lead us to Nature, and in our age to metaphysical Nature, to the invisible awful facts, to moral abstractions, which are . . . [Nature's] essence and soul. (*W* 12:314–15)

9. Johann Gottlieb Fichte, "Erste Einleitung in die *Wissenschaftslehre,*" *Sämmtliche Werke* 1:434; Johann Wolfgang Goethe, "Gespräche aus den letzten Lebensjahren," *Gedenkausgabe der Werke, Briefe und Gespräche* 23:817.

10. Northrop Frye, *Anatomy of Criticism*, 332.

11. Friedrich Nietzsche, *Jenseits von Gut und Böse* §17, *Sämtliche Werke* 5:31.

While writing *Emerson's Ethics*, I tried to be faithful to the spirit of this statement. Since my book is not an intellectual *biography*, I have made but minimal reference to Emerson's character, life, and historical circumstances. Instead I have focused on his ideas themselves and on the intellectual context in which they achieved definition and depth.

1

Beginnings

Emerson's interest in ethics bore literary fruit early. In his late teens he produced two essays (both submitted as Bowdoin Prize dissertations at Harvard), "The Character of Socrates" (1820) and "The Present State of Ethical Philosophy" (1821), that encapsulate his earliest substantial confrontations with questions of ethical theory and practice. For the student of Emerson's ethics, these essays are valuable on several grounds. Not only are they important for the insight they provide into the early thought of a great moralist, but they also already show Emerson's unwillingness or inability to conform to the expectations of his intellectual environment. To a considerable degree, to be sure, these essays reflect the moral thought and assumptions prevalent in young Emerson's academic world, thus helping us to understand where he started, so to speak, as an ethical thinker. But especially in his second essay, as Evelyn Barish has shown, he also repeatedly disappointed his audience both conceptually and methodologically, though it is hard to gauge how conscious he himself was of this fact. His ignoring Christ as an exemplar of superior ethics, his intellectual flirtation with Hume, his omission of any reference to Locke, and his methodological preference for near-enthusiastic claims over scholarly demonstration already suggest the independent-minded and assertive Emerson of later years.[1] In ethics as in any other area of thought that preoccupied him, Emerson would eventually articulate views that were unmistakably Emersonian. Thus these early essays, by revealing what he did owe to the ethical thought of his day, also better enable us to

1. Evelyn Barish, *Emerson: The Roots of Prophecy,* 102–4. On Emerson's confrontation with Hume in "The Present State of Ethical Philosophy," see also John Michael, *Emerson and Skepticism: The Cipher of the World,* 40–42.

appreciate the intellectual distance he had to travel before he could make contributions that were significantly his own.

I

Although products of a very youthful mind, Emerson's Bowdoin Prize dissertations are remarkable for the number of major issues in ethics they confront. In both "Socrates" and in the early pages of "Ethical Philosophy," Emerson succeeded in identifying principles and characteristics of Greek moral thought that are as interesting and controversial today as they were to him and his contemporaries. Emerson recognizes, for instance, the pervasive intellectualism of Greek ethics, which considered insight or its lack, knowledge or its absence to be the cause of virtue or vice. Virtue is the necessary enactment of one's insight into or knowledge of the good, whereas vice results from erroneous views about what is good. Since all humans strive for what they perceive to be good, vice can be interpreted only as an error in perception. The different ethical systems developed by the Greeks were all, in Ernst Cassirer's words, "expressions of one and the same fundamental *intellectualism* of Greek thought. It is by rational thought that we are to find the standards of moral conduct, and it is reason, and reason alone, that can give them their authority." As a result, we have Plato denying the possibility of deliberate wrongdoing and Socrates insisting that there is no such thing as *akrasia* (weakness of will). Greek ethics did not problematize the will as such.[2] Its corruption did not become a real issue in ethical theory until Augustine.

Grasping all this, Emerson praises Socrates for his great "prudence . . . in the philosophical signification of the term" (*CHS* 77), thus showing his awareness that philosophically, "prudence" is but the Ciceronian translation *(prudentia)* of *phronēsis,* a term denoting to Plato moral wisdom in general and to Aristotle practical wisdom, that is, "a truth-attaining rational quality, concerned with action in relation to things that are good and bad for human beings."[3] Emerson further

---

2. Ernst Cassirer, *The Myth of the State,* 81. Plato, *Laws* 731C, 860D; *Protagoras* 352A–358D. Aristotle devotes Book Seven of the *Nicomachean Ethics* mainly to a critical examination of *akrasia.* Nicolai Hartmann, *Ethik,* 573–74.

3. Cicero, *De officiis* 1.43; Plato, *Symposium* 209A; Aristotle, *Nicomachean Ethics* 6.5.4. The quotation is from H. Rackham's translation of the *Nicomachean Ethics* (Loeb Classical Library).

stresses the primacy of knowledge when he says that Socrates "directs his disciples to know and practise the purest principles of virtue" (*CHS* 79), or when, commenting on the most uncompromisingly intellectualist of the Greek ethical schools, he writes that "the Stoics exhibited rational and correct views of ethics" (*EP* 104). Emerson rightly concludes that the Stoics were not only the culmination but also the conclusion of Greco-Roman intellectualism in ethics: "With Seneca and Marcus Antoninus [i.e., Marcus Aurelius] closes the line of ancient moralists, and with them the chief praise of human ingenuity and wisdom" (*EP* 105).

Emerson also understood that according to Greek ethics the individual moral life involved rational detachment or disengagement from the self, or, what amounts to the same thing, rational self-objectification. Such disengagement and objectification were a prerequisite for ethical self-control. Emerson praises Socrates for his ability "to investigate his own character, to learn the natural tendency and bias of his own genius, and thus to perfectly control his mental energies" (*CHS* 67). Ethical self-control involved discovering and maintaining a valid hierarchy among the elements constituting the self. Just as, according to Plato, bodily health consists in some elements properly ruling the others, so virtue consists in our identifying the right order among the principles that guide our actions.[4] In the Greek view the highest such principle was, of course, reason; when dominant, reason established the proper ethical hierarchy. Emerson's Socrates was able to "mould . . . the roughest materials into form and order" and to "create [his] own virtues, and set them in array to compose the aggregate of character" (*CHS* 73).

A similar sense of right order informs Emerson's discussion of the passions. He avoids the Stoics' suppression of them and, in Aristotelian fashion, he recognizes their value when confined to their proper function. Victory over the passions is not for Emerson a Stoical freeing oneself of them, but a bringing them into "such subjection as to be subservient to the real advantage of the possessor" (*CHS* 75). Socrates wisely "endeavored to subdue his corporeal wants so far as to make them merely subservient to the mental advantage, yet never carrying it to anything like that excess of Indian superstition which worships God by outraging nature" (*CHS* 92).

4. Plato, *Republic* 444D-E.

The rational moderation reflected in this last statement was central to Greek ethics. Aristotle famously asserted that moral virtue consisted in hitting the mean between two extreme courses of action, while Plato's Diotima insisted that moderation *(sōphrosunē)* was one of the two virtues representing prudence *(phronēsis)* in by far its highest and noblest form. (The other was justice.)[5] More intriguing perhaps in Emerson's last-quoted statement is the invocation of nature as a moral norm ("outraging nature"). In the next sentence he refers to Indian asceticism as an *"unnatural* expression of courage" that has been wrongly called "an assertion of the dignity of man" (*CHS* 92–93; emphasis added). Obviously young Emerson was already looking for a foundation for ethics less tradition-bound than culture or custom. This concern is also apparent in his only significant negative comment on Socrates: "In treating of things which are *just,* by which he meant *virtuous,* he declares all things to be just which are agreeable to the laws. Modern improvement acknowledges this to be a flimsy and fallacious criterion, which must necessarily vary under every different government" (*EP* 102–3). Socrates' stress on law-abidingness as the only defense against individual inclination and social and political anarchy is here misinterpreted by Emerson as sanctioning Protagorian moral relativism. Socratic goodness is ultimately "something eternal and immutable" to which we gain access through "insight into principles," through "direct personal insight into the structure of the universe and man's place in that structure."[6] My concern is not, however, with noting Emerson's misinterpretation of Socrates, but with pointing out Emerson's early impatience with what he regarded as an ethic deriving its authority from convention or tradition and his appeal to "nature" as an alternative source of ethical legitimacy. Elsewhere, moreover, he took a less critical view, acknowledging that Socrates was the first thinker to have rooted "moral science" in "the relations which bind man to the universe about him" (*EP* 98–99, 101).

The equation of righteousness and justice with cosmic order and physical laws was already suggested by Parmenides, almost a century before Plato. For Plato himself, ethics was inseparable from a vision of order—not just the order within the soul already commented on, but,

---

5. Aristotle, *Nicomachean Ethics* 2.6–9; Plato, *Symposium* 209A.
6. A. E. Taylor, *Plato: The Man and His Work,* 246–47, 131.

more fundamentally, in Charles Taylor's words, "the order of things in the cosmos, [which] is related to the right order of the soul as whole is to part, as englobing to englobed." Or as Anders Hallengren puts it, since Plato and other Greek thinkers held that "reason is present in the order of nature," they interpreted human rationality as "an active sharing of the ordering principle of the universe." From such views arose the "Law of Nature," a phrase coined by Plato *(kata nomon ge ton tēs phuseōs)* but as a concept given real moral significance by Aristotle and especially by the Stoics, for whom living in accordance with nature became the paramount ethical obligation.[7]

No term in Western culture has had a richer and more complex semantic history than "nature," and the complexity is only barely reduced when we confine "nature" to its meanings in ethics. Emerson frequently confronted "nature" in the course of his ethical thinking. At this very early stage he simply adopted the Stoic view that for humans to live truly in accordance with nature they must obey the law of *human* nature, and—since in its essence human nature partakes of the cosmic *logos*, the rational principle governing the universe—thus obey the law of reason. Socrates, as interpreted by Emerson, demonstrated obedience to the law of nature thus conceived. Although resorting to "harsh discipline" to subdue "his corporeal wants," Socrates, as already indicated, did not fall into the "excess" and "superstition" that "outrag[e] nature" but remained humanly natural, that is, rational, and in this way he became a champion of "the dignity of man" (CHS 92–93).

Emerson's negative but very interesting comments on Aristotle further clarify his early ethical thought: "Aristotle pursues different views of morals from the moderns, and exhibits unexpected trains of ideas, unconnected, indeed, by philosophical association; he occupies himself long and tediously in ascertaining definitions and in drawing the boundary lines of moral and mathematical philosophy" (EP 103–4). Aristotle originated the distinction between theoretical reason *(nous theoretikos)* and practical reason *(nous praktikos)*,[8] and he considered ethics to fall within the purview of the latter. Whereas for Plato there

7. Aristophanes, *Clouds*, ed. K. J. Dover, 245, note to line 1292. Charles Taylor, *Sources of the Self: The Making of the Modern Identity*, 122; Hallengren, *The Code of Concord*, 354. Plato, *Gorgias* 483E; Aristotle, *Nicomachean Ethics* 5.7.

8. Lewis White Beck, *A Commentary on Kant's "Critique of Practical Reason,"* 37.

was a scientific (mathematical, geometrical) absoluteness about ethics, for Aristotle ethics is rooted in the changeable world of human experience. For him not just the conventional societal law but also the natural moral law, though valid everywhere, is subject to what today we might call, roughly, "evolutionary change" (Aristotle's principle of *entelekheia*). He can say, therefore, that although rules of natural justice have universal validity, they are not absolute.[9]

Given this general stance, it is not surprising that, as Emerson points out, Aristotle endeavored to separate ethics from mathematics—for the Greeks the paradigmatic science of absolute principles. In the words of Albert Jonsen and Stephen Toulmin, Plato interpreted "moral discernment" as "an unwavering vision of eternal universal Truth," and he presented "moral knowledge as a sub-species of formally demonstrable, or 'geometrical,' knowledge and end[ed] by treating Ethics as a theoretical Science." Aristotle, by contrast, was unable to regard ethics as a science in this sense. He insisted that there was a categorical difference between the "timeless, intellectual grasp of scientific ideas and arguments" and "timely, personal wisdom about moral or practical issues."[10] Aristotle can consequently be considered an intellectual ancestor of casuistry (in the nonpejorative sense of this much-abused term), as Jonsen and Toulmin have demonstrated. As is obvious from the passage quoted earlier, Emerson showed little appreciation for the Aristotelian approach to ethics. Regarding Aristotle's attempt to found ethics as unsystematic and even unphilosophical ("trains of ideas, unconnected . . . by philosophical association"), he, like most of those he called "the moderns," much preferred Plato's more grandiose, absolutist views, in comparison with which Aristotle's careful definitions seemed, moreover, pedestrian.

Emerson remained a lifelong Platonist in his commitment to an absolutist foundation for ethics. Whereas Aristotle rooted ethics in human experience and wisdom (*his* kind of concrete universals), Plato based ethics on an ideal, perfect, eternal, unique "Form of the Good" (*hē tou agathou idea*), which, in A. E. Taylor's words, "is the supreme value and the source of all other values."[11] Emerson's

9. Aristotle, *Nicomachean Ethics* 5.7.
10. Albert R. Jonsen and Stephen Toulmin, *The Abuse of Casuistry: A History of Moral Reasoning*, 62, 65.
11. Plato, *Republic* 505A; A. E. Taylor, *Plato*, 289.

early allegiance to this Platonic view is obvious when he says that an important contribution of Socrates/Plato "should not be forgotten in ethical history,—that from him is derived the modern custom of grounding virtue on a single principle" (*EP* 102). Emerson is, moreover, quite right about this "modern custom." As Charles Taylor puts it, "There has been a tendency to breathtaking systematization in modern moral philosophy. Utilitarianism and Kantianism organize everything around one basic reason."[12]

Emerson also recognizes that Socrates made ethics into a philosophical discipline, into a well-defined subject of rational inquiry: his was the first intellect "qualified to institute and methodize the science of morality" and thus to give it a distinct place "in the circle of human knowledge" (*EP* 98, 104). Emerson regards Socrates, however, not just as a great philosopher but also as a noble human being worthy of the veneration and love of posterity. Moved by the "grandeur of soul" of Socrates, Emerson, the young Unitarian, is "irresistibly led to bestow upon the pagan the praise of a perfect man" (*CHS* 88). The ancient world has given us Socrates as "a model of moral perfection which the wise of any age would do well to imitate" (*CHS* 59). At this stage in Emerson's career, imitation of others and even hero worship constitute values and are, consequently, important in his ethical thinking. The image of Socrates bequeathed to us by history is a good that can evoke our love or enthusiasm and inspire us to efforts at self-ennoblement. The very presence of that image in our mental life is already a good: it is culturally enriching, if nothing else (cultural enrichment is itself part of "the good life," and in this sense ethically relevant). But more importantly, what evokes our love or admiration because of the qualities it represents also evokes our desire to be like it, and thus it impels us to imitation of it. Nobody is morally *obliged* to imitate Socrates, but we all have a moral obligation to improve ourselves, and if imitation of Socrates can become a means to that end, the ethical significance of such imitation becomes all the more obvious.

The trait that Emerson admired most in Socrates was his independence from circumstances—an independence so complete as to seem preternatural. In Socrates' case, "exemption from the influence of circumstances in the moral world is almost like exemption from the

---

12. C. Taylor, *Sources of the Self*, 76.

law of gravitation in the natural economy" (*CHS* 74). Charles Taylor has stressed that an important aspect of ethical life concerns our sense of our own dignity, that is, our sense of the "attitudinal" respect (as different from, say, respect for our rights) we command, or fail to command, in the world in which we live.[13] We can locate this sense of dignity in such things as our power in society, our indifference to such power, our professional competence, our philosophical detachment, our financial success, or our self-sufficiency. Like Kant and Thoreau, Emerson located his dignity in self-reliance and self-sufficiency. Given the poverty and the precarious social position of his family during his youth, he not surprisingly found Socrates' indifference to circumstances an ideal worth pursuing.

II

Emerson devotes the remaining pages (106–35) of "The Present State of Ethical Philosophy" to a rapid survey of developments in moral philosophy subsequent to the Greeks and to an examination of major questions confronting moral philosophers in his day. Some of the problems examined by the Greeks keep recurring, and inevitably so. As Alasdair MacIntyre has reminded us, the history of philosophy— moral and other—is in some measure "doomed to repeat it[self] . . . because the sources of so many philosophical problems lie so close to permanent characteristics of human nature and human language."[14] In Emerson's words, "The truths of morality must in all ages be the same; the praise of its teachers consists in the ability manifested in their development" (*EP* 112). To young Emerson, the greatest such teachers of modern times were Ralph Cudworth, Samuel Clarke, Richard Price, Joseph Butler, Adam Smith, Thomas Reid, William Paley, and Dugald Stewart. The last three especially appear to Emerson to represent the utmost in modern speculation on the subject of ethics (*EP* 111– 12, 119).

Plato's solution to the problem of the supreme principle of morality, or the foundation of ethics, was not quite satisfactory: his absolute

---

13. C. Taylor, *Sources of the Self*, 15.
14. Alasdair MacIntyre, ed., *Hegel: A Collection of Critical Essays*, 219.

"Form of the Good" proved unconvincing to his most brilliant pupil, Aristotle, and to many subsequent thinkers. The Fathers of the Church did not succeed in clearing up the confusion; as Emerson sees it, they "did little to settle the foundations of morals" (*EP* 106). Real progress proved elusive until much later, when

> by the rapid advancement of the collateral philosophy of the mind by the spring imparted by Bacon and Descartes, ethical specu- lations were matured and improved. It was useless to disclose defects in the culture of the moral powers till the knowledge of the mental operations taught how they should be amended and regulated. (*EP* 109)

Emerson is here drawing our attention to the predominance of epis- temology in modern philosophical thought and to the effect of that predominance upon ethics. His linking, in an epistemological argu- ment, of Bacon the empiricist and Descartes the rationalist may at first seem surprising, but he obviously thought of Bacon in a general sense as one of the great emancipators of the human mind—the Bacon who promised in the preface of his *Instauratio Magna* that his work would be "infiniti erroris finis et terminus legitimus," "the end and appropriate termination of infinite error." It was presumably a similar view of Bacon that induced Kant, though certainly no Baconian, to choose a passage from this same preface as the motto for the second edition of his *Critique of Pure Reason*. Bacon appealed to critical thinkers of many stripes because, as Douglas Bush said, "his analysis of the permanent sources of uncritical credulity [the 'idols'] . . . is a landmark in the intellectual development of mankind."[15]

Descartes, however, is far more important to Emerson's argument. He is called the father of modern philosophy precisely because he planted the standard of truth firmly within the mind and its rational processes. Unlike Hegel, who stresses in his *Phenomenology of Spirit* that certainty is incompatible with truth, Descartes holds that *the* criterion of truth is certainty, but that the only thing we can be certain about is our mental life and, a fortiori, our mind's clear and distinct ideas. In Richard Rorty's words, "indubitability" is for Descartes "*a criterion*

---

15. Francis Bacon, *Instauratio Magna*, "Praefatio," in Bacon, *Novum Organum*, 168; Douglas Bush, *English Literature in the Earlier Seventeenth Century*, 277.

of the mental"; it is no longer the mark of any externally derived "truth." Cartesian philosophy inaugurated the "change from mind-as-[outer-directed]-reason to mind-as-inner-arena." Certainty rather than wisdom "became philosophy's subject, and epistemology its center."[16] Or as Charles Taylor explains this development, in Cartesian philosophy

> rationality is no longer defined substantively, in terms of the order of being, but rather procedurally, in terms of the standards by which we construct orders in science and life. For Plato, to be rational we have to be right about the order of things. For Descartes rationality means thinking according to certain canons. . . . Rationality is now an internal property of subjective thinking, rather than consisting in its [correct] vision of reality.[17]

This "inward turn" had profound implications for ethics. To quote Charles Taylor once more, "the move from substance to procedure, from found to constructed orders, represents a big internalization relative to the Platonic-Stoic tradition of ethics." Emerson grasped that it was the Cartesian "philosophy of the mind" and "the knowledge of the mental operations" resulting therefrom (*EP* 109) that advanced ethics by establishing it on the only basis acceptable to moderns, namely, the mind itself. Whether subsequent moral philosophers were Cartesians or not was irrelevant to this decisive "inward turn" of moral thinking. Hobbes (who knew Cartesian philosophy well and who submitted to Descartes his objections to the latter's *Meditationes de prima philosophia*) not only located the source of ethics in the self but also traced moral motivation to selfishness or self-interest, thereby provoking a horrified response that affected moral philosophy for a century or more. Young Emerson dutifully chastises "the malevolent spirit of Mr. Hobbes," the originator of "an important controversy which has been much agitated among modern philosophers,—whether benevolence or selfishness be the ground of action" (*EP* 110). When referring to "benevolence," Emerson is presumably thinking of such critics of Hobbes as the third Earl of Shaftesbury and Francis Hutcheson. But the point to remember here is that the defenders of benevolence as the source of moral motivation rooted ethics as deeply in the self as did Hobbesian egoism.

16. Richard Rorty, *Philosophy and the Mirror of Nature*, 58, 61.
17. C. Taylor, *Sources of the Self*, 156.

More than the traditional Christian virtue of charity, "benevolence" draws attention to personal inclination and subjective feeling. It is part and parcel of eighteenth-century sentimentalism, a term signifying, in Norman Fiering's words, "the emphasis in . . . eighteenth-century British literary and philosophical culture on the constructive role of the affections and passions (in French, *sentiment*, feeling) in the moral life." The real destroyer, however, of Hobbesian ethics, according to Emerson, was the Cambridge Platonist Ralph Cudworth, who in his *Treatise concerning Eternal and Immutable Morality* (not published until 1731) "attacked the system of Hobbes . . . with ability and success, and modern opinion has concurred in his boldest positions" (*EP* 111). But as G. R. Cragg points out, interiorization prevailed also here: the Cambridge Platonists regarded morality "as an integral law of man's being and not as an arbitrary imposition from without"; "Cudworth in particular" insisted that "self-determination . . . was fundamental to any genuine morality."[18]

The high point of Emerson's rapid historical survey is his claim that the "fundamental principles" of ethics "are taught by the moral sense" (*EP* 112). He thus introduces a moral faculty and a source of moral authority that will achieve crucial importance in his ethical thought. The term "moral sense" was first used by Shaftesbury and given conceptual depth by Hutcheson. It was thus first the property, so to speak, of the ethical sentimentalists. Hutcheson emphatically associates the moral sense with the mind's nonrational faculties. Indeed, D. Daiches Raphael says, Hutcheson "never considers the possibility that immediate apprehension can be a rational faculty." Instead he considers the moral sense to be, in Fiering's words, "a capacity for immediate, involuntary (or, in theological terms, irresistible), nonpropositional recognition of virtue," or in Richard Price's simpler language, "a feeling of the heart" rather than "a perception of the understanding."[19]

The moral sense did not remain, however, the monopoly of the sentimentalists. Thomas Reid, founder of the Scottish Common Sense school, used the terms "moral sense" and "moral sentiment" to refer

18. C. Taylor, *Sources of the Self*, 156. Norman Fiering, *Jonathan Edwards's Moral Thought and Its British Context*, 10. G. R. Cragg, *From Puritanism to the Age of Reason*, 48–49.

19. D. Daiches Raphael, *The Moral Sense*, 16, 29. Fiering, *Jonathan Edwards's Moral Thought*, 129–30. Price is quoted in Raphael, *The Moral Sense*, 104; his statement, though accurate as a description of Hutcheson's position, is intended to be critical.

to a faculty that he also called "conscience" and "reason." As this last term would lead one to expect, Reid strongly objected to the reduction of the moral sense to feeling. Even "moral *sentiment*" meant to him primarily a judgment, though a judgment *accompanied* by emotion.[20] Reid was a rational intuitionist who held that all humans are innately endowed with a moral sense that gives them inward access to true (i.e., objectively real) moral principles and enables them to apprehend these principles intuitively (i.e., through an immediate, noninferential cognition of them as self-evident). Although Reid did object to what he regarded as the extreme rationalism of a moral philosopher such as Samuel Clarke, he himself considered *reason* (in its intuitive, not its discursive mode) rather than sentiment to be ethically determinative.[21] In this respect he is aligned not only with the greatest eighteenth-century ethical intuitionist, Richard Price, but also with the ethical intuitionism of the Cambridge Platonists.

In various ways all these intuitionists played a part in Emerson's intellectual development. Daniel Howe notes, however, that the rational moral sense of Reid and his Scottish Common Sense followers, most notably Dugald Stewart, was "almost certainly a more influential concept in America" than the sentimental moral sense of Shaftesbury and Hutcheson.[22] At any rate, young Emerson's definitions reflect a rational bias. He speaks of "the *decision* of the moral faculty, which is recognized as an original principle of our nature,—an intuition by which we directly *determine* the merit or demerit of an action" (*EP* 116; emphasis added); he refers to "the moral sense, or, as others term it, the decisions of the understanding" (*EP* 130). At this point Emerson has not yet adopted the Coleridgean (Kant-inspired) desynonymization of "reason" and "understanding," which will profoundly affect his concept of the moral sense or, as he will prefer to call it, the "moral sentiment."[23]

20. Raphael, *The Moral Sense*, 152–53.

21. Ibid., 166–67.

22. Daniel Walker Howe, *The Unitarian Conscience: Harvard Moral Philosophy, 1805–1861*, 48–49.

23. On Emerson's relation to the "moral sense" tradition, see also Merrell R. Davis, "Emerson's 'Reason' and the Scottish Philosophers"; Whicher, *Freedom and Fate*, 175–76; Porte, *Emerson and Thoreau*, 68–92; J. Edward Schamberger, "The Influence of Dugald Stewart and Richard Price on Emerson's Concept of Reason: A Reassessment"; David M. Robinson, *Apostle of Culture: Emerson as Preacher and Lecturer*, 50–55, and Robinson's "The Sermons of Ralph Waldo Emerson: An Introductory Historical Essay," *CS* 1:7, 24–28.

Some general comments about "modern ethics" provide additional insight into Emerson's moral thinking at the time. He points out that "the moderns have made their ethical writings of a more practical character than the sages of antiquity" (*EP* 114), thus signaling his recognition that in their response to the two traditional concerns of normative ethics—value (the nature of the good life) and obligation (the content of right action)—many moderns have emphasized the latter to the point of virtually ignoring the former. The ancients often debated questions of "only speculative importance," such as the advantages of "solitude or society" for the life of virtue (*EP* 114). The moderns lay down "maxims in morals" to support the translation into practice of their "systems of . . . duties," and they "introduce demonstrations from mathematical analogy" (*EP* 115). Regarding this last point, Emerson has in mind the "moral arithmetic" of Bentham (*EP* 130) and probably also the algebraic formulae in Hutcheson's *Inquiry into the Original of our Ideas of Beauty and Virtue* (1725). In fact, quantification and mathematical procedures had become quite common in seventeenth- and eighteenth-century treatises on ethics, the most famous example being, of course, Spinoza's *Ethica ordine geometrico demonstrata* (1677).

As these names suggest, not every modern philosopher considered duty to be the paramount concern of ethics. But Emerson is right when he implies that those "modern systems of ethical philosophy" in which duty is central are indebted to our Judeo-Christian heritage: they "found . . . these duties on the will of the Creator" (*EP* 115–16). In the Judeo-Christian tradition the highest mode of being that is attainable by a human is the doing of one's duty, that is, living in conformity with the will of God as revealed in His commandments. Greek ethics, by contrast, was above all concerned with the human's attainment of *eudaimonia* ("happiness"). As Ludwig Edelstein puts it, "The fundamental problem of all Greek philosophy . . . is the question concerning the *summum bonum;* and the answer of the Stoa like that of all systems, classical and Hellenistic alike, is that the highest good of life is *eudaimonia.*"[24] Once duty becomes paramount in ethics, happiness becomes inevitably secondary: doing one's duty for duty's sake comes to rank higher morally than living in a manner conducive to the

24. Ludwig Edelstein, *The Meaning of Stoicism*, 1.

attainment of a good (for instance, happiness). Emerson, moreover, regarded the eudaimonistic argument as flawed for another reason: "In ascertaining the will of God [ethics] does not always proceed on the principle that the greatest possible happiness is intended, for that this is true, we cannot know" (*EP* 116).

Emerson is here cautiously distancing himself from the opinion advanced by many eighteenth-century thinkers that God's primary concern is the happiness of His creatures and that, consequently, ethical life consists above all in the pursuit of one's own and the promotion of others' happiness. Garry Wills has shown how pervasive a role the striving for happiness played in eighteenth-century moral thought. Some moralists clearly anticipated the utilitarians. Francis Hutcheson, after all, coined the basic utilitarian formula: "That action is best which accomplishes the greatest happiness for the greatest numbers." Emerson doubts such claims not only on account of our ignorance concerning God's will, but also because the history of ethics is riddled with "disputes on the nature of happiness." The ancient speculations on the subject he finds largely "futile." The "most ingenious" modern theory is Hume's, which "certainly discovers great philosophical sagacity" (*EP* 120–21). Emerson recognizes precisely what the modernity of Hume's theory consists in: "Old systems indicated some one external quality or affection of the mind as happiness; the present plan discovered it in the condition of mind, without regard to the particular objects of contemplation" (*EP* 121). As Allen Wood has pointed out, Greek ethics from Socrates through the Stoics took for granted the objectivity of happiness. One's happiness consisted in one's orientation toward a mode or category of life that was thought to be objectively valuable, for example, the life of virtue, a life in harmony with the laws of the universe, living in accordance with "nature," or a life of detachment from the pains and pleasures of this world. Modern ethics, by contrast, has made happiness much more "subjective" in both content ("Happiness consists in a subjective state of mind, such as pleasure or satisfaction") and determination ("My conception of happiness has an irreducible role to play in determining the actual content of my happiness").[25]

25. Garry Wills, *Inventing America: Jefferson's Declaration of Independence*, 149–64, 248–55. D. Daiches Raphael, ed., *British Moralists 1650–1800*, 1:284. Allen W. Wood, *Hegel's Ethical Thought*, 53–55.

Emerson recognizes the subjectivity in the modern conception of happiness not only in his comments on Hume, but also when he speaks more generally of ethics offering "sentiments and precepts which promote the happiness of man [and] whose exercise generates pure and tranquil enjoyment" (*EP* 134). He insists, however, that all the "ingenious" theorizing of the moralists is unlikely to bring us any closer to ending "the disputes on the nature of happiness" that "have been always connected with this science [i.e., ethics]" (*EP* 119–20). In fact, modern theorizing has left the nature of happiness more open to question than ever.[26] As Kant said, all humans desire happiness yet nobody really knows what it is because "all elements belonging to the concept of happiness are empirical, that is, they must be derived from experience, whereas the idea of happiness demands an absolute totality, a maximum of well-being" far beyond any experience (which is by definition specific, limited, and in any case often disappointing) and consequently not humanly determinable.[27]

Emerson considers virtue to have been as controversial a concept in the history of ethics as happiness (*EP* 119–20). For him virtue consists in the performance of duties, and such performance derives its legitimacy from "a conformity to the law of conscience" (*EP* 115, 121). The entire debate about virtue, "from Socrates to Paley," amounted to little more than "a dispute about words" because all moralists ultimately meant the same thing by "virtue," namely, "conformity to the law of conscience" (*EP* 121). But the status and role of conscience had themselves become matters of dispute. David Hume, having relegated morality to the domain of feeling, turned moral judgment into an expression of sentiment and denied the objectivity of moral values. According to Hume,

> Morality . . . consists not in any *matter of fact,* which can be discover'd by the understanding. . . . Morality is not an object of reason. . . . [A] vice entirely escapes you, as long as you consider the object. You never can find it, till you turn your reflexion into your own breast, and find a sentiment of disapprobation, which arises in you, towards this action. Here is a matter of fact; but 'tis

26. Wood, *Hegel's Ethical Thought*, 63–66.

27. Immanuel Kant, *Grundlegung zur Metaphysik der Sitten, Gesammelte Schriften* 4:418.

the object of feeling, not of reason. It lies in yourself, not in the object. So that when you pronounce any action or character to be vicious, you mean nothing, but that from the constitution of your nature you have a feeling or sentiment of blame from the contemplation of it. Vice and virtue, therefore, may be compar'd to sounds, colours, heat and cold, which, according to modern philosophy, are not qualities in objects, but perceptions in the mind.[28]

Not surprisingly, Emerson condemns Hume's attempts "to represent the eternal truths of morality as involved in the same gloomy uncertainty with which he would envelop all knowledge" and to reduce "the laws of morals [to] idle dreams and fantasies." Fortunately, Emerson points out, to "this outrage . . . to this pernicious ingenuity has been opposed the common-sense philosophy . . . which aims at establishing a code of propositions as axioms which no rational being will dispute" (*EP* 121–22). Most important for ethics among the Common Sense philosophers' axioms was the objectivity of moral principles. According to Daniel Howe, the principles known through the moral sense "were regarded . . . as objective truths," and for this reason "intuitions of moral values were entitled to be termed genuine 'perceptions,' not mere subjective 'sensations.' "[29] Robert D. Richardson rightly claims that throughout his long career Emerson remained convinced that such "perceptions" were "inarguable" and provided "self-evident" truth. By "self-evident" he did not mean obvious or superficial, but he referred to something that quite literally provided its own fundamentally inarguable evidence.[30] In sum, moral principles are ontically real in the world in which humans live and move and have their being.

Emerson also addresses "the rights of man," the most significant of which, from the point of view of modern ethics, are "the rights of person and property, implying the right of self-defence" (*EP* 116–17). Emerson's formulation recognizes the intimate connection between "rights" and "personhood." Being a person *means* having certain rights—an idea traceable to Roman law but given its first influential modern expression by Hugo Grotius, who interpreted natural-law

28. David Hume, *A Treatise of Human Nature*, 468–69.
29. Howe, *The Unitarian Conscience*, 56.
30. Richardson, *Emerson: The Mind on Fire*, 538, 563.

ethics as a matter of rights, of individual rights: the natural law is "a body of rights . . . which has reference to the person. In this sense a right becomes a moral quality of a person, making it possible to have or to do something lawfully."[31] Grotius thus defines "person" as a moral agent deriving his or her legitimacy not from the state or society but from "natural law." As an individual moral agent, the person is superior to the state: *it* will have to derive *its* legitimacy from the consent of such moral agents. Given the often-conflicting claims of the individual and society and the ever-lurking danger of political oppression, it was "natural" that the individual's most fundamental rights were considered to be those of self-preservation and freedom, that is, maintaining one's life and liberty vis-à-vis the state, both of which rights are covered by Emerson's "right of self-defence."

Emerson felt no need to spell out the individual's rights to life and liberty, not only because these rights are contained in the very concept of personhood, but also because in the nomophilosophical terminology of his age "property" (in Emerson's words, "the rights of . . . property"—*EP* 116–17) often designated life and liberty in addition to material possessions. John Locke's *Second Treatise of Government* (1689) provided the *locus classicus:* "Man . . . hath by Nature a Power . . . to preserve his Property—that is, his Life, Liberty and Estate." In Emerson's day, Hegel elaborated this idea in his *Philosophy of Right (Grundlinien der Philosophie des Rechts,* 1821). As Allen Wood aptly summarizes, Hegel "treats all abstract right as a right of property, even the right to our own life and body, the right over our inner life and conscience, and the right to a social status as free persons." Being "property," all these rights are ipso facto things, objects to be possessed; possessing them is what constitutes personhood. Put differently, personhood consists in one's being, uniquely, a *subject:* in the context of rights, only the person has subject-status (turning a person into an object of rights is tantamount to destroying his or her personhood, as in slavery); everything else has the status of object. In Hegel's words, "only personhood *(Persönlichkeit)* gives a right to things *(ein Recht an Sachen)* . . . [and] this right to things *(Sachenrecht)* is the right of personhood as such *(das Recht der Persönlichkeit als solcher).*"[32]

31. Hugo Grotius, *The Law of War and Peace* 1.1.4.
32. John Locke, *The Second Treatise of Government* §87. Wood, *Hegel's Ethical Thought,* 96. Georg Wilhelm Friedrich Hegel, *Grundlinien der Philosophie des Rechts, Werke* 7:99.

Defining rights in terms of persons (rather than in terms of religious, political, social, or cultural hierarchies) helps universalize the former and thus equalize the latter. Emerson appreciates the "leveling principle" in ethics, which "makes void the distinctions of intellect and the pride of erudition" and without which "the universe would present an aristocracy odious to God and man" (*EP* 117). Emerson's identifying intellect and erudition as antithetical to the "leveling principle" of ethics is most significant. Intellectual elitism was inherent in the Greek association of ethics with philosophical knowledge. Aristotle, for instance, held that the ability to choose the mean between two opposite extremes of attitude or conduct was a virtue appropriate to ordinary people, but that the highest virtue, and hence the highest form of happiness, consisted in a life of contemplation, which was accessible only to persons of intellect and wisdom. The Stoics are rightly honored for having advanced the doctrine of universal brotherhood, of the fundamental equality of all humans. Yet in developing their moral ideal of the sage, they revealed a quite unsympathetic attitude toward common mortals. As Herschel Baker comments, "Obviously, few could be sages, and in their moral rigidity the Stoics . . . despised the mass of mankind." The pride, arrogance, and exclusivism inherent in their notion of the perfect sage exposed them to devastating criticism from one of Emerson's favorite authors, Plutarch. Because of their reliance on knowledge as the basis of virtue, Kant considered all Greek systems of ethics to be guilty of such intellectual elitism. He himself, by contrast, asserted the value and correctness of the fundamental moral insights of common humans, whom he always considered most worthy of respect (*achtungswürdigste*). *Their* moral insights, Kant believed, usually have more value than those of philosophers, who are all too often misled by arrogance and confused thinking.[33]

For this democratization of ethical authority, Emerson needed no instruction from Kant. Reid and his Scottish associates had developed

33. Aristotle, *Nicomachean Ethics* 10.7–8. Herschel Baker, *The Image of Man*, 77; Plutarch, *Moralia* 75A-86A ("Quomodo quis suos in virtute sentiat profectus"). Immanuel Kant, *Kritik der reinen Vernunft* B xxxiii; *Grundlegung zur Metaphysik der Sitten, Gesammelte Schriften* 4:404. Although I use the *Gesammelte Schriften* for all citations from Kant, I follow traditional scholarly practice in making page references to either the first (A), or the second (B), or both editions (A/B) of the *Critique of Pure Reason* (1781, 1787).

a similar position. They were, after all, the apostles of *common* sense. As Daniel Howe remarks, "Their philosophy was, in a way, a 'no-philosophy' or an 'antiphilosophy'. . . . Philosophy, they decided, was not really useful. The important philosophical truths were obvious. . . . 'I despise Philosophy, and renounce its guidance,' cried Reid; 'let my soul dwell with Common Sense.' "[34] What common sense taught, among other things, was that the fundamental principles of ethics were intuitively available to all, and that every human had the capacity to act in accordance with those principles. Ordinary people had as much moral wisdom and potential as any moral philosopher. Emerson comments amply upon this ethical "egalitarianism":

> In every family of ordinary advantages in the middle ranks of life the great questions of morality are discussed with freedom and intelligence, introduced as matters of speculation but as having foundations of certainty like any other science. In the lowest orders of the people the occurrences of the day are debated, the prudence or folly of politicians and private conduct examined, and all with a reference to know the principles of ethical science. Anciently, such views were confined to small circles of philosophers. . . . This diffusion of the knowledge accumulated upon these topics, although it does not multiply new terms of technical value nor unfold delicate discoveries to the subtle metaphysician, is yet the true and best interest of philosophy; for it marks the boundary line of truth and speculation, it settles the foundations of the science to be in the opinions of men, and thus confers the only legitimate immortality upon its constitution and results. (*EP* 126–28)

What gives distinction to humans on the moral level is not, therefore, intellect or genius but what Emerson calls "worth," a quality inherent in the moral life (*EP* 118). Many personal qualities such as intelligence and artistic talent are valuable, and their value is determined externally (for instance, in the marketplace of ideas or of aesthetic taste). Only the moral life has intrinsic value, that is, worth—what the younger Seneca called *dignitas* (worthiness) as opposed to *pretium* (price).[35] The only aim ultimately appropriate to the moral life

34. Howe, *The Unitarian Conscience,* 31.
35. Seneca, *Epistulae Morales* 71.33.

is, therefore, the intrinsic one of achieving maximum worth, that is, approximating perfection (cf. "Be ye therefore perfect, even as your Father which is in heaven is perfect"—Matthew 5:48). For Emerson, the essential role of moral philosophy is to help humans advance toward perfection: ethics is "a science whose very object is to perfect the nature of man" (*EP* 130). Indeed, the achievement of human perfection will mean the demise of ethics as a philosophical discipline: "Should these eras of perfection which imagination anticipates arrive, we must cease to speculate with any reference to the progress of science; if science can sustain such an advancement, it must terminate here" (*EP* 131–32). As Kant pointed out, moral imperatives can have relevance only for *imperfect* rational beings, that is, for humans as they are presently constituted. Humans would be unaware of moral imperatives if their will and inclinations were not at variance with their sense of duty; absolute congruence between them would obviate the very notion of obligation.[36]

Since perfection is not yet, Emerson recognizes the need for advances in moral philosophy. At this early stage, he believes that the only hope for progress in ethics lies with "the school in which Reid and Stewart have labored." The Scottish Common Sense philosophers made a fruitful start, but their "reasonings as yet want the neatness and conclusiveness of a system" (*EP* 130, 122–23). "System" is not an ideal one associates with the mature Emerson, but at this point he, like his teachers and contemporaries, was convinced that any important theoretical endeavor needed to be translated into systematic form. Jonsen and Toulmin have shown that the ideal of system dominated Western intellectual life in the later seventeenth and the eighteenth century; Thomas McFarland has noted "the omnipresence of system" well into the nineteenth century: "Always it was to system, to the architectonic harmonizing of various elements, that thought bent its energies."[37] By way of illustration from the field of ethics I might point to the greatest work on the subject in mid-nineteenth-century Germany, *System der Ethik* (1851) by Immanuel Hermann von Fichte, son of a more famous father (Johann Gottlieb Fichte) who himself had

---

36. Kant, *Grundlegung zur Metaphysik der Sitten, Gesammelte Schriften*, 4:414.
37. Jonsen and Toulmin, *The Abuse of Casuistry*, 275–78; Thomas McFarland, *Coleridge and the Pantheist Tradition*, xxxix.

written *Das System der Sittenlehre (The System of Ethics)* half a century earlier (1798). When calling for a true system of ethics, Emerson was giving voice to a common aspiration of his day. He recognizes that "to exhibit a system of morals, entire and in all its parts, requires a powerful faculty of generalization." The ultimate generalization in ethics is to establish one universal principle to which every part of the discipline can be systematically related. Emerson calls upon moral philosophers, therefore, to "look no longer for many ultimate principles . . . [but to] persevere in accurate classifications" (*EP* 108, 130). The hoped-for outcome will be a "code of moral maxims" endowed with a systemic authority that "no rational being will dispute" (*EP* 122, 130).

Until ethics reaches this point of "self-evidence," it will remain a discipline clouded by uncertainty. Emerson repeatedly draws attention to the present state of our ignorance. As already indicated, "we cannot know" that God intends the greatest possible happiness for His creatures. When Emerson asserts that the human is a free agent, he adds, "at least to all the purposes of which we have any conception." More generally he states that "the end of all human inquiry is confessedly ignorance" (*EP* 116, 123). Since Plato, almost every great moral philosopher has acknowledged the indefinability of key concepts and other obstacles on the road to understanding. Kant opened the first edition of his *Critique of Pure Reason* with the observation that it was the peculiar fate of human reason to be impelled to ask questions that it cannot answer.[38] The resulting uncertainty, of course, is what has made the history of thought exciting and fruitful. Emerson's reason was also impelled to ask questions to which it found no satisfactory answers. But no matter how tentative, Emerson's answers were responses to questions he asked afresh, and *that* made them in his view superior to any "answers" provided by predecessors. In ethics as in every other field to which he directed his attention, Emerson endeavored to think his own thoughts, and in so doing he enriched his intellectual heritage rather than merely absorbing it.

38. Kant, *Kritik der reinen Vernunft* A vii.

2

Metaethics

*E*merson's position as a moralist is more readily understood if some important distinctions within ethics are kept in mind. The basic distinction is that between normative ethics and metaethics. The former accepts ethics as a given and attempts to relate it to human life and conduct. As the name suggests, normative ethics intends to provide guidance, and it does so in two areas: value and obligation. "Value" covers such questions as: What is the nature of the good life? What makes life meaningful, fulfilling, worth living? "Value" refers to all those things that it is *good* to *be*.[1] "Obligation" prescribes what one should *do*, how one should *act*. It concerns the rightness or wrongness of actions, the performance of duties. The rightness of an obligatory action is determined either teleologically or deontologically. For tele-ologists (also called consequentialists) an action is right if it aims at or achieves a result regarded as desirable in itself. The result, in other words, has priority in the determination of rightness. An example would be utilitarianism, where the aimed-at result ("the greatest happiness of the greatest number") becomes the criterion by which the rightness of an action is measured: rightness depends on the degree in which the action is productive of happiness. Deontology (derived from *deon*, neuter present participle of the Greek impersonal verb *dei*: "one must") rejects such consequentialism. It considers the rightness of an action to depend on the action's conforming to a purely *intrinsic* (that is, without regarding consequences) standard or principle. In Kant's view, for instance, an action is right only if it conforms to the moral law, whose obligatoriness is revealed to us in our awareness of the demands

1. Cf. C. Taylor, *Sources of the Self*, 79.

of duty. Kant's uncompromising adherence to the deontological view may be judged from his claim that for an action to be morally right it is not sufficient that it be *pflichtmäßig* ("in accordance with duty," but possibly inspired also by other considerations, such as goals or consequences): the action must be performed *aus Pflicht* ("for the sake of duty," "from a motive of duty").[2]

Normative ethics takes ethics for granted and deals with its content and relevance from within the field, so to speak. Metaethics, on the other hand, deals with questions *about* ethics—questions concerning such matters as the metaphysical and epistemological status of ethics, the foundation of ethics, the meaning of ethical terms, the nature of ethical judgments, and the justification of ethical claims. Whereas normative ethics makes, in Bernard Williams's words, "substantive claims about what one should do, how one should live, what [is] worthwhile," metaethics "concern[s] itself with the status of those claims."[3] Are such claims, for instance, susceptible to knowledge, and if so, what is the nature of ethical knowledge? And do such claims concern properties that are "objective," that are ontologically real, or does, say, "goodness" not exist apart from its being thought or felt as such? Responding to a query of a fellow passenger during his homeward voyage from Europe in 1833, Emerson confronted some basic metaethical questions:

> Yesterday I was asked what I mean by Morals. I reply that I cannot define & care not to define. It is man's business to observe & the definition of Moral Nature must be the slow result of years, of lives, of states perhaps of being. Yet in the morning watch on my berth I thought that Morals is the science of the laws of human action as respects right & wrong. Then I shall be asked—And what is Right? Right is a conformity to the laws of nature as far as they are known to the human mind.—These for the occasion but I propound definitions with more than the reserve of the feeling abovenamed—with more because my own conceptions are so dim & vague. (*JMN* 4:86)

The present chapter will examine Emerson's metaethics, and subsequent chapters will treat the areas of normative ethics that were

---

2. Kant, *Grundlegung zur Metaphysik der Sitten, Gesammelte Schriften,* 4:397–99.
3. Williams, *Ethics and the Limits of Philosophy,* 72.

most important to him. Needless to say, metaethics and normative ethics are not entirely separable. In the above quotation, Emerson's "I cannot define & care not to define" reflects a metaethical assumption that the ultimate questions concerning ethics are beyond human *understanding,* and this assumption has obvious implications for Emerson's normative ethics: the moral law we have to obey confronts us on the level of the Reason (through the "moral sentiment"), not on the level of the Understanding (empirically). Whereas the Understanding explains, the Reason—in its practical (moral) rather than its theoretical (epistemological) function—commands with an authority transcending explanation. Conversely, normative considerations can affect metaethics. Emerson believes humans have the duty to increase their knowledge. Hence (in the above quotation), all metaethical indefinability notwithstanding, "It is man's business to observe" and to strive for definition. In fact, Emerson sometimes considers metaethics a major concern of normative ethics, as when he suggests that man's highest duty is to "revere the law & study the foundation principles of Morals" (*JMN* 2:137). Obligation extends here not only to revering the moral law, which is purely a matter of normative ethics, but also to such a metaethical pursuit as the study of "the foundation principles of Morals." Emerson believes that the diligent study of such metaethical problems will provide some answers. Although "morals [moral laws] do not change . . . the *science* of morals does advance; men discover truths & relations of which they were before ignorant; therefore, there are discoveries in morals" (*JMN* 3:61).

I

Emerson's metaethical efforts were directed primarily toward establishing the autonomy of ethics vis-à-vis religion and toward defining the relations between ethics and nature and between ethics and knowledge. In addressing himself to the connection of religion and ethics, Emerson responded to a problem that had become increasingly troublesome in the century before him. The eighteenth century is rightly called the golden age of moral philosophy, an age in which a host of thinkers confronted afresh important questions in ethics and which witnessed such signal achievements in the field as those of Butler, Price, Hume, Kant, and Fichte. But as Laurence Lockridge points out, "the deepest motive for the eighteenth-century absorption in moral philosophy is the growing anxiety about the legitimacy of theological sanctions." When increasing doubt called into question the religious bases of ethics, humans confronted a universe in danger of becoming valueless and morally indifferent. Hence the desire for a "Morality [that] might be built up on its own foundation." This search for an "independent" ethic or, in Lockridge's words, "this pursuit of the ethical as a counter-measure to the waning of faith," lost none of its urgency when the Enlightenment gave way to the Romantic Age.[4]

These developments affected America no less than they did Europe. As Daniel Howe comments, "moral philosophy was, in a sense, the successor of theology. The prominence of moral philosophy in antebellum American education apparently reflected a desire to supplement religious sanctions with natural bases for values." In New England there occurred "a change in man's very attitude toward theology. The emphasis on ethics rather than dogma, which the eighteenth-century Liberals pioneered, was one of the mainstays of nineteenth-century Unitarianism." Indeed, the Unitarians insisted that "dogma was subordinate to ethics."[5]

In his early theorizing on the subject, Emerson at times considered ethics to be a personal God's gift to humankind. In "The Present State of Ethical Philosophy," human duties are held to derive from "the will of the Creator as expressed in the constitution of the world, and in revelation" (*EP* 116). Although Emerson might have sounded a little more like a Christian and a little less like an exponent of natural religion if he had put "revelation" ahead of "constitution of the world," the Christian orthodoxy of his view is not actually impaired by his not limiting God's expression of His will to revelation. Emerson is simply voicing the traditional "Two Books" concept, which for centuries was a commonplace among Christian theologians, philosophers, and poets.[6] To quote one of Emerson's favorite authors, Sir Thomas Browne: "There are two bookes from whence I collect my Divinity; besides that written one of God, another of his servant Nature, that universall and publik

---

4. Laurence S. Lockridge, *The Ethics of Romanticism*, 21.
5. Howe, *The Unitarian Conscience*, 3, 7, 100.
6. Ernst Robert Curtius, *European Literature and the Latin Middle Ages*, 319–23.

Manuscript, that lies expans'd unto the eyes of all." Cotton Mather, invoking the authority of the fourth-century St. John Chrysostom, expressed the same view in his preface to *The Christian Philosopher.* In the twelfth century the severely orthodox St. Bernard of Clairvaux put the matter most tersely, declaring unhesitatingly that *Natura Codex est Dei* (Nature is the Book of God).[7] Emerson was, therefore, on solid Christian ground when he found in nature the same personal God that he found in the Bible, and it was the personal God thus twice revealed that at this stage he considered "the Founder of the Moral Law" (*JMN* 2:5). Indeed, the moral law owes its existence to "the eternal character of the Deity"; it derives "from a *Mind,* of which it is the essence. That Mind is God" (*JMN* 2:49). Why should one obey the law of God? Emerson gives a classic Christian answer:

> You are not your own, but belong to another by the right of Creation. This claim is the most simple, perfect, and absolute of all claims. . . . God is [man's] Maker and made those very rights which he possesses. . . . Hence, the first ground of moral obligation consists in this, that, the Being who ordained it, is the Source, the Support, & the Principle of our existence. (*JMN* 2:121–22)[8]

This kind of derivation of the moral law from God ultimately proved unacceptable to Emerson's developing thought for three reasons: (1) it conveyed the moral law "externally" (through revelation or the book of nature); hence (2), it conveyed the moral law empirically (through the senses and the understanding) rather than transcendentally; (3) it presupposed a personal God, a God having such attributes of personality as law-giving, and a God thus conceived became increasingly problematic for Emerson. The mature Emerson ceased regarding dogmatic religion as a source of ethics. Foundationally, dogmatic religion and ethics seemed to him incompatible. As we learn from *Nature* (1836), "Ethics and religion differ herein; that the one is the system of human

7. Sir Thomas Browne, *Religio Medici, Works,* 1:24–25; Cotton Mather, *The Christian Philosopher,* 17–18; St. Bernard is quoted in Basil Willey, *The Eighteenth Century Background: Studies on the Idea of Nature in the Thought of the Period,* 42.

8. Emerson's reasoning on this point is identical with John Calvin's. See Eric Murphy Selinger, " 'Too Pathetic, Too Pitiable': Emerson's Lessons in Love's Philosophy," 177n36.

duties commencing from man; the other, from God. Religion includes the personality of God; Ethics does not" (*CW* 1: 35). It is noteworthy that in this passage Emerson has virtually translated religion into ethics: *both* are now a "system of human duties," and nothing more. Emerson does not mean to privilege the religious system over the purely ethical one by grounding the former in a personal God. By the mid-1830s he had come to regard the attribution of personality to God as misguided anthropomorphism and as conducive to idolatry (*JMN* 5:38, 467), and he had, after some hesitation, embraced pantheism.[9]

Several years before *Nature*, Emerson had already reversed the priority involving religion and ethics. Far from ethics needing religious sanction and definition, religion appeared increasingly to Emerson to derive its value from the degree to which it became ethics. From an 1833 journal entry we learn that Christianity "rests in the broad basis of man's moral nature & is not itself that basis" (*JMN* 4:92). A year later Emerson wrote that "Spiritual Religion . . . simply describes the laws of moral nature as the naturalist does physical laws" (*JMN* 4:364). The primacy or, to quote from the title of one of Emerson's lectures, "the sovereignty" of ethics remained a vital principle in his mature thought, acting as a solvent of religious dogma—as is obvious, for instance, in the Divinity School "Address" (1838). He continued to insist that "the progress of religion is steadily to its identity with morals" (*W* 10:208). He often expressed himself on this subject fervently, as when he exclaimed in a late lecture called "The Preacher": "Anything but unbelief, anything but losing hold of the moral intuitions, as betrayed in the clinging to a form of devotion or a theological dogma" (*W* 10:229). By 1859 he expected that religious formalism and dogma would soon be a thing of the past, both locally and universally. He called Unitarianism "a mere spec of whitewash, because the mind of our culture has already left it behind," and he saw Unitarianism's loss of vitality as occurring within a larger context of religious decline brought on by a more deeply experienced morality: "Nobody . . . longer holds the Christian traditions. We rest on the moral nature, & the whole world shortly must" (*JMN* 14:283).

9. For the sources and characteristics of Emerson's pantheism, see my *Emerson's Modernity and the Example of Goethe*, 28–30, 38–40.

Emerson's grand alternative to God and religion as foundations of ethics is, of course, the moral sentiment, which dispenses with any external or empirically derived authority. In his early thought Emerson did regard the moral sentiment as itself something with which a personal God had endowed the human soul, but the inward and ideal nature of this endowment proved so completely absorbing to Emerson's intellect that God's role inevitably attenuated even before God's personality dissolved into Emerson's pantheistic One-in-All. As early as 1822 Emerson spelled out some basic characteristics of the moral sentiment:

> This Sentiment which we bear within us, is so subtle and unearthly in its nature, so entirely distinct from all sense and matter, and thence so difficult to be examined, and withal so decisive and invariable in its dictates—that it clearly partakes of another world than this. . . . This Sentiment differs from the affections of the heart and from the faculties of the mind. . . . And the golden rules which are the foundation of its judgements we feel and acknowledge, but do not understand. (*JMN* 2:49–50)

Emerson here recognizes not only that the moral sentiment is absolute in its authority, but also that it is a sentiment sui generis: it cannot be understood or explained through analogy with such categories as "affections of the heart" and "faculties of the mind." In the following years and decades Emerson devoted much effort, conceptual and rhetorical, to elucidation of the moral sentiment. For reasons to be examined later in this chapter, he was bound never to succeed completely; but although he failed in definition, he did provide a considerable amount of descriptive material that significantly enriches the reader's appreciation of the moral sentiment.

A primary concern of Emerson's was to establish the universal authority of the moral sentiment, or what amounts to the same thing, the universality of the moral law. He was convinced that the moral law would command real respect and authority only if it were perceived to be normatively universal. If the moral law were not universal, it would emerge in human consciousness only as a congeries of subjective, relativistic, and inconsistent ethical judgments. In fact, it would cease to be a law at all: for Emerson, as for many other moral thinkers, the very concept of "law" implies universal applicability, in ethics just as much as in physics.[10] Emerson asserted the universality of the moral law by making ethics part—the essential part—of the nature of things. He equated ethics with Being. As Evelyn Barish points out, from his early years he cherished a phrase borrowed from his aunt Mary Moody Emerson, "Morals [are] coeval with existence."[11] For Emerson the structure of the universe is moral, "all things are moral." The moral law "lies at the centre of nature and radiates to the circumference" (*CW* 1:25–26). Attributing "self-existent excellence" to the moral law and calling it the "causing force" and the "supreme nature which lurks within all," Emerson expresses a fundamental principle first articulated by Plato in the *Phaedo* and in Book Six of the *Republic*, namely, that the moral law, or as Plato's Socrates phrases it, "the good and the ought" *(to agathon kai deon)*, is the essence (in the various philosophical meanings of this term) of reality (*CS* 2:8; *CW* 1:182).[12]

Morality is consequently also the essence of human nature. Emerson considers morality *the* defining characteristic of our humanity. To be human means to be morally implicated. Wanting to emphasize this point, he almost rivals Cotton Mather in the use of italics: *"The perception of right and wrong, the perception of duty* [is the] part of our nature [that] is the sovereign part. It is the distinctive part. He that had it not, would not be man" (*CS* 2:30). "Perception" is an important term here in that it points, as we saw in chapter 1, to the objective status of the moral law, a status already implied by the moral law's universality. Although *accessible* only through individual consciousness, the moral law is not therefore its *product*. As an idealist Emerson remained, also in ethics, an objective idealist (like Schelling and Hegel, for instance): the moral law has ideal self-existence; it has (like Platonic Ideas) ontic reality.[13] Urging self-trust in a lecture on ethics, Emerson therefore stresses that self-trust is "not a faith in man's own whim or conceit as if he . . . acted on his own private account, but a perception that the mind common to the Universe is disclosed to the individual through his own nature" (*EL* 2:151). Human nature, as Emerson never tires of

10. For a detailed discussion and evaluation of this principle in ethics, see Reiner Wimmer, *Universalisierung in der Ethik.*

11. Barish, *Emerson: The Roots of Prophecy*, 101.

12. Plato, *Phaedo* 99C; A. E. Taylor, *Plato*, 287–89.

13. For the distinction between objective and subjective idealism, see Vittorio Hösle, *Die Krise der Gegenwart und die Verantwortung der Philosophie*, 46–47, 205–13.

insisting, is the actualization of Soul, Mind, or Universe in self. This
is worth remembering when one reads statements like "Conscience—
Virtue . . . have . . . their foundation in the nature of man," or "Ethics
result . . . from [man's] constitution" (*JMN* 3:68; 12:57), or some of
the more extreme assertions in "Self-Reliance." Emerson never lost
sight of what he considered the essential fact: "There exists a Universal
Mind which imparts this perception of duty" (*JMN* 15:470).

Emerson comments on the moral sentiment most informatively in
the Divinity School "Address." His key statement is philosophically
revealing: "The intuition of the moral sentiment is an insight of the
perfection of the laws of the soul. These laws execute themselves. They
are out of time, out of space, and not subject to circumstance" (*CW*
1:77). As a cognitive faculty, the moral sentiment clearly belongs with
the Reason rather than the Understanding. Insight is gained through
intuition, not through sense perception or ratiocination. Having no
phenomenal existence ("out of time, out of space"), the moral law
("the laws of the soul") is not accessible empirically and provides
no data for analysis. Transcending all experience (a point Emerson
repeats when he says that the moral law is "not subject to circumstance"), the moral law can be grasped only transcendentally. The
moral sentiment intuits the moral law as absolute (it has "perfection")
and autonomous, in the strict sense of "self-legislative": there is no
higher law, and there is no agent or causality external to the law
("these laws execute themselves"). The moral sentiment apprehends
this "self-execution" of the moral law as conscience. Just as the Unitarians identified conscience with the moral sense,[14] Emerson identifies conscience with the moral sentiment. Emersonian conscience,
therefore, is not grounded in culture, experience, or psychology, but
in one's transcendental self: "In the soul of man there is a justice
whose retributions are instant and entire" (*CW* 1:77–78). The very
absoluteness and immediacy (in the sense of "unmediatedness") of
this justice defy discursive analysis. The moral sentiment/conscience
simply *is* as a constitutive fact of our humanness.

A related metaethical issue concerns the status of the Good. As a
pantheist, the mature Emerson was ipso facto a monist, and he therefore emphatically rejected any theory granting evil a status equal to

14. Howe, *The Unitarian Conscience*, 54, 58, 59.

that of good. The Manichaean view, for instance, which held that evil is an independent, absolute principle opposed to the good, represented the kind of metaphysical dualism that Emerson found unacceptable. He regarded *absolute* evil or *essential* evil as a self-contradictory concept. Evil as such cannot *be:* "That pure malignity exists, is an absurd proposition" (*JMN* 5:266; 8:183). Emerson instead interpreted evil as *privation,* a view first given prominence by Plotinus, for whom evil was absolute want *(penia panteles),* the complete absence of good *(apousia agathou),* the total privation *(steresis)* of Being.[15] Plotinus was thus able to maintain his doctrine of the One from which all things emanate without weakening its monistic character and without making the One the source of evil. Regarding the One, Being, and the Good as synonymous, Plotinus insisted that since evil is the nonexistence of the Good, evil is non-Being, nonentity. This doctrine proved attractive to anyone wanting to deny evil the status of ultimate principle, whether to avoid dualism or for other reasons. St. Augustine, for instance, considered the will as such to be good, and he interpreted moral evil as "a privation of right order" in the will. Frederick Copleston comments:

> This doctrine of evil as a privation was the doctrine of Plotinus, and in it Augustine found the answer to the Manichees. For if evil is a privation and not a positive thing, one is no longer faced with the choice of either ascribing moral evil to the good Creator or of inventing an ultimate evil principle responsible for evil. This doctrine was adopted by the Scholastics generally from Augustine and finds adherents among several modern philosophers of note, Leibniz, for example.[16]

Emerson also was a modern exponent of this originally Plotinian doctrine. His view that "the world is not the product of manifold power, but of one will, of one mind" made it inevitable that he should have regarded "whatever opposes that will" not as a positive principle but as the very absence of such a principle: only "Good is positive. Evil is merely privative, not absolute. . . . All evil is . . . nonentity. Benevolence [Latin *benevolentia:* "*good*-will"] is absolute and

15. Plotinus, *Enneads* 1.8.3; 1.8.11.
16. Frederick Copleston, *A History of Philosophy,* vol. 2, pt. 1:100.

real" (*CW* 1: 78). For Emerson, in brief, "Goodness & Being are one" (*JMN* 8:183).

This doctrine helps explain one of Emerson's most striking metaethical statements—a statement that Barbara Packer has described as "surely one of the more audacious gestures in American literature":[17]

> We believe in ourselves, as we do not believe in others. . . . It is an instance of our faith in ourselves, that men never speak of crime as lightly as they think. . . . The act looks very differently on the inside, and on the outside. . . . Murder . . . is an act quite easy to be contemplated, but in its sequel, it turns out to be a horrible jangle and confounding of all relations. . . . For there is no crime to the intellect. That is antinomian or hypernomian. . . . It leaves out praise and blame, and all weak emotions. . . . Saints are sad, because they behold sin, (even when they speculate,) from the point of view of the conscience, and not of the intellect; a confusion of thought. Sin seen from the thought, is a diminution or *less:* seen from the conscience or will, it is pravity or *bad*. The intellect names it shade, absence of light, and no essence. The conscience must feel it as essence, essential evil. This it is not: it has an objective existence, but no subjective. (*CW* 3:45)

Throughout this passage the implicit identification of Being or essence with subject and of subject with thought (intellect) entails the relegation of evil to a realm that is accessible only empirically—the world of phenomena, of others, of our own emotional and psychological states; a world, in sum, that is in Emerson's view epistemologically, and therefore ontologically, less real than the world of ideal subjectivity. Evil partakes of the reality of that less real world—the world in which we "speak," in which acts are perceived ("on the outside") and have frightening consequences ("horrible jangle and confounding of all relations"), in which society's laws prevail and its judgments ("praise and blame") affect us through our "weak emotions." None of these things, however—as we also learn from Emerson's poem "Brahma" (*W* 9:195)—has *essential* reality. To the intellect, there is no crime or law (it is "hypernomian"); the intellect names evil "no essence." The saints are confused when they allow their emotions ("conscience," "will") concerning evil to shape their thoughts ("when

---

17. B. L. Packer, *Emerson's Fall: A New Interpretation of the Major Essays*, 175.

they speculate") on the subject. The conscience *feels* evil "as essence"; however, there *is no* "essential evil." Evil, in sum, "has an objective existence, but no subjective." Both "objective" and "subjective" in the last sentence may be somewhat misleading to present-day readers. By "objective" existence Emerson means that, to the subject, evil is phenomenal and experiential, and thus not part of the subject's essence. Since he associates subject with Being or essence, he obviously intends "subjective" here to mean "essential"—a meaning of the term supported by the *Oxford English Dictionary* (second edition) and attested by examples from the seventeenth through the end of the nineteenth century. The *OED*'s second definition of "subjective" provides a helpful gloss indeed on Emerson's use of the term: "Pertaining to the subject as to that in which attributes inhere; inherent; hence, pertaining to the essence or reality of a thing; real, essential." Emerson has often been criticized for his supposedly superficial sense of evil. As I hope to have shown, his convictions concerning the status of evil were an integral part of a complex and well-considered metaethical argument.[18]

II

The editors of Emerson's *Early Lectures* suggest that his interest in natural science in the early 1830s was "perhaps the principal agent in his shift from a theological to a secular base for his moral philosophy" (*EL* 1:1). Whereas religion confronted Emerson with doctrines and forms that he had come to regard as local and temporal, as historically and culturally specific, nature appeared to be the material representation of that universality which he regarded as a sine qua non for the validity of the moral law. For Emerson the idealist, mind does not conform to nature, but nature conforms to mind—a view obviously reflecting Kant's Copernican revolution in epistemology. Nature as such does not, however, conform to any *finite* mind, but to what Emerson variously calls Mind, Soul, or Spirit. Not having risen to consciousness (yet), Nature is, pantheistically speaking, God objectified, whereas the human mind, though limited by individuality, is God achieving

18. For an important different interpretation of the passage discussed in this paragraph, see Robinson, *Emerson and the Conduct of Life*, 67–68.

(limited) self-awareness. In nature the human individual encounters, therefore, his or her potential universality objectified; nature thus suggests to the individual the need to realize in consciousness the universality that is Spirit: "The world . . . is a remoter and inferior incarnation of God, a projection of God in the unconscious. . . . Its serene order is inviolable by us. It is therefore, to us, the present expositor of the divine mind" (*CW* 1:38–39).

Nature's "serene order" is but another name for its lawfulness. Because of its inescapable lawfulness, nature can figure for Emerson as a type of the absoluteness of the moral law as perceived by the moral sentiment. Studying nature, consequently, amounts to studying one's own moral nature: "I would learn the law of the diffraction of a ray because when I understand it, it will illustrate, perhaps suggest, a new truth in ethics" (*JMN* 4:322). Emerson here expresses a generally Romantic position of profound epistemological and moral significance. In the Hegelian view, for instance, "natural science is implicitly the effort of consciousness to discover itself in Nature."[19] Emerson agreed: since "the laws of nature preexisted in [the] mind" (*EL* 2:221), and since we can, therefore, ultimately encounter only ourselves in nature, he concluded that "the ancient precept, 'Know thyself,' and the modern precept, 'Study nature,' become at last one maxim" (*CW* 1:55). In this context, Hegel's claim that the best possible elucidation of the freedom of the will is provided by the law of gravity makes perfect sense. Freedom "is just as fundamental a determinant of the will (*Grundbestimmung des Willens*) as gravity is a fundamental determinant of bodies (*Grundbestimmung der Körper*)." Gravity is a necessary, not an accidental, predicate of bodies; similarly, freedom is a necessary, not an accidental, predicate of the will. Just as to the modern student of nature bodies without gravity are inconceivable, so is (to Hegel and many moderns) a will without freedom "a meaningless term" (*ein leeres Wort*).[20] Emerson relished the fact that freedom is "necessary"— as necessary as gravity: "We are made of contradictions,—our *freedom* is *necessary*" (*JMN* 9:335; also 11:76, 161). Or as he puts it in "Fate": One cannot "blink the freewill. To hazard the contradiction,—freedom is necessary. If you please to plant yourself on the side of Fate, and

19. G. R. G. Mure, *The Philosophy of Hegel*, 153n1.
20. Hegel, *Grundlinien der Philosophie des Rechts*, *Werke*, 7:46.

say, Fate is all; then we say, a part of Fate is the freedom of man" (*W* 6:23). In sum, the lawfulness of the physical universe illustrates ethical freedom, which is "the *law* of moral agents in the universe" (*EL* 2:201; emphasis added). Or as Emerson put it more generally, echoing Mme. de Staël, "The axioms of physics translate the laws of ethics" (*CW* 1:21, 249).

Nature is not mere law, however. It is, in Kant's formulation, "the existence of things as determined by universal laws."[21] It is phenomena—sensuous objects—governed by law, and these provided Emerson with an inexhaustible source of symbols for specific moral truths. As he said in a sermon of 1832, "it is *moral nature*, which affords the key by which the works of nature are to be read. They seem all to be hieroglyphicks containing a meaning which only that can decipher" (*CS* 4:144). The editors of the *Early Lectures* remind us that the tendency to interpret natural objects as symbols of moral truth characterized Emerson's thought to the end of his intellectually active life (*EL* 1:3). He regarded the moral law as "the pith and marrow of every substance, every relation, and every process" (*CW:* 1:26), and he insisted that only the symbolic imagination can detect the moral law within the natural fact. Read symbolically, natural facts provide moral enlightenment: "The moral influence of nature upon every individual is that amount of truth which it illustrates to him" (*CW* 1:26).

III

Emerson endeavored to clarify not only the relation of ethics to nature, but also that of ethics to knowledge. Early in his career, he sometimes adopted the Greek view and made morality dependent upon knowledge. In the manner of Socrates, whom in a sermon he called "the wisest certainly of all the pagans that preceded our Saviour," Emerson equated wickedness with ignorance and traced all fraud, pride, selfishness, and envy to "false views of our nature and interest" (*CS* 1:192, 79, 128, 163, 199). As might be expected, he paraphrased the Socratic position at considerable length in his chapter on Plato in

---

21. Kant, *Grundlegung zur Metaphysik der Sitten, Gesammelte Schriften*, 4:437; *Kritik der praktischen Vernunft, Gesammelte Schriften*, 5:43.

Representative Men (*CW* 4:36, 41, 47). But when in his mature years Emerson, speaking in his own name, sometimes made moral progress contingent upon deeper insight, he did little more than express the obvious point that more advanced knowledge of what is right refines one's sense of moral obligation. Put bluntly, Emerson but restated the commonsensical notion that one cannot experience as a moral obligation something one does not or cannot *know* to be a moral obligation.

Very early, Emerson began to move to another view of the relation between ethics and knowledge—a view best described as Kantian. Since Kant plays a significant part in the argument of this book, the availability (in more than one sense) of his thought to Emerson needs to be considered. Scholars have argued at length about the extent of Emerson's knowledge of Kant's works, the quality of his sources of information on Kant, and the degree to which he understood Kant. David Van Leer, in addition to making his own contribution to the debate, has provided a helpful survey of the scholarship on the subject.[22] It is unlikely that the argument concerning Emerson's indebtedness to Kant will become any less inconclusive than it is at present. As Van Leer points out, "there is no way of proving the two facts that would be most revealing—that Emerson did not read a text or that he did understand it." For Van Leer, what really matters is not Emerson's knowledge of or familiarity with Kantian concepts, but his understanding of them; "for questions of understanding," Van Leer concludes, "any study of the genesis of thought is irrelevant." The study of Emerson's Kantian sources is "a lost cause" since it cannot "address the real issue of Emerson's philosophical understanding."[23]

This conclusion seems unduly categorical. There may, indeed, be no way of proving that Emerson understood Kantian philosophy, but is Kant for that reason irrelevant to him? If evidence of real understanding were a prerequisite for discussion, would one be able to discuss any thinker's Kantianism? Who, after all, has understood Kant? Fichte would have us believe that not even Kant understood Kant. Exegesis of Kant has been a staple of philosophical scholarship for two centuries, and there is no consensus anywhere in sight. Any student of, say, the

22. David Van Leer, *Emerson's Epistemology: The Argument of the Essays*, 2–8, 209–13.
23. Ibid., 6.

Kritik der reinen Vernunft is likely to be baffled by a text in which "there is hardly a technical term which is not employed . . . in a variety of different and conflicting senses." If Kant scholars are unable to convince each other of the "correctness" of their respective understandings of Kant, such "correct" understanding is certainly not to be looked for among creative interpreters like Coleridge, Carlyle, and Emerson. But the absence of such understanding does not make these writers' responses to Kant's thought irrelevant to *our* efforts to understand *them*. Coleridge's maxim is to the point: "Until you understand a writer's ignorance, presume yourself ignorant of his understanding."[24]

A more fruitful approach to the question of Kant's significance for Emerson is suggested by James Engell and Walter Jackson Bate in their edition of Coleridge's *Biographia Literaria*: "Kant, as the founder and central figure of the critical philosophy, touched almost every important intellectual topic of the period. Coleridge could not—nor could anyone else—take up issues and ideas raised and introduced by the new philosophy without everywhere encountering Kant."[25] When Emerson examined the mind's constitutive role in our experience of the world, when he confronted the mind's epistemic limitations, when he struggled with the threat of solipsistic idealism, when he had the sense of living in two worlds—the ideal and the actual—that often seemed unrelatable to each other, he was responding, however indirectly, to problems that, for his day, had been defined above all by Kant. Kant's importance to our understanding of Emerson is not limited, therefore, to what can be shown—on the basis of external or internal evidence—to have been Emerson's firsthand knowledge of Kant. Emerson also exemplifies Kantian positions without always being aware of their specific Kantianism; or sometimes he may not have made his awareness explicit. In such cases, Emerson's ideas often gain focus and clarity when read in the light of theoretical insights or interpretive analogues provided by Kant.[26]

24. Heinrich Heine, *Zur Geschichte der Religion und Philosophie in Deutschland, Sämtliche Schriften*, 3:608. Norman Kemp Smith, *A Commentary to Kant's "Critique of Pure Reason,"* xx. Samuel Taylor Coleridge, *Biographia Literaria*, 1:232.

25. Coleridge, *Biographia Literaria*, 1:cxxv.

26. Excellent illustrations of this approach to Emerson's Kantianism are Stanley Cavell, "Thinking of Emerson," *The Senses of Walden*, 123–38, and "Emerson, Coleridge, Kant," *In Quest of the Ordinary: Lines of Skepticism and Romanticism*, 27–49.

Emerson's introduction to Kant came as early as 1822, apparently through Dugald Stewart (*L* 7:118). Reading Stewart on Kant is now a rather painful experience, but his self-confessed inadequacies as an interpreter of Kant and his exploitation of secondary sources without much sense of their reliability or authoritativeness did not prevent his making available, however rudimentarily, some basic Kantian notions that made Emerson's mind more readily receptive to Kantian ideas in years to come. By means of quotations and linking commentary, Stewart referred to such ethically relevant matters as the world of freedom versus the world of necessity and the problems involved in the human's presence in either world; the practical reason's supplementing the theoretical reason's inadequacy in establishing such ideas as freedom, God, and immortality; and the primacy of morality among human concerns. As early as 1823, such Kantian theorizing began to bear fruit in Emerson's own moral thinking, as evidenced, for instance, by *JMN* 2:82–83 (see below). Henry A. Pochmann recognized the essential Kantianism of this passage, but having dismissed Stewart's nearly thirty pages as "incomparably bad as a commentary on Kant," he failed at this point to consider the Scot as an intermediary and was thus not quite able to account for an Emersonian statement that, "when reduced to essentials, will be recognized as Kant's practical philosophy."[27] As Emerson matured philosophically, Kant became increasingly important to his ethics, and his encounters with Kantian thought became, naturally, more complex and meaningful.

When considering the Kantian aspect of Emerson's ethics, it is also important to remember that the statement quoted from Engell and Bate is as relevant to ethics as to epistemology. Kant accomplished a "Copernican Revolution" in both fields. He was the greatest moral philosopher of modern times—indeed, the greatest since antiquity. He wrote, as Bernard Williams has concluded, "the most significant work of moral philosophy after Aristotle" (Williams is referring to the *Grundlegung zur Metaphysik der Sitten* [1785]—*Groundwork of the Metaphysic of Morals)*. In the moral thought of Emerson's day, Kant was

---

27. See Henry A. Pochmann, *German Culture in America: Philosophical and Literary Influences, 1600–1900*, 86, 120, 159, 166; also Barish, *Emerson: The Roots of Prophecy*, 167–70; Dugald Stewart, *Dissertation Exhibiting the Progress of Metaphysical, Ethical, and Political Philosophy*, in *Collected Works*, 1:408–10, 412.

preponderant and inescapable. The Harvard Unitarians worried about the "moral tendency" of Kantianism, while Transcendentalists such as Frederic Henry Hedge rejoiced in "the moral liberty proclaimed by [Kant] as it had never been proclaimed by any before." And no matter how intrigued Emerson was by Kant's contributions to epistemology, he was primarily interested, as René Wellek has pointed out, in Kant's moral philosophy.[28]

At present I am concerned with Kant's significance to Emerson's metaethical conception of the relationship between ethics and knowledge. In Emerson's view, this relationship involves three aspects, all of them prominent in Kant's moral theory: (1) the primacy of ethics (or of the practical reason), (2) the cognitive function of the practical reason, and (3) the inexplicability of the moral law.

As already indicated in chapter 1, Aristotle originated the distinction between theoretical (or speculative) and practical reason and brought ethics within the purview of the latter. This distinction—though not necessarily the use to which Aristotle put it—was maintained by medieval and modern philosophers.[29] To cite a few authors known to Emerson, Cudworth distinguished within "the understanding, both speculative understanding, or the soul, as considering about the truth and falsehood of things, and the practical, considering their good and evil, or what is to be done and not done." According to Hume, "Philosophy is commonly divided into *speculative* and *practical*; . . . morality is always comprehended under the latter division." Reid insisted that "to judge of what is true or false in speculative points, is the office of speculative reason; and to judge of what is good or ill for us upon the whole, is the office of practical reason."[30] Given this long-established distinction, Emerson could in his first book simply refer to "Reason, both speculative and practical, that is, philosophy and virtue" (*CW* 1:36) and assume that his readers needed no further explanation.

Kant is unique in the tenacity, depth, and detail of his inquiries into the theoretical (speculative) and the practical reason. Putting matters

28. Beck, *A Commentary on Kant's "Critique of Practical Reason,"* 21–23, 179, 199. Williams, *Ethics and the Limits of Philosophy,* 55. Howe, *The Unitarian Conscience,* 79–81; Frederic Henry Hedge, ["Coleridge"], 126. René Wellek, *Confrontations,* 193.

29. Beck, *A Commentary on Kant's "Critique of Practical Reason,"* 37.

30. Raphael, ed., *British Moralists 1650–1800,* 1:131 (Cudworth), 2:269 (Reid); Hume, *A Treatise of Human Nature,* 457.

as briefly as possible, one can say that whereas the first *Critique* (*Kritik der reinen Vernunft,* 1781) was a critical examination and refutation of the pretensions of the pure theoretical reason (its claims to metaphysical knowledge), his second *Critique* (*Kritik der praktischen Vernunft,* 1788) was a critical examination and refutation of the pretensions of the empirical practical reason—and, per contra, a defense of the absolutist claims of the pure practical reason. According to Kant, pure reason, in its theoretical function, can give us no *knowledge* of the objects that speculative metaphysics has traditionally claimed to be able to give us knowledge of, since a basic ingredient of all theoretical knowledge—sensibility—is lacking. Since God, for example, transcends all sensible experience, the theoretical reason, while enabling us to *think* God, cannot enable us to *know* God, or even to know whether there is a God. Like soul, freedom, immortality, holiness, and such, God is an "Idea of the Reason," to which nothing in our experience can possibly correspond. This absolute transcendence, while depriving us of knowledge of the objects of these Ideas, also guarantees that the Ideas are indeed products of the Reason, since they could not possibly have been suggested by our (nonexistent) experience of their objects. But though not derived empirically, Ideas of the Reason are not innate ideas. They are regulative or heuristic concepts inevitably arising from the very nature of the Reason—from the Reason's relentless drive toward absoluteness, completeness, finality, and unity, the lack of which leaves the Reason forever unsatisfied.[31]

In its practical function, on the other hand, pure reason rules absolutely and universally. Pure practical reason is the a priori (that is, nonempirical), unconditioned legislative faculty through which humanity imposes the moral law upon itself. Only pure reason can be the source of a formal (without specific, experience-derived content), absolute, universally binding moral law. And since the moral law is

---

31. Kant often used "speculative reason" as synonymous with "theoretical reason," but he sometimes limited "speculative reason" to the metaphysical pursuits of the theoretical reason (Beck, *A Commentary on Kant's "Critique of Practical Reason,"* 23–24; Roger J. Sullivan, *Immanuel Kant's Moral Theory,* 301n7). I see no point in maintaining this distinction in a general discussion like the present, and I shall throughout use "theoretical" since this term was clearly for Kant the more comprehensive one (see, e.g., *Kritik der reinen Vernunft* A 634/B 662 ad fin.). Kant, *Kritik der reinen Vernunft* B xxvi, A 327/B 383–84, A 323/B 380, A 327/B 384, A 642–68/B 670–96, A 670–71/B 698–99, A 797–98/B 825–26.

given to us *qua* rational beings by our own reason, we are, literally speaking, autonomous. Our highest function as rational beings is to obey the categorical commands of our own reason. All other sources of the moral law Kant rejected as heteronomous: they put human reason in the position of having to obey a law that it has not prescribed to itself. Moreover, because such sources involve empirical elements, their claims to universal validity must, by definition, be disallowed. This is true even of God as source of the moral law. Since we cannot know God (see above), every age fashions the God best suited to its religious and intellectual resources and needs, as for instance, in Kant's day, the God "according to Crusius and other theological moralists"—in other words, the anthropomorphized God "experienced," analyzed, and taught by eighteenth-century German theological scholarship.[32] Similar problems vitiate attempts to found the moral law on nature, tradition, or society, all of which are accessible only empirically. Kant is equally firm in his rejection of any source involving subjective or affective—hence, again, empirical—elements, such as our own "nature," desires (as in philosophical hedonism), or psychological makeup. Involving our *experience* (of our desires, for instance), such sources are inherently limited and cannot possibly originate a universally binding moral law.

Since one of Kant's heteronomous targets was the moral sense *(das moralische Gefühl, nach Hutcheson)*,[33] he would no doubt also have rejected Emerson's moral sentiment. He would have found Emerson, at one and the same time, too empirical in his derivation of what is morally right ("No law can be sacred to me but that of my nature. . . . the only right is what is after my constitution, the only wrong what is against it"—CW 2:30) and too much of an intuitionist, a thinker granting ontic reality to transcendent moral principles that reason perceives but does not originate. But such fundamental differences notwithstanding, Emerson, as I shall try to show, is often remarkably Kantian in his views of the theoretical and the practical reason.

The dominant tradition in Western philosophy had identified the highest form of the good life as the life of thought, of contemplation. In this regard Kant, as Roger Sullivan has stressed, accomplished

---

32. Kant, *Kritik der praktischen Vernunft, Gesammelte Schriften,* 5:40.
33. Ibid.

> another Copernican revolution: He stood the traditional doctrine
> on its head by insisting that moral practice . . . has supreme value.
> It is "to be esteemed beyond comparison" as far more valu-
> able than anything else, including theoretical understanding. . . .
> Kant . . . argued that of itself theoretical activity is neither uncon-
> ditionally nor intrinsically good; it is valuable only insofar as it
> enhances moral practice . . . [34]

The primacy of morality (the practical reason) over the theoretical
reason is a principle Emerson insists on over and over again, often
in terms strongly reminiscent of Kant. A few examples must suffice:
"Intellectual nature does not take the first rank in the scale of excellence. . . . Our understandings have an ultimate aim beyond their
own perfection—viz to be employed about moral excellence" (*JMN*
2:149). Or in a letter: "The moral is prior in God's order to the
intellectual. . . . to the moral nature belongs sovereignty" (*L* 1:450).
Or as he put it in a sermon, "There are many faculties in the mind
but the highest faculty is the conscience" (*CS* 2:193). There is no
doubt whatsoever in Emerson's mind that "the Moral Sentiment is
the highest in God's order" or that "Ethics stand when wit fails" (*JMN*
5:362, 344). Explaining, in his splendid essay "Circles," that there
are "degrees in idealism," Emerson insists that in its highest form
idealism "shows itself ethical and practical" (*CW* 2: 183). Assertions
like these lend support to Cornel West's claim that Emerson's thought
"prefigures" such dominant characteristics of American pragmatism as
its "evasion of epistemology-centered philosophy," its "unashamedly
moral emphasis," and its "unequivocally ameliorative impulse."[35]

34. Sullivan, *Immanuel Kant's Moral Theory*, 97. For detailed discussion, see Sullivan, 95–113; also Beck, *A Commentary on Kant's "Critique of Practical Reason,"* 249–
50. David Jacobson's fine argument in *Emerson's Pragmatic Vision: The Dance of the
Eye* is somewhat marred by his persistent misreading of Kant's position concerning
practical vs. theoretical reason and by his consequent misinterpretation of Emerson
as anti-Kantian in this respect. Jacobson refers to Emerson's "dismissal of the Kantian
privileging of theoretical reason" (15); to Emerson's "relegation of theoretical reason
to a secondary role," thereby differentiating his thought "from Kant's system" (33); to
Emerson's "repudiat[ion of] Kant's rationalism," a repudiation involving his rejection
"of the limitation theoretical reason places on practical reason" and his liberating
"practical reason . . . from . . . the dominance of theoretical reason" (34; see also 60).
Since Kant himself asserted the primacy of the practical over the theoretical reason,
Emerson's attitude on this point was hardly anti-Kantian.

35. Cornel West, *The American Evasion of Philosophy: A Genealogy of Pragmatism*, 9,
5, 4.

Kant also speaks of the pure practical reason as a superior *cognitive* faculty. While the pure theoretical reason is incapable of providing us with any knowledge of noumenal reality, we do have cognitive access to that reality through the pure practical reason. We cannot know what ultimately *is,* but we do know what ultimately *ought to be done.* Through the absolute *ought,* that is, through the moral law, the practical reason brings us face to face with a reality that owes nothing to the phenomenal world. The ultimate Law does not originate in the world of sensibilia or experience; it confronts us with an absolute fact of reason. Pure practical reason is noumenal reality brought to our awareness as absolute Law—as moral law, as imperative, as obligation.[36]

The pure practical reason extends its cognitive function by assuming three postulates—God, freedom, and immortality—as necessary to the proper functioning and ultimate efficacy of the moral law. From the standpoint of practical reason, Kant insists, a postulate is a mode of knowledge "not inferior in degree to any other knowledge *(Wissen),* although in kind it is wholly different." Again, none of these postulates is an object of *theoretical* knowledge and hence none of them is susceptible of proof (each is an Idea of the Reason), but the pure practical reason conceives of them as implementally necessary to the moral law. Take freedom, for example. Kant's claim that we cannot *know* what freedom is or *know* that we are free is amply supported by the fact that the question of moral freedom (freedom of the will) has been one of the most hotly debated issues in the history of Western thought, with philosophers and theologians as often as not inclining to the view that we are not free. Emerson rightly concluded that "it is an old dispute which is not now and never will be totally at rest, whether the human mind be or be not a free agent" (*JMN* 2:58). But reason, Kant holds, would be inconceivably self-contradictory if it were to impose upon itself—upon us as *rational* beings—commands it could not possibly execute. Since reason "commands that such [actions] should take place, it must be possible for them to take place." Our ability to obey the moral law, to act in accordance with the commands of the pure practical reason, brings with it a consciousness of freedom—freedom to act "rationally" and thereby freedom from

36. Kant, *Kritik der praktischen Vernunft, Gesammelte Schriften,* 5:43.

habit, inclination, temptation, or any other empirical factor. Although theoretically undefinable and unprovable, freedom enters our consciousness, and this fact exemplifies once again the cognitive role of the practical reason. In Roger Sullivan's words, "the positive assurance of our freedom rests epistemologically on the prior appearance in our awareness of the Categorical Imperative and its more particular commands." Or as Kant himself puts it, "the moral law is the only condition under which we can become *aware* of freedom." Freedom is inherent in the moral law. Without freedom the pure reason could not be "practical," that is, *morally* binding. Freedom thus becomes the defining trait of humanity under the law of reason. For Kant, in sum, freedom and morality are mutually implicative, as Dugald Stewart did not fail to notice. Kant was, in Stewart's words, "deeply impressed with a conviction . . . that morality and the freedom of the human will must stand or fall together."[37]

Emerson often contrasts the epistemological limitations of the theoretical reason (his theoretical skepticism) with the cognitive assurances provided by the practical reason. In the early journal passage Pochmann already recognized as essentially Kantian (see above), Emerson, having duly appreciated the claims of theoretical skepticism, concludes:

> But it is in the constitution of the mind to rely with firmer confidence upon the *moral principle*, and I reject at once the idea of a delusion in this. This is woven vitally into the thinking substance itself. . . . Upon the foundation of my *moral sense*, I ground my faith in the immortality of the soul. (*JMN* 2:83)

This passage not only stresses the superior cognitive status of the moral principle or the moral sense, but it also calls to mind one of Kant's postulates of the practical reason. Emerson often also regards the idea of God as a product of the practical reason: "He who does good, in the moment that he does good, has some idea of God," or expressed without qualification, "We form just conceptions of [God] by doing

---

37. Immanuel Kant, "Was heißt: Sich im Denken orientiren?" *Gesammelte Schriften*, 8:141. Kant, *Kritik der reinen Vernunft* A 807/B 835. Sullivan, *Immanuel Kant's Moral Theory*, 321n6; Kant, *Kritik der praktischen Vernunft, Gesammelte Schriften*, 5:4n. Stewart, *Dissertation*, 1:410.

his will. Obedience is the eye that sees God" (*CS*: 3:52, 4:134). The cognitive range of the practical reason is apparent when Emerson claims that "Obedience is the eye which reads the laws of the Universe" (*JMN* 3:269). In fact, "as [the] demands of duty are complied with the soul is rewarded by a better knowledge" (*CS* 4:140). This knowledge is also self-directed: it is through the moral sentiment that "the soul first knows itself" (*CW* 1:79). In sum, "the moral sense is the proper keeper of the doors of knowledge" (*JMN* 3:269). Emerson thus seems to have reinterpreted St. Anselm of Canterbury's famous *credo ut intelligam* ("I believe so that I may understand")[38] along Kantian or "practical" lines. Searching for some insight into the mystery of God, St. Anselm regarded faith as a prerequisite for understanding: faith provided the correct point of view, so to speak. Emerson's prerequisite for insight, on the other hand, is obedience to the moral law. For him it is morality that provides the correct point of view: "Goodness is the right *place* of the mind. . . . Man . . . must be set in the right place to see or the order [of the whole] will become confusion to his microscopic optics" (*JMN* 3:269). This morality-based epistemology informs Emerson's argument most strikingly in *Nature*, where "the redemption of the soul" supplies the correct point of view. Without such redemption, "the axis of vision is not coincident with the axis of things, and so they appear not transparent but opake" (*CW* 1:43).

Like Kant, Emerson insists that freedom, the sine qua non of morality, is "known" through the practical, not the theoretical reason:

> We know that we are free to all the purposes of moral account-ability. . . . When we say that we are free we rest on a conviction that is too mighty for reason and must stand whether reason can sanction it or no. We feel in every action that we may forbear, that we are unquestioned masters of our own purposes. . . . Our whole worth depends upon our freedom. A man is respectable only as far as his actions are his own. (*CS* 2:71)

By "reason" in this passage, Emerson obviously means the theoretical reason. It is interesting to note that theoretical ignorance is actually

---

38. "Neque enim quaero intelligere ut credam, sed credo ut intelligam" ("I do not, in fact, seek to understand in order that I may believe, but I believe so that I may understand.")—St. Anselm, *Proslogion, Opera Omnia*, 1:100.

a condition of the exercise of moral freedom. According to Kant, metaphysical arrogance distorts the claims of the reason, in the process weakening the legitimate demands of the pure practical reason and giving rise to every imaginable form of anti-moral, because dogmatically binding, superstition or unbelief. Hence Kant's famous claim that he had to destroy knowledge (that is, metaphysical pseudo-knowledge) in order to make room for faith (faith in such postulates of the practical reason as God, immortality, and freedom).[39] Coleridge adopted this view: for him also, our acquisition of true metaphysical knowledge (if such a thing were possible) would have destroyed our moral freedom. He puts it best in a statement that Emerson seems to echo. Discussing the existence of God, Coleridge writes: "It could not be intellectually more evident without becoming morally less effective; without counteracting its own end by sacrificing the *life* of faith to the cold mechanism of a worthless because compulsory assent."[40] Commenting on immortality, Emerson writes in the same vein:

> If a greater knowledge of the future state were given us, it would destroy our freedom, and so make us incapable of virtue. . . . If the mist of our ignorance should roll away . . . we should be bribed to goodness. We should be frighted from crime. We should have no choice in our action; no liberty; no virtue. (CS 2:178)

In addition to the primacy of the practical reason (or pure reason in its practical function) and the cognitive role of the practical reason, there is a third aspect to the relation of ethics to knowledge, namely, the inexplicability of the moral law itself. In Kant's view, to explain anything is to bring it within the framework of the laws governing phenomenal experience. What has no empirical reality for us is not susceptible of explanation. Kant often refers to Ideas of the Reason as "mere Ideas" precisely because they have no empirically accessible content and are, therefore, unknowable and inexplicable.[41] As a product of pure reason, the moral law is part of what Kant variously calls the "noumenal" (as opposed to "phenomenal"), "intelligible" (as

39. Kant, *Kritik der reinen Vernunft* B xxx.

40. Coleridge, *Biographia Literaria,* 1:203.

41. See, e.g., *Kritik der reinen Vernunft* A 328–29/B 384–85; *Grundlegung zur Metaphysik der Sitten, Gesammelte Schriften,* 4:459.

opposed to "sensible"), or "thinkable" (as opposed to "knowable") world. Our *actions* in response to the moral law, like all actions, inevitably occur in the phenomenal world, but the law itself—absolute, unconditioned, universally binding—not only is not derived from experience but transcends all possible experience and has, consequently, no *knowable* content. We become aware of the law not as knowable object but as absolute command, as moral obligation. The law is thus for us a "practical," not a "theoretical," reality.

Emerson's views reveal a similar combination of moral absoluteness and theoretical agnosticism. Commenting upon the moral sentiment, he declares: "An eternal, uniform necessity at the heart of being requires ever the good act at the hands of each soul. The sentiment is the ultimate fact, and cannot be defined. . . . It is the law of soul" (*EL* 2:345). In another discussion of the moral law, he tells his audience: "You cannot conceive yourself as existing . . . absolved from this law which you carry within you. It can't be defined but it is understood by us all" (*CS* 2:31). By "understood" Emerson obviously means "familiar to us through our moral sense," as opposed to "definable," that is, "subject to intellectual determination." Emerson's attitude here resembles St. Augustine's toward time: Augustine said that he was aware of time but could not answer any questions concerning it. In other words, he could not translate his experience of time into theoretical statement.[42] The law of ethics, Emerson writes elsewhere, "cannot yet be stated, it is so simple" (*EL* 1:370)—so *absolutely* simple (Latin *simplex:* uncompounded, one) as to be untranslatable into predicates, inaccessible to analysis. Emerson's connecting simplicity with ineffability may be due in part to the influence of Mary Rotch, a Quaker who made a deep impression on him in the early 1830s. As he noted in his journal, Mary Rotch was spiritually guided by something that was neither an "impression" nor an "intimation" nor an "oracle": "It was none of them. It was so simple it could hardly be spoken of" (*JMN* 4:263).[43] Theoretical unknowability is also in Emerson's mind when he draws his audience's attention to the fact that moral

42. "Quid est ergo tempus? Si nemo ex me quaerat, scio; si quaerenti explicare uelim, nescio" ("What, then, is time? When nobody asks me, I know; when I want to explain it to someone asking me, I don't know.")—St. Augustine, *Confessions* 11.14 (17).

43. For an insightful discussion of Mary Rotch's effect on Emerson, see Richardson, *Emerson: The Mind on Fire,* 157–63.

problems such as "the origin of evil" and "human liberty" have baffled thinkers through the ages; consequently, "it is fair to conclude that here lies a great question, to settle which the human understanding is perhaps inadequate" (*CS* 2:46). Through the moral sentiment, the human confronts the *ought*—absolute as command but, we are told once more, theoretically ungraspable: "*He ought.* He knows the sense of that grand word, though his analysis fails entirely to render account of it" (*CW* 1:77). *How* the moral sentiment commands, "we pretend not to define. . . . It passes understanding" (*W* 10:98). We only know *that* it commands. For Emerson the moral law, in short, is the *ens realissimum* ("most real being"). Its reality is unconditioned and self-derived, and, while transcending our understanding, to us humans inescapable.

Emerson's most purely Kantian text on this subject is to be found in his 1835 formulation of what he called "the First Philosophy" (*JMN* 5:270–73)—a label intended to stress the intrinsic importance of what he was trying to say ("First Philosophy" translates Aristotle's *prōtē philosophia*, Aristotle's own term for what was later called his metaphysics):[44]

> By the First Philosophy, is meant the original laws of the mind. It is the Science of what *is*, in distinction from what *appears*. It is one mark of them that their enunciation awakens the feeling of the Moral sublime. . . . These laws are Ideas of the Reason, and so are obeyed easier than expressed. They astonish the Understanding and seem to it gleams of a world in which we do not live. (*JMN* 5:270)

"Ideas of the Reason," laws commanding obedience but defying articulation and even understanding, part of a world transcending our experience but awakening "the feeling of the Moral sublime"—the Kantian flavor is unmistakable.[45] Emerson apparently owed his Kantian "Ideas

44. Emerson apparently derived the Aristotelian term, in its Latin form (*prima philosophia*), through Francis Bacon (*JMN* 3:360). Aristotle, Bacon, and Emerson use "first philosophy" in very different senses, but for all three the term designates what they consider most important or most fundamental in human thought. It is also noteworthy that the father of modern philosophy, Descartes, titled his philosophical masterpiece *Meditationes de prima philosophia* (1641).

45. For Kant's association of the moral law with the sublime (*das Erhabene, die Erhabenheit*) see, e.g., *Kritik der praktischen Vernunft, Gesammelte Schriften* 5:85–89, 117.

of the Reason" to the mediation of Coleridge. A couple of months before writing his "First Philosophy" statement, he remarked in his journal: "I should be glad of a Catalogue of Ideas; objects of the Reason, as Conceptions are objects of the Understanding. Mr. Coleridge names . . . God, Free will, Justice, Holiness, as Ideas in Morals" (*JMN* 5:29). Emerson here not only revealed his awareness of the Kantian distinction between Ideas of the Reason and Concepts of the Understanding, but as the editors of the *Journals* indicate (*JMN* 5:29n86), he *added* "God" to Coleridge's list of Ideas (which he found in *The Friend*), thus making it all the more completely Kantian.

Daniel Howe notes that the Harvard Unitarians were deeply committed to belief in a personal and supernatural God, whose existence they "proved" through the teleological argument (the argument from design). Kant rejected all "proofs" of the existence of God—whether ontological, cosmological, or physico-theological (as he called teleological)—and made God, as already indicated, a postulate of the practical reason.[46] "This," Howe comments, "was too much for a Harvard Unitarian to swallow; God could not be a mere hypothesis."[47] Emerson apparently had no such theological qualms. He regarded the attribution of personality to God as evidence of a confusion of planes, that is, of an Idea of the Reason being reduced to the level of sensibilia: "The Ideas of the Reason assume a new appearance as they descend into the Understanding. Invested with space & time they walk in masquerade. It [the Understanding] *incarnates* the Ideas of Reason. Thus the gods of the ancient Greeks are all Ideas" (*JMN* 5:272; emphasis added). Similarly, "Heaven is the projection of the Ideas of Reason on the plane of the Understanding" (*JMN* 5:273). The Divinity School "Address" was Emerson's strongest protest against such a confusion of planes, which in his view resulted in Christianity having become mythological, like "the poetic teaching of Greece and of Egypt, before." There is, simply, "no doctrine of the Reason which will bear to be taught by the Understanding" (*CW* 1:81). Stripped of anthropomorphic and other pictorial associations, the God of the Divinity School "Address" is law, practically commanding but theoretically unknowable, accessible not through doctrine or dogma but

---

46. Kant, *Kritik der reinen Vernunft* A 592/B 620-A 630/B 658.
47. Howe, *The Unitarian Conscience,* 76–80.

through the moral sentiment (*CW* 1:81). Emerson never abandoned this conviction. As he put it in a late lecture, "The populace drag down the gods to their own level. . . . God . . . [is] known only as pure law. . . . Every nation is degraded by the goblins it worships instead of this Deity" (*W* 10:104). Like Kant, Emerson wants to remove all pseudo-knowledge of God; his pantheistic God is quite as much a transcendent Idea as is the personal God *postulated* by the Kantian practical reason and thus equally defies conceptualization. Emerson's pantheistic God arises in human consciousness first and foremost as all-pervasive lawfulness.

Stephen Whicher remarked that Emerson's was a mind "precipitated into originality . . . by contact with 'modern philosophy.' "[48] Emerson's receptivity to Kantian ideas in ethics not only distinguished him from his philosophically more conservative Unitarian contemporaries but also was an important aspect of his creative engagement with modern thought—an engagement that helped make him perhaps intellectually the most fascinating figure in our literature.

48. Whicher, *Freedom and Fate*, 181.

3

Self-Realization

*W*hereas on the metaethical level Emerson is an intuitionist, on the level of normative ethics he espouses a position best characterized as self-realizationism. In chapter 2, I pointed to the distinction between teleological and deontological theories in normative ethics. Self-realizationism is most aptly described as a modified form of teleological ethics. The basic similarity between self-realizationism and standard teleological ethics consists in their both judging actions in the light of ends to be achieved. They both regard the consequences of an action—its promotion or realization of some good—as the defining criterion of the action's moral value. They are thus both at variance with deontological ethics, which considers actions to be right (or wrong) "in themselves," that is, in the light of some absolutist notion of duty or obligation. Still, there is a significant difference between teleological and self-realizationist ethics. A teleological theory presupposes a relatively clear sense of the end aimed at, whether this be the *eudaimonia* of Aristotle, the *apatheia* of the Stoics, the *ataraxia* (imperturbability) of Epicurus, or "the greatest happiness of the greatest number" of Francis Hutcheson and the Utilitarians. Self-realizationist ethics, while goal-directed by definition, is less certain about the "content" of the goal because it lacks adequate knowledge about the latent, yet-to-be-explored-and-developed "content" of the self. In other words, in self-realizationist ethics humans are *in search of* the self that they are duty-bound to realize, and they have, consequently, no clear idea of the end to be achieved. Self-realization, to be sure, *is* the end, but in view of the indeterminacy of the self before its realization, this end is indefinite. It is also, obviously, an end forever unattainable: no degree of self-realization can ever be assumed to have realized the full potential of the self. This is all the more so since the self is no objective substance but is constituted, to a significant degree, by a process of self-interpretation and self-articulation, as Emerson well understood: "The man is only half himself, the other half is his expression" (*CW* 3:4). Such a process is unending: every self-interpretation, every self-articulation adds to the self, constitutes a new aspect of the self—which calls for further interpretation and new attempts at articulation. Unendingly, "we study to utter our painful secret" (*CW* 3:4).

Ethical labels often obscure more than they clarify, as a result of either jargonistic excess (the current affliction) or lack of specificity. Laurence Lockridge's witty question highlights the former problem: "Was Aristotle an act-utilitarian cognitivist non-definist, or something worse?"[1] The term "self-realizationism," on the other hand, is definitionally weak because it seems to lack specificity: students of ethics have used it to designate the most varied ethical orientations. Broadly speaking, one might claim that all ethics is concerned with human self-realization, in the sense that all schools of ethics have been concerned with promoting that which is "best" in and for us, and thus with bringing our ideal human self-image, however defined, as close to reality as possible. In this broad sense, Socrates, Aristotle, the Stoics, Thomas Aquinas, and Shaftesbury, to name but a few, are all self-realizationists.

As my opening remarks suggest, I am using "self-realizationism" in a narrower sense, limiting it to the ethical thought of those for whom the very notion of "self" had become problematical. The first thinkers fully to confront the crisis of the self were the post-Kantian idealists and, in literature, the Romantics. It was not until the Romantic age, in other words, that self-realizationism truly came into its own as an ethical theory. It then not only gained in definition and depth but also acquired a special urgency. The impact of democratic and egalitarian ideals, the growth of mass culture, the increasing complexity and interdependence of modern life, urbanization and industrialization, nascent socialism, and, on a more speculative level, historicism—all contributed to what Emerson called the "fading" of

1. Lockridge, *The Ethics of Romanticism,* 139.

"our pretension . . . of self-hood" (*W* 6:320). Reaction to these threats to the integrity and viability of the self took various forms, such as compensatory hero worship, the cult of the rebel, one-man reform like Thoreau's, cosmic self-assertion à la Whitman, or advocacy of a return to nature in order to find one's true self in solitude. Emerson's anti-historicist gesture is significant in this context. In his lecture series on "The Philosophy of History," as his editors point out, he "invert[ed] the organic theories of the day to merge history into the individual rather than to merge the individual into the process of history" (*EL* 2:3). But the reaction that really concerns me here is the ethical one: self-realizationism. Understanding its true significance requires a closer look at the predicament of the self, as Emerson perceived it.

Most striking about Emerson's treatment of questions concerning the self, personal identity, the "I—this thought which is called I" (*CW* 1:204), is the frequency with which he confesses that they pass all understanding. He gave all but aphoristic expression to his sense of the mystery of the self in an 1837 journal entry: "Hard as it is to describe God, it is harder to describe the Individual" (*JMN* 5:337). Emerson's eloquence about the importance, the supremacy, the centrality of the self is matched by an equally eloquent skepticism, as when he calls the self the human's "Unknown Centre" or considers the self to be rooted in "that Fact which cannot be spoken, or defined, nor even thought." And yet, as every reader of Emerson knows, this unknown self is the source of all moral empowerment. From it "follows easily [man's] whole ethics. . . . The height, the deity of man is to be self-sustained" (*CW* 1:203–4). In "The American Scholar," Emerson emphasizes the supreme duty of self-trust, which he considers the source of all virtues (*CW* 1:63). But why should we trust the self? "For this self-trust, the reason is deeper than can be fathomed,—darker than can be enlightened" (*CW* 1:65).

This imbalance between the richness of moral self-reference and the poverty of self-knowledge is a characteristic Emerson's thought shared with that of many of his contemporaries. It is traceable to that radical desubstantialization of the self in eighteenth-century thought, for which Hume and Kant were chiefly responsible. Hume denied substance to the self and considered personal identity a mental fiction. "There are some philosophers," Hume writes, "who imagine we are every moment intimately conscious of what we call our SELF; that we feel its existence and its continuance in existence; and are certain, beyond the evidence of demonstration, both of its perfect identity and simplicity." However, he continues, "when I enter most intimately into what I call *myself*, I always stumble on some particular perception or other, of heat or cold, light or shade, love or hatred, pain or pleasure. I never can catch *myself* at any time without a perception, and never can observe any thing but the perception." The question of identity is not, therefore, a relevant philosophical question at all. It is a linguistic or, as Hume puts it, a "merely verbal" question. In sum, "all the nice and subtle questions concerning personal identity . . . are to be regarded rather as grammatical than as philosophical difficulties."[2]

Kant in his turn denied substance to the self. The "I" has no content. It is not a subject of experience. It functions merely, Kant says, as "a transcendental subject of the thoughts." As such, it "equals X," that is, "this I, or he, or it (the thing) that thinks"—a statement that clearly anticipates Nietzsche's unsettling critique of the notion that the predicate "think" presupposes "I" as subject. We become aware of this "I" only through its predicates, that is, through our thoughts. We can never have the least awareness of an "I" in isolation from the thoughts it thinks. The "I" itself is no concept, but "a mere consciousness accompanying all concepts" (*ein bloßes Bewußtsein, das alle Begriffe begleitet*). Kant calls the a priori form or structure enabling the "I" to unify the manifold of perception into an object of thought "the transcendental unity of apperception" (*die transscendentale Einheit der Apperception*). In other words, there can be no object of thought, no concept, without a corresponding "objective unity of consciousness"—"unity," because only through what can be united in *one* consciousness can there be an "I think" at all; "objective," because, as H. J. Paton puts it, "the self-consciousness of thinking is only a consciousness of the principles (or conceptions) in accordance with which it functions."[3] Unlike Hume, for whom the self is "nothing but a bundle or collection of different perceptions, which succeed each other with an inconceivable rapidity, and are in a perpetual flux and movement," Kant thus maintains the

---

2. Hume, *A Treatise of Human Nature*, 251–52, 262.
3. Kant, *Kritik der reinen Vernunft* A 345–46/B 404, B 139; Nietzsche, *Jenseits von Gut und Böse* § 17, *Sämtliche Werke*, 5: 31; H. J. Paton, *The Categorical Imperative: A Study in Kant's Moral Philosophy*, 237.

unity of the subject. However, as already indicated, the Kantian "I think" provides no insight into the "I" beyond pointing to its necessary logical function. In sum, Kant emphasizes that even though my "I" is a constant in all my thinking, it does not at all follow that my "I" has independent existence or substance *(daß ich als Object ein für mich selbst bestehendes Wesen oder Substanz sei).*[4] On this last point, Kant is in complete agreement with Hume.

Hume and Kant between them, Stanley Cavell suggests, shattered all hope of success for Emerson's (or, for that matter, any other Romantic's) attempts at "a resubstantializing of the self." Kant's influence proved especially decisive. Chief, and most problematic, among his legacies to Romanticism was precisely, in the words of Philippe Lacoue-Labarthe and Jean-Luc Nancy, the "weakening of the subject," the anguished response to which was perhaps best captured by Teufelsdröckh's "unanswerable question: Who am *I*; the thing that can say '*I*'?" Yet, as Lacoue-Labarthe and Nancy also point out, the Romantic "weakening of the subject is accompanied by an apparently compensatory 'promotion' of the *moral subject*." Here again, Kant showed the way. According to Bernard Williams, "this transcendental *I*, which is [merely] formal in the case of thought in general, is made by Kant to do much more in relation to morality."[5] It is in the context of morality that the "I" becomes truly a person.

Personhood is, however, a Kantian "Idea of the Reason," and as such it transcends all our experience and cannot, therefore, become an object of theoretical knowledge. But although theoretically empty, Ideas of the Reason, as we saw in chapter 2, have great regulative or heuristic value, especially in relation to moral thought. As Roger Sullivan points out, "Since moral reasoning is concerned with the way we *ought* to behave, our moral life is defined by a whole range of standards or ideals or models of perfection, none of which is or can be found . . . in the world of theoretical experience."[6] Personhood is such a standard or ideal. Lewis White Beck (who prefers the term "personality") puts

---

4. Hume, *A Treatise of Human Nature*, 252; Kant, *Kritik der reinen Vernunft* B 407.

5. Cavell, *In Quest of the Ordinary*, xii. Philippe Lacoue-Labarthe and Jean-Luc Nancy, *The Literary Absolute: The Theory of Literature in German Romanticism*, 30–31; Thomas Carlyle, *Sartor Resartus*, 53. Williams, *Ethics and the Limits of Philosophy*, 211n18.

6. Sullivan, *Immanuel Kant's Moral Theory*, 18.

it thus: "Personality . . . is an Idea of reason, and personality is not a given. We are persons, but no finite sensuous being is fully adequate to the Idea of personality. In human nature, considered empirically, we find at most only a 'predisposition to personality.' " Although as an Idea of the Reason personhood does not contribute to our theoretical self-*knowledge*, it is, in Kant's words, "necessary and sufficient to practical [i.e., moral] use." And as Beck concludes, this practical role leads to "a richer conception of personality than that of the transcendental unity of apperception."[7]

This promotion of the "moral subject" characterizes the thought of many of Kant's successors. Fichte, centering his entire philosophical system in the "absolute ego," conceived of that ego as positing itself through activity. The Fichtean ego is not a "being," but an endless striving toward self-realization through overcoming the non-ego, itself posited by the ego and constituting an "other," "limitation," or "obstacle" that provides *necessary* scope for the ego's self-realizationist striving. The moral implications are obvious. Windelband summarizes Fichte's position thus: "The inmost essence of the ego . . . is its action, directed only toward itself, determined only by itself,—the *autonomy of the ethical reason.* . . . The I is the ethical will, and the world *is the material of duty put into sensuous form.*" In a similar vein Coleridge considered "the free-will" to be "our only absolute *self*"; as he told Emerson when they met in 1833, "the will [is] that by which a person is a person" (CW 5:6). Carlyle raised the moral self by reinterpreting Kant's pure reason as "the moral intuition of the world of eternal values." Emerson, in his turn, conceived of the self primarily in moral terms. He is eloquent about self-trust, self-reliance, self-dependence, and self-culture, but he has little to say about self-knowledge beyond asserting that it is unattainable. In his search for a morally competent self he is even willing to accept foundations for it that some of his predecessors had declared invalid. Hume, for instance, had considered and rejected memory as a source of personal identity.[8] But

7. Beck, *A Commentary on Kant's "Critique of Practical Reason,"* 227; Kant, *Kritik der reinen Vernunft* A 365–66.

8. Wilhelm Windelband, *A History of Philosophy,* 2:594. Coleridge, *Biographia Literaria,* 1:114. For an erudite discussion of Coleridge's "will" in the context of relevant German thought from Böhme through Schelling, see McFarland, *Coleridge and the*

for Emerson, "Memory . . . is the thread on which the beads of man are strung, making the personal identity which is necessary to moral action" (*W* 12:90). He was, to the mind of his contemporaries, on surer and philosophically more respectable ground when he claimed that "man is man by virtue of willing, not by virtue of knowing and understanding" (*CW* 4:70). He was as convinced as Coleridge that "the will . . . is the seat of personality," that "the will constitutes the man" (*CW* 4:54; *W* 10:91).

Recognizing that the self is theoretically indefinable compounds the problem of teleological indeterminacy that, as already indicated, seems inescapable in self-realizationist ethics. Yet, since actions have to be judged in the light of the end to be achieved, there is a need for criteria beyond the obvious and indefinite one according to which an action is right or wrong on the basis of its advancing or impeding the self in its progress toward self-realization. Emerson the intuitionist (metaethically speaking) perceives two absolute values inherent in the transcendent Self: *harmony* and *universality*. For the individual, subjective, empirical self, both are ideals—ultimately unattainable but to be striven for—and criteria by which to judge actions. The individual has to approximate, to the highest degree possible, the transcendent entity that Emerson variously calls Self, Soul, Spirit, or God, and he or she does so by striving for the harmony (which Emerson sometimes also calls symmetry) and the universality that are constitutive of the Self transcendentally conceived.[9] Self-realization thus amounts to the

---

Pantheist Tradition, 328–30. Carlyle, *Sartor Resartus,* 65n4. Hume, *A Treatise of Human Nature,* 261–62.

9. It should be obvious by now that I am using "transcendent" and "transcendental" in the loose Emersonian rather than the strict Kantian sense of these terms. Put as simply as possible, Kant used *transscendental* to refer to knowledge concerned not with objects, but with our mode of cognition of objects so far as this is possible a priori; he used *transscendent* to designate cognitive principles *(Grundsätze)* directed (fruitlessly) to what lies beyond the limits of possible experience *(Kritik der reinen Vernunft* B 25, A 296/B 352, A 327/B 384). Emerson's "transcendental" and "transcendent" have little connection with either Kantian term. Emerson uses "transcendental" as virtually synonymous with "intuitive" and "transcendent" to designate what is accessible only through intuition (in the exalted Emersonian, not the humble Kantian, sense of "intuition," i.e., through immediate, noninferential, suprarational apprehension; Kant, by contrast, considered intuition *[Anschauung]* to be purely sensuous *[sinnlich]*—*Kriktik der reinen Vernunft* A 35/B 52, B 148–49, 159, 302n). In "The Transcendentalist," Emerson attributed to Kant the notion that *"Transcendental* forms" are "intuitions of the mind" and traced to "the extraordinary profoundness and precision" of Kant's thought

self striving to become the Self, and more fully than anything else, such striving confronts the individual with "the moral fact of the Unattainable, the flying Perfect . . . at once the inspirer and the condemner of every success" (*CW* 2:179).

Emerson regarded discord and dissonance as inherent in our awareness of our own individuality. As conscious individuals we cannot help realizing that our very self-definition involves separation, alienation, and disharmony, and this realization is as necessary to our self-concept as it is painful. In "Experience," Emerson stated our problem in all its poignancy and finality: "It is very unhappy, but too late to be helped, the discovery we have made, that we exist. That discovery is called the Fall of Man" (*CW* 3:43). Years later he speculated: "It may be that we have no right here as individuals; that the existence of an embodied man marks fall & sin. . . . We have stopped, we have stagnated, we have appropriated or become selfish. . . . It is for this reason that we are dualists . . . and [confront] the inexplicable jangle of Fate & freedom, matter & spirit" (*JMN* 14:337). Human striving for harmony is a never-ending effort to overcome the duality, the discordance at the heart of our experience, and this striving takes place on three levels: *conscience, character,* and *culture.*

Emerson identifies conscience with the moral sentiment and with "the moral reason of man" (*CS* 1:116; 3:19), and given his belief in the primacy of the moral (or practical) reason, he not surprisingly considers conscience to be determinative of individual identity. Conscience dominates all the powers of the mind and "gives to all these powers the unity of one moral being" (*CS* 1:117). Conscience also gives access to transcendent reality: "this Conscience, this Reason . . . is the Presence of God to man" (*CS* 4:175). Through conscience as a cognitive faculty the individual achieves identification, albeit partial, with God. Emerson here embraces the ancient idea, stated aphoristically by Heraclitus and more poetically by Plotinus, that all knowledge presupposes a certain similarity between the knower and the object of knowledge.[10] In Emerson's words, "You cannot form an idea of that

---

the prestige of Kantian terminology, so that "whatever belongs to the class of intuitive thought, is popularly called at the present day *Transcendental*" (*CW* 1:207).

10. For Heraclitus, see *CS* 3:190n3; for Plotinus, *Enneads* 1.6.9. Plotinus' statement was apparently a favorite among the Romantics. Coleridge quoted it in its original

to which there is nothing resembling in yourself," or "What is unlike us, we cannot perceive" (*CS* 3:181, 190). But since the identification of the individual self with God is incomplete, the self experiences transcendent reality "in the form of a law" (*CS* 3:43), that is, as a moral imperative commanding ever-closer identification. As already indicated, the very concept of obligation, of "ought," makes sense only in reference to a self that is finite and imperfect. Conscience commands precisely because it is that "something in us which is higher and better than we" (*CS* 4:175).

Conscience is thus inevitably a cause of disharmony, of a divided self in which one part legislates for and commands the other. We have an example here of the mind interiorizing the master-slave relationship and thus transforming itself into what Hegel famously called "the unhappy consciousness" *(das unglückliche Bewußtsein)* and Emerson "the double consciousness" (*CS* 4:215).[11] There are, Emerson says, "two selfs . . . within this erring, passionate, mortal self, sits a supreme, calm, immortal mind, whose powers I do not know, but it is stronger than I am, it is wiser than I am" (*CS* 4:215). Another way of expressing this self-division is to make conscience the seat of guilt. By its very nature, guilt manifests the self's awareness of the discrepancy between what is and what ought to be. Guilt derives from the felt contrast between the self as ideal perceiver of law and the self as inadequate executor of law. The perfection of the moral law is a source of joy when accepted theoretically, but it stands as a perpetual reproof to practical ability: "Pleasant it is to the soul, painful it is to the conscience to recognize . . . the fixed eternity of moral laws" (*JMN* 3:286).

One possible road to harmony, obviously, is for the self to act in obedience to the moral law. Emerson regards conscience as the faculty of not only moral cognition but also moral motivation. Conscience "is not a simple perception that one action is good and another evil and ending there," but "it *includes a command to adopt or to reject;*—to perform one action, and to forbear another" (*CS* 1:191). The exact relationship, however, among conscience, motive, and act troubled

---

Greek at the end of chapter 6 of *Biographia Literaria,* and it inspired poetic renderings by Blake *(For the Sexes: The Gates of Paradise,* Frontispiece, *Poetry and Prose,* 568) and Goethe ("Zahme Xenien" iii, *Gedenkausgabe* 1:629).

11. Georg Wilhelm Friedrich Hegel, *Phänomenologie des Geistes,* 158.

Emerson as much as it did his Unitarian contemporaries.[12] He had, furthermore, serious doubts about the moral quality of human motives and about the moral status of action as such.

Emerson's doubts about motives arose from his sense of human self-opaqueness, of the difficulty of our reading completely and correctly our own consciousness. David Robinson claims that Emerson's "fundamental moral principle" was "disinterestedness"—that is, "the willingness to elevate principle over self-interest"—so that, paradoxically, in Emerson's "philosophy of self-culture, self-sacrifice was the highest achievement of the self," and "selfless devotion to another . . . becomes a culmination of the culture of the individual." I am troubled by this claim because Emerson strikes me as a little too "Nietzschean" to see much virtue in selflessness; but even if one accepted it, the fact remains that we can never be really sure about the purity of our motives, that is, about the degree to which our actions are dictated by our sense of moral obligation versus the degree to which they are dictated by prudence or self-interest. Believing that our motives are purely moral is probably but one more example of our infinite capacity for self-delusion, "so difficult is it to read our own consciousness without mistakes" (*JMN* 4:312). From this point of view even the self-abnegation of the saint is suspect: does he or she sacrifice so much here on earth *for the sake of* a much more attractive posthumous reward? Does the Christian martyr court martyrdom (thus evincing perhaps, as Nietzsche suggested, displaced suicidal tendencies) *for the sake of* eternal bliss? Even a qualified "yes" in answer to these questions would introduce an element of self-interest detracting from the moral purity of the saint's and martyr's lives or actions. While still a clergyman, Emerson acknowledged that "it is most true that holding the belief of the immortality of the soul, we cannot sever our interest from our duty" (*CS* 2:31); throughout his intellectual career, he recognized the near impossibility of disentangling the pursuit of virtue from considerations of personal advantage (however defined—happiness, health, economic independence, etc.). Such perplexities of the spirit drove Spinoza to the drastic conclusion that he who truly loves God "cannot seek that God should love him in return." They also induced Jonathan Edwards's disciple Samuel Hopkins to express

---

12. Howe, *The Unitarian Conscience,* 56–64.

the notorious view that the believer shows truly devout disinterestedness by being content to be damned for the glory of God—a view that Emerson considered "an extravagance" and an "absurdity," yet having an undeniable element of the "generous and sublime" in it (*CS* 2:33).[13]

Emerson was also keenly aware of the frequent lack of correspondence between motive and action. In 1832 he even considered writing a book whose third chapter was to be devoted to defending the proposition "That good motives are at the bottom of [many] bad actions" (*JMN* 3:316; the square brackets are Emerson's). Conversely, "good actions may be done from bad motives" (*CS* 2:46). The discrepancy between motive and action and its attendant moral confusion explain why conscience expresses itself more clearly and emphatically in the negative, that is, commanding the *omission* ("thou shalt not") rather than the commission ("thou shalt") of an action. As Emerson says, "we can all feel we are rather commanded what not to do than urged to any performance" (*CS* 1:193). A command in the negative (e.g., "thou shalt not steal") is clear and does not allow motives to come into play: we are told *not* to act. A command in the positive (e.g., "thou shalt help the poor") is vague (*how* should one help the poor?), and its execution is "corruptible" by impure motives (does one help the poor out of self-interest, out of a desire, for instance, to help prevent social unrest, which might threaten one's socially and economically privileged position?).[14] Action has the further drawback of imposing limitations upon the freedom inherent in conscience as moral lawgiver. Like its ontological and epistemological parallels (Spirit and Reason), conscience (the moral sentiment) is free of the limitations characterizing the inferior realms of Nature, Understanding, and conventional morality. Action is an irruption of freedom into the realm of necessity—the realm of Nature, natural law, phenomena—and thus inevitably partakes of its limitations. The "perfect freedom" that Emerson claims to be "the only counterpart to nature" (*JMN* 14:53) is

13. Robinson, *Emerson and the Conduct of Life*, 137, 110, 166. Friedrich Nietzsche, *Die fröhliche Wissenschaft* § 131, *Sämtliche Werke*, 3:485. Baruch Spinoza, *Ethica* 5.19. On Hopkins, see Fiering, *Jonathan Edwards's Moral Thought*, 351.

14. For interesting Kantian parallels to Emerson's argument, see Sullivan, *Immanuel Kant's Moral Theory*, 50–54.

inevitably compromised through the fusion of conscience and nature in moral *action*.

Although necessary to harmonious self-realization, as will become clearer when we discuss character and culture, moral action does not enjoy the high status that Emerson grants to moral principles. His commitment to an idealistic ethic made his preference for the purity of principle over the mixed nature of action inevitable. He gives voice to this preference with unrelenting frequency. "In the eyes of God," he assures his audience, "not the *actions* but the *principles* of moral beings are regarded. . . . Principles are important . . . actions have no other importance than that derived from the principle" (*CS* 1:179). What matters is the moral status of the principles motivating actions, not the actions "for themselves" (*CS* 1:181). Hence when moral littleness prevails, it "consists in the purpose not in the act" (*CS* 2:153). Such emphasis on the motivating principle precluded Emerson's seeing much merit in standard teleological ethics: if actions are unimportant in themselves, neither do they derive importance from "their effects on the world" (*CS* 1:181). The well-informed moralist "does not judge of actions, by their effects, but by their principle" (*CS* 1:200). On the same grounds Emerson dismisses "mere bene*ficence*," which is "good for nothing without it is accompanied by bene*volence* or the will to do good" (*CS* 2:134; emphasis added). In sum, since "the merit of all action is measured by the principle" and since all action "governed by any less than the highest [principle]" is morally flawed, we need to embrace "this duty of steady Reflection upon the principles by which we should live" (*CS* 2:73, 127).

By thus emphasizing the primacy of principle and making the inner determinations of conscience the primary focus of moral life, Emerson embraces an ethical position that is, once again, remarkably similar to Kant's. For Kant, moral life was primarily a matter of "intention," "mental disposition," "the inner legislation of reason," and not of "performances in the world." The worth of the good will, for example, "cannot be diminished or increased, and cannot be outweighed or dimmed, either by any consequences or by the varying contexts in which it may be found." We should strive, of course, to carry out the decisions of conscience (such endeavor proves the depth of our inner commitment), but what really matters is the quality, the purity of our intentions, whether or not we succeed in realizing them. Equally inner-directed, and equally Kantian, is Emerson's emphasis on reverence or respect, on "the sincere veneration . . . of duty," "this devout reverence of Duty," as an important factor in moral life (*CS* 4:139). Kant defined duty as "the requirement to act out of respect for the law" *(die Nothwendigkeit einer Handlung aus Achtung fürs Gesetz)*; indeed, he regarded such respect as the one unexceptionable motive to moral action. But since, in Kant's view, the moral law is a product of our reason, the truly moral person acts out of respect for himself or herself as a rational being. As moral self-legislator the human, *qua* rational being, possesses absolute worth and intrinsic dignity *(dignitas interna)*, which imbue him or her with the highest self-respect *(die höchste Selbstschätzung)*, with feelings of profound reverence *(reverentia)* toward himself or herself. Such reverence is, in fact, a duty, as is implied by the Kantian definition of duty given above.[15]

Although as an ethical intuitionist Emerson does not embrace Kant's vision of human reason as purely self-legislative, he is as committed as Kant to the view that humans derive their true worth and dignity from their definition as moral beings. Is it not "the noblest attribute in us," Emerson asks rhetorically but emphatically, *"that we are capable of being addressed on the ground of moral principles?"* (*CS* 3:65). Like Kant, furthermore, Emerson believes that self-reverence is not only inspired by this "noblest attribute" but also commanded as a duty. Without self-reverence, without respect for our inward dignity as moral beings, we could not possibly obey the moral law. Emerson, therefore, makes self-reverence the basis of all other duties. Clearly, his ethical intuitionism did not preclude his according self-reverence as great an importance in his moral thought as had resulted from reason's absolute autonomy in Kant's ethics: "The authority of conscience and the love of truth in us is the manifestation of [God]; and therefore let each man . . . *hold his own nature in a reverential awe"* (*CS* 2:254). Kant, of course, would have objected to the terms "God" and "nature" in this statement: he would have regarded both as proof of Emerson's having embraced heteronomy in his moral thinking. As we saw, Kant's entire

---

15. Sullivan, *Immanuel Kant's Moral Theory,* 66–67; Paton, *The Categorical Imperative,* 37. Kant, *Grundlegung zur Metaphysik der Sitten, Gesammelte Schriften,* 4:400; *Kritik der praktischen Vernunft, Gesammelte Schriften* 5:78; *Die Metaphysik der Sitten, Tugendlehre* §11, *Gesammelte Schriften,* 6:434–36.

endeavor was directed to liberating the moral law from any "extrinsic" authority and basing it firmly in autonomous (self-legislative) human reason. Still, the point at issue here is self-reverence, and its degree or intensity is in no way dependent, it appears, on how the moral self is constituted—whether it equals pure practical reason, as in Kant, or involves moral intuitions and man's moral "nature," as in Emerson.

Emerson was aware that "reverence thyself" was an ancient maxim (*CS* 1:163 and n3). He associated it with the Stoics, as in his 1837 lecture on "Ethics": "the sufficient rule of all Ethics is comprised in the Stoical precept, Reverence Thyself" (*EL* 2:152). A year later this became, in the Divinity School "Address," "the great stoical doctrine, Obey thyself" (*CW* 1:82). Stoic ethics held indeed considerable appeal for Emerson. It anchored moral responsibility and moral authority firmly within the individual. According to Ludwig Edelstein, the Stoic knew "that even in the last extremity of moral action he and his reason must be the sole point of reference." Such views resulted, as Herschel Baker points out, "in a strong assertion of personality."[16] But Emerson also sensed the limitations of Stoic self-reverence: as a modern thinker, he found the Stoics lacking in true inwardness, in real self-reflexivity. The Stoics, after all, rooted their ethics in their vision of the cosmos; they made their ethics dependent upon their physics. Such outward orientation proved increasingly unacceptable as Western thought devoted itself to the exploration of an ever-richer, deeper, more complex and problematic human subjectivity (examples are numberless; suffice it to mention St. Augustine, Montaigne, Puritan introspection, and Rousseau). Emersonian self-reverence is thus very different from the Stoical variety, and Emerson knew that on this subject his thought was attuned to that of a philosopher who, though like Emerson respectful of the Stoics, had departed from them radically: "Kant . . . searched the Metaphysics of the Selfreverence which is the favourite position of modern ethics" (*JMN* 9:62).

Unfailing and all-encompassing reverence for oneself as a moral being would result in moral perfection—in a life brought "into harmony with . . . conscience" and in a conscience "put . . . into harmony with the real and eternal" (*CS* 4:206, 235). Another name for this

16. Edelstein, *The Meaning of Stoicism*, 90; Baker, *The Image of Man*, 79.

state would be holiness, which Emerson defines as "the state of man under the dominion of the moral sentiment" (*EL* 2:340). But the very fact that Emerson regards self-reverence as a duty shows, of course, that the dominion of the moral sentiment is incomplete. Though "the good man reveres himself, reveres his conscience" (*CS* 1:163), he is "the good man" precisely because he endeavors to do his duty, an endeavor that would be meaningless on the part of the holy (perfect) man. The conscience even of the good man glimpses harmony only through its unceasing efforts to overcome *dis*harmony. The principle of compensation—"the great law of Compensation in our moral nature" (*JMN* 4:313–14)—plays so prominent a part in Emerson's ethics because he regards conscience as being perpetually in the process of trying to recover its moral "balance." Conscience is endlessly "self-retributive"; indeed, "every moment is a judgment day, because, every act puts the agent in a new condition" (*JMN* 4:46).

There is, however, "a deeper fact in the soul than compensation, to wit, its own nature." In language reminiscent of Meister Eckhart, Böhme (whom Emerson usually calls Behmen), and Schelling, Emerson speaks of the soul as "the aboriginal abyss [the *Abgrund, Ungrund, Urgrund,* or just plain *Grund* of the Germans] of real Being." He also refers to the soul as "Essence, or God." Put differently, "the soul *is*"; it is "the whole"; it equals "Being" (*CW* 2:70). Emerson then tries to establish that Being is harmony, and he does so through a claim that reads like a reply to Spinoza's famous doctrine that all affirmation is negation (in the sense that all affirmation, definition, determination, or identification implies contrastive negation; any concept or thing is what it is by virtue of its *not* being any other concept or thing). According to Emerson, "Being is the vast affirmative, excluding negation" (*CW* 2:70). By denying to Being negation, "the awesome power of the negative" (*die ungeheure Macht des Negativen*), as Hegel called it, Emerson precludes the possibility of any dialectic within Being. Being enjoys the stasis inherent in absolute harmony. Emerson expresses this simply but conclusively: "Being is . . . self-balanced" (*CW* 2:70). His favorite metaphor for the state of moral perfection is health, and since (in ethical contexts) he adopts the Platonic view of health (see chapter 1), he thereby again emphasizes that the essence of perfection is harmony. Plato had adopted the theory of Alcmaeon that "health depends on the . . . 'constitutional balance' between the constituents of the organism." In *The Republic* he established a clear parallel between health as physical harmony and virtue as spiritual harmony.[17] Emerson readily shared such views: "The health which we call Virtue is an equipoise" (*W* 11:392).

The individual conscience recognizes the harmony that is Being as its perfect "other" and as its spiritual destination. The problem, as Thoreau said, is "how to . . . actually migrate thither."[18] At present, Emerson suggests, this end is attainable only in those rare states of absolute identification of self with Being and attendant "loss" of self. Examples would be ecstasy, as in the "transparent eye-ball" experience in *Nature*, in which state the soul beholds "virtue, and not duties" (*CW* 1:10, 131); prayer, rightly conceived, which is "the soliloquy of a beholding and jubilant soul . . . the spirit of God pronouncing his works good" (*CW* 2:44); and the absolute subjection of self to moral principle: "If a man is at heart just, then in so far is he God; the safety of God, the immortality of God, the majesty of God do enter into that man with justice" (*CW* 1:78). Such states, of course, are as rare as they are transcendent. As Emerson says, "Our faith comes in moments; our vice is habitual" (*CW* 2:159).

17. For Emerson's awareness of Schelling's *Grund* and *Abgrund*—"the Ground or Abyss which Schelling so celebrates"—see *JMN* 6:312, 9:223. Much earlier, at the age of nineteen, Emerson spoke of "that Platonic dream, that the soul of the individual was but an emanation from the Abyss of Deity" (*JMN* 2:6). Both "emanation" and "Abyss" indicate that this statement is Gnostic and Plotinian rather than Platonic. Christian Gnostics like Valentinus (100–165) spoke of God as the unknown Deep or Abyss *(buthos)* which "realizes" itself through a hierarchically ordered series of thirty emanations. Similarly, the One *(to hen)* of Plotinus, from which everything rational, spiritual, and material emanates, is absolutely inconceivable. It is "something" of which nothing whatsoever can be predicated, and it is therefore truly *abusson* (literally, bottomless; hence, unfathomable: a conceptual abyss). This Neoplatonic idea became one of the sources of Christian "negative theology," which holds that God can be "defined" only through the negation of what is conceivable. God is, for instance, *in*visible, *un*imaginable, *in*effable, time*less*, *un*limited, *un*created—in a word, "absolutely and intrinsically other than and opposite of everything that is and can be thought" (Rudolf Otto, *The Idea of the Holy*, 29; also 179–86). On the multiple ancient sources of "negative theology," see Windelband, *A History of Philosophy*, 1:237–38. Alfred Doppler provides a wide-ranging discussion of the abyss motif in "Das Motiv des Abgrunds," *Der Abgrund des Ichs*, 9–35. Baruch Spinoza, "Epistola 50," *Opera*, 4:240. Only Spinoza's "God" precludes negation because his "God" is "infinite existence," i.e., existence without any limitation and thus without any scope for negation. "God," in sum, is absolute affirmation. See *Ethica* 1.8. Hegel, *Phänomenologie des Geistes*, 29. A. E. Taylor, *Plato*, 194; Plato, *Republic* 444C–E.

18. Henry David Thoreau, *Walden*, ch. "Higher Laws," ad fin.

The pursuit of harmony is also an imperative on the level of character. The cultivation of character ranked high among the moral concerns of Emerson's day. His one-time ministerial colleague, Henry Ware, Jr., managed to become a best-selling author with his handbook, *On the Formation of the Christian Character* (1831).[19] This preoccupation with character was an expression of the strongly ethical tendencies within Unitarian piety. And as Daniel Howe points out,

> If there were a single conception that dominated Harvard Unitarian thought . . . it was the conception of harmony. The Unitarian conscience was not a repressive, but an expressive faculty: not to crush, but to harmonize, regulate, and balance, was the task of the ruling power. . . . Unitarian preachers . . . frequently led their congregations in the contemplation of the balanced character of a virtuous man. . . . When they rejected the doctrine of innate depravity, Unitarians were led to espouse the view that sin consisted of a breakdown in the internal harmony.[20]

Although the mature Emerson was less concerned with the religious factors shaping the Unitarian conception of the *Christian* character, he was as committed as his Unitarian contemporaries to the conception of character as harmony. For him, the building of character was but another means of self-realization, of striving toward the harmony of Self. Character, therefore, as Barbara Packer rightly says, meant much more to Emerson than the *ēthos* bequeathed to him and to his classically educated contemporaries by the Greek (and Roman) rhetoricians.[21]

The primary locus of character, in Emerson's view, is the will. His close identification of character with will can be easily documented. For instance, in an 1838 journal entry he states: "*Will* or Reality reminds you of nothing else. It takes place of the whole creation" (*JMN* 7:146; emphasis added). Transferred to "Self-Reliance," this passage reads: "*Character*, reality, reminds you of nothing else; it takes place of the whole creation" (*CW* 2:35; emphasis added). Since will and character share reality and centrality in the same degree, and since both

19. Howe, *The Unitarian Conscience*, 106–8; Robinson, *Apostle of Culture*, 26, 32; Robinson, "An Introductory Historical Essay," *CS* 1:7.

20. Howe, *The Unitarian Conscience*, 60.

21. Packer, *Emerson's Fall*, 182.

are expressions of the practical Reason's self-actualization, Emerson saw no harm in using "will" and "character" interchangeably. Indeed, "a grand will . . . when legitimate and abiding, we call *character*" (*W* 8:117).

The Emersonian will is not purely conative; it has also an intellectual determinant. The will has to be guided by the mind's perception of truth or rightness, which perception is then actualized through the conative faculty of the mind. Both components, the intellectual and the conative, are equally necessary to the making of the will (*W* 6:29). Without perception, the will would not rise above the level of blind instinct; without conation, the will would be still-born. The Emersonian will is perhaps best described as "Reason-determined conation."

Responsive to the Reason, the will discovers itself to be at variance with nature (thought of as a system of causality) and fate (which is but a name for as yet "unpenetrated causes"—*W* 6:32), and in the process discovers its freedom, that is, its independence from the world of necessity, whether actual ("nature") or presumptive ("fate"). The will is not mechanically determined but is spontaneous, in the sense of being able to introduce actions into nature not dependent upon natural causation (*EL* 3:144). As humans, "we are not creatures of necessity, but creatures of free will"; therefore, we are not condemned to move "like the silent orb we tread upon, in one eternal round" (*CS* 2:52). Our moral constitution lifts us out of the phenomenal world in which we have our physical existence. The human "has his life in Nature, like a beast: but choice is born in him. . . . He chooses,—as the rest of the creation does not" (*W* 10:91–92). Schiller remarks that a starving human experiences hunger as intensely as does a starving animal (and thus participates in the world of nature or necessity), but that whereas the starving animal is ineluctably driven by its nature to satisfy its craving for food (and thus remains in the world of nature or necessity), the human can choose to continue starving, thereby asserting his or her independence from that world (and thus attaining the level of morality or freedom).[22] Agreeing that morality "implies freedom and will," Emerson was as insistent as Schiller that we should

22. Friedrich Schiller, "Über Anmut und Würde," *Werke*, 4:176.

strive to make the will truly free by liberating it "from the sheaths and clogs of organization" (*W* 10:91; 6:36).

One way of accomplishing this liberation is by transforming the world of blind necessity as much as possible into a realm of rational (Reason-determined) freedom. Brute necessity (afflicting us with "the pain of an alien world; a world not yet subdued by the thought"—*CW* 1:106) must be made to yield to rational vision. It must be made to reflect the order and harmony inherent in the Reason. This end can be accomplished only by sublating the world of perfect causality by "a will as perfectly organized," that is, by a will realizing the "perfect freedom" that is but another name for the moral law: "It is the perfection of free agency to . . . find our perfect freedom a perfect law" (*JMN* 14:53; *CS* 3:71). And no matter what the order of magnitude, a victory of the will always amounts to making Reason and rational law prevail over necessity. Emerson's commitment to the (moral, free) will as a "harmonizing" force in a disturbingly "alien world" is his way of expressing the deeply felt human need for some form of ultimate harmony. The human intellect, Iris Murdoch says, "is naturally one-making. To evaluate, understand, classify, place in order of merit, implies a wider unified system. . . . We fear plurality, diffusion, sense-less accident, chaos, we want to transform what we cannot dominate or understand." Similarly, Thomas McFarland regards the "complete" philosophical systems produced or attempted by many of Emerson's contemporaries as "a reflection, in the special realm of philosophy, of a universal concern, the need to harmonize."[23] The mature Emerson had little patience with "systemgrinder[s]" of any kind (*JMN* 5:75; *W* 12:11–13), but in his interpretation of the moral life as an attempt to impose a world of freedom, and therefore the (practical) Reason, upon the world of necessity, he gave voice to the same human desire to create a "harmonious" world, a world in which the human spirit could recognize the harmony of the Reason, and thus itself.

This commitment to the harmony inherent in the Reason also explains why Emerson prefers the "quality" of the good will to the actions resulting from such will. Action, to be sure, plays a more important part on the level of character than on that of conscience.

---

23. Iris Murdoch, *Metaphysics as a Guide to Morals*, 1–2; McFarland, *Coleridge and the Pantheist Tradition*, xxxix.

Nevertheless, action is always partial, conditional, affected by the limitations both of the agent and of the phenomenal world in which it takes place. Action restricts, as Goethe said;[24] it implies roads not taken. In Emerson's words, "A certain partiality, a headiness, and loss of balance, is the tax which all action must pay" (*CW* 4:154). Like Kant, therefore, Emerson is more concerned with the quality (goodness, spontaneity) of the will as such, and he regards a will thus qualified as "the best account of virtue at which we are at present able to arrive" (*EL* 3:144). Kant said that the only thing in the world, or even outside the world, conceivable as good without limitation is the good will, but he added that the good will is good not through what it achieves but through being what it is in itself: it is good "through willing alone."[25]

For Emerson also, "it is more important that these victories [of the good will] should be won by the mind than that the events should turn up as we desire" (*CS* 2:106). What matters is "the feeling of duty," which is synonymous with "Virtue" (*CS* 2:34). Only virtue thus defined is, according to Emerson, "free" and "absolute." It is also "self-existent" (*CS* 2:74). It thus also becomes synonymous with the practical Reason, and consequently Emerson finds it possible to claim that virtue always "subordinates [the world] to the mind" (*CW* 1:36). But this subordination is achieved ideally rather than actually. When Emerson speaks of the omnipotence of the "virtuous will" (*JMN* 4:257; 7:183), when he grants the will the power to chain "the wheel of Chance" (*CW* 2:50), he asserts an ideal and therefore, in his view, a real rather than a merely actual truth. Emerson here shows himself an exponent of the moral philosophy of his age, which, he claims, "recedes to grounds more and more purely ideal and at last entrenches man in the *sentiment* of Duty as the only reality" (*EL* 3:308; emphasis added).

This whole argument notwithstanding, action does play an important part in Emerson's ethic of character, but his commitment to the pursuit of the harmonious self emerges also here in his tendency to interpret action as primarily a matter of overcoming disharmony. Action is an attempt to overcome obstacles within (suffering, unhappiness)

24. Johann Wolfgang Goethe, *Wilhelm Meisters Lehrjahre* 8.5, *Gedenkausgabe*, 7:590.
    25. Kant, *Grundlegung zur Metaphysik der Sitten*, *Gesammelte Schriften*, 4:393–94, 399–400.

and without (nature, society) that both impede and invite the self's attainment of wholeness, of moral and spiritual health. Obstacles are a necessary antithesis in the self's endless dialectical striving for harmony. Emerson repeatedly emphasizes the will's need to be "educated" through struggle, and he therefore stresses such qualities of character as courage, perseverance, and resilience. David Robinson is certainly right in stressing that Emerson's position exemplifies the Unitarian doctrine of probation, which held that "life was a testing ground for the cultivation of character." The Unitarians had, in fact, "translated the question of salvation into one of character development."[26]

Emerson also reflects a generally Protestant ethic according to which moral improvement is the fruit of struggle against the evils of this world, as opposed to the view of the medieval Church that moral perfection was attainable primarily through renunciation of the world and avoidance of its temptations. *Areopagitica*, which Emerson called "the most splendid" of Milton's prose works (*EL* 1:147), expresses this Protestant ethic in a passage that Emerson repeatedly echoes:

> I cannot praise a fugitive and cloister'd vertue, unexercis'd & unbreath'd, that never sallies out and sees her adversary, but slinks out of the race, where that immortall garland is to be run for, not without dust and heat. Assuredly we bring not innocence into the world, we bring impurity much rather: that which purifies us is triall, and triall is by what is contrary. That vertue therefore which . . . knows not the utmost that vice promises to her followers, and rejects it, is but a blank vertue, not a pure.[27]

Emerson agreed. He insisted that "man should be acquainted with vice, and earn the crown of virtue in overcoming it" (*CS* 2:152). Even if the adult could regain the blank innocence of early childhood, he would but return to an inferior, premoral state, a state precluding "temptation, and therefore . . . virtu[e]." The reward of moral struggle "will not be innocence, it will be something far more glorious, it will be virtue" (*CS* 2:172, 174). We cannot even *imagine*, Emerson says, "the highest good . . . as existing without evil." What is dialectically

26. Robinson, *Emerson and the Conduct of Life*, 11; "An Introductory Historical Essay," *CS* 1:5.
27. John Milton, *Areopagitica, Complete Prose Works*, 2:515–16.

necessary to our imagining, is equally so to our acting: "without evil there can be no such thing as virtue, which consists in overcoming evil" (*CS* 3:58). To prepare for such struggles, we need to (in language echoing Milton's) "breathe and exercise the soul," we need to acquire an "athletic virtue" (*CW* 2:154; *CS* 2:74). Every victory obtained over the disruptive force of evil is one step closer to harmony of character, or as Emerson puts it, "to simplicity of character,—to that unity of purpose and word and action, that is in God, and in the children of God" (*CS* 2:175).

At present, however, we fail to live up to that vision of harmony and unity. The will is often directed to narrow ends. Our very prayers are "a disease of the will." They are prayers of petition, they crave, and thus they evidence our lack of faith in our higher Self: "As soon as the man is at one with God, he will not beg" (*CW* 2:44–45). Moreover, by obeying inclination rather than duty, the will reveals its adherence to the world of necessity rather than to the realm of moral freedom. For this reason, Emerson says that though the will is strong, "Trust is stronger"—trust in the moral order that alone should dictate the direction of the will (*EL* 3:312). Once again, it appears that Emerson is writing in the optative mood: character is a desideratum; it is a goal to be pursued endlessly. The harmonious self has never been realized. Although it is easy to find "men of great gifts," there have never been any truly "symmetrical men." Even Shakespeare suffers from "halfness" (*CW* 3:134; 4:124). Yet the ideal keeps beckoning with never-diminishing force: "The least hint sets us on the pursuit of a character, which no man realizes" (*CW* 3:133).

The third level on which the pursuit of harmony is a moral imperative is that of culture, which to Emerson meant essentially self-culture, that is, the full, harmonious development of one's latent capacities in order to achieve as nearly perfect a realization as possible of one's human potential. Emerson's concept of self-culture had its roots in Unitarian thought, as David Robinson has shown; it also owed much to the ideal of self-culture *(Bildung)* that dominated the classic age of German literature (ca. 1775–1830) and that was exemplified for New Englanders primarily by the works and personality of Goethe. But as one would expect, Emerson put his own interpretation upon self-culture. For the Germans, self-culture was a *cultural ideal;* for Emerson, it was a *moral obligation*—indeed, the fundamental moral obligation. Although this moral emphasis aligns him with the Unitarian position, Emerson's pantheism led to a very different sense of self and self-culture. Unitarian humanism, as Robinson insists, "was indeed Christian humanism, essentially because the Unitarians accepted the biblical revelation as the basis of their faith." Although, stimulated by the example of Christ, the Unitarians might strive for "Likeness to God" (to quote the title of one of William Ellery Channing's sermons), they never lost sight of the ontic distinction between God and man. The mature Emerson insisted on *complete* self-culture precisely because that is the only way of performing one's duties to God pantheistically conceived. The pantheistic God, to be sure, achieves self-realization in Nature, but only in humans does God's self-realization rise to consciousness, to self-awareness. The self-culture of humans thus becomes the conscious self-realization of God. Only humans, therefore, can experience self-realization as a moral obligation. As Kant said, the concept "ought" is meaningless when applied to Nature.[28] Nature is inescapably "law-abiding"; it truly (more than Martin Luther at Worms) "cannot do otherwise." The human, on the other hand, perceiving self-realization as the highest good, apprehends striving for the most complete self-culture as a duty—and for that very reason retains the freedom to choose not to engage in such striving.

Emerson leaves no doubt about his post-Unitarian (or generally post-Christian) orientation when it comes to matters of self-culture. "There are innocent men," he says, "who worship God after the tradition of their fathers, but their sense of duty has not yet extended to the use of all their faculties" (*CW* 1:43–44). Or disagreeing with the Shorter Catechism (whose well-known opening Question and Answer are: "What is the chief End of Man?" / "Man's chief End is to Glorify God, and to Enjoy Him for ever."), Emerson writes: "His own Culture,—the unfolding of his nature, is the chief end of man. A divine impulse at the core of his being, impels him to this. . . . The true culture is a discipline so universal as to demonstrate that no part of a man was made in vain" (*EL* 2:215). Measured by this standard, Jesus fell far short of "true culture": "Perfect in the sense of complete man

---

28. Robinson, *Apostle of Culture*, 22. Kant, *Kritik der reinen Vernunft* A 547/B 575.

he seems not to me to be, but a very exclusive & partial development
of the moral element. . . . a perfect man should exhibit all the traits
of humanity" (*L* 1:451). Jesus has not "fulfilled all the conditions of
man's existence, [nor] carried out to the utmost, at least by implication,
all man's powers." Consequently, there can be no *imitatio Christi* for
a person striving for self-culture as defined by Emerson: "Do you ask
me if I would rather resemble Jesus than any other man? If I should
say Yes, I should suspect myself of superstition" (*JMN* 5:71–72). It is
obvious that such views reflect a position much closer to Goethean
Bildung (itself connected with Goethe's pantheism) than to Unitarian
self-culture.

Emerson, nevertheless, remained committed to a more specific
morality than did Goethe. Anything at all contributing to the full
and harmonious development of our humanity Goethe considered
to be moral. It was moral *because* it was a factor in our human
development.[29] Emerson, equally committed to full human development, nonetheless wanted that development to be guided by a sense of
what was morally "right," and on this point he found Goethe wanting.
During his first Italian journey, Goethe apparently considered it part
of his education to study classical sculpture while in the arms of his
well-proportioned Roman mistress.[30] Noting this fact in his journal,
Emerson, while praising Goethe's commitment to "self-cultivation,"
deplored his inability "to perceive the right of his moral sentiments to
his allegiance." As a result, Goethe, while capable of saying "all his fine
things about *Entsagen* [renunciation, self-denial]," often appears to be
no better than another Earl of Rochester (*JMN* 4:301). Or as Emerson
put it with revealing bluntness a few months later (November 20,
1834), in a letter countering Carlyle's "apotheosis" of his "eminent
friend Goethe," "the Puritan in me accepts no apology for bad morals
in such as *he*" (*CEC* 107). Clearly, Emersonian self-culture had a
moral emphasis absent from Goethean *Bildung*—or rather, the moral
provenance was different in each case. For Emerson, self-culture had
to meet certain criteria derived from the moral sentiment; in Goethe's

29. For Goethe's comprehensive understanding of the term *ethisch* (ethical, moral),
see Dorothea Kuhn, *Empirische und ideelle Wirklichkeit: Studien über Goethes Kritik des
französischen Akademiestreites*, 134, 289n2.

30. Johann Wolfgang Goethe, *Römische Elegien* 5.7–10, *Gedenkausgabe*, 1:167.

view, the ideal of *Bildung* produced the moral criteria by which one should measure the rightness of one's actions. Moreover, whereas for Goethe *Bildung* was an end in itself, Emerson wants us to do our duty to ourselves so that we may become "mightier moral agents." Still, like Goethe, he recognizes that "we shall not have done our duty to ourselves until we have carried all our powers to the highest perfection those powers can reach" (*CS* 1:209). In fact, a person whose development is "partial" as a result of his or her cultivation of "particular faculties" and neglect of others is "in a degree depraved" (*CS* 2:227). Emersonian self-culture, in other words, has both instrumental and intrinsic value: on the one hand, it fits us to become "mightier moral agents" (*CS* 1:209), but on the other, a failure in self-culture is *in itself* a moral failure.

Emerson's moral emphasis in relation to self-culture explains his repeated insistence that there can be no full intellectual development without a parallel development of the moral faculty. Once again, his concern with harmonious self-realization is patent here. He wants no separate cultivation of intellect and virtue because he is convinced that both can advance only in tandem. But given the intellectualist illusions of his age, he often feels the need to give morality pride of place, as when he says that "moral superiority explains intellectual," or that "the Intellect is the head of the Understanding but is the feet of the Moral Power" (*JMN* 10:135, 355). Emerson's real point, however, is that there exists "an intimate interdependence of intellect and morals," that "the intellect and the moral sentiment . . . in the last analysis can never be separated" (*W* 6:217; 8:302). Both morals and intellect "ennoble" humans, but only if they unite in one human being do we have someone "truly great" (*W* 8:317). At the highest level, intellect and morality harmonize to the point of becoming one and the same: "the intellect in its purity and the moral sense in its purity are not distinguished from each other" (*W* 12:417).

Since self-culture involves the fullest possible realization of all one's powers, action plays a more important part here than it does on the level of conscience or even of character. Emerson stresses the need for self-expression in word and deed, for creativity and productivity, for work. Only through our efforts to make recalcitrant material (of whatever kind—language, nature, society) vehicular to our thought or will can our latent powers be evoked and exercised: "By doing his own work, [man] unfolds himself" (*CW* 2:83). In the process we acquire greater self-knowledge, which is further enhanced by the objectification of the inner self that is inherent in all expression. Expression means "embodiment of . . . thought" (*W* 7:38). Thought arises "to the end that it may be uttered and acted" (*W* 7:39), and in its objectified form it is a mirror to the mind whence it arose. We need expression because self-knowledge is an ideal and an imperative, and without expression we continue to be burdened with the "painful secret" of our inarticulate self (*CW* 3:4). Expression helps us understand what we are and thus helps to make us real to ourselves.

Emerson's interest in work goes far beyond its economic and social significance. Its most important aspect is the "ethical instruction" it provides. Its true benefits are "knowledge and virtue," which, rather than "wealth and credit," are productive of real power (*EL* 2:126–27). Only he "can become a master, who learns the secrets of labor." Even "the seer himself" suffers "some loss of power and of truth" through "separation from labor" (*CW* 1:152–53). Emerson confesses to feeling some shame before the workers on whom he has to depend for commodities and material comfort. He feels inadequate when confronting the practical abilities of his ploughman, woodchopper, or cook. They "have got the education, I only the commodity"; they have "some sort of self-sufficiency," while he must endure his continuing dependence on them (*CW* 1:150). All this sounds remarkably like the master-slave relationship to which Hegel devoted some of his most interesting pages.[31] In Hegel's view, the master is ultimately reduced to inauthenticity and self-emptiness precisely because his continuing dependence on his bondman has denied him the moral and spiritual education inherent in labor. The bondman, by contrast, achieves authentic individuality through his work. Labor not only enables him practically but also leads to self-discovery because his spirit reveals itself in the transformative effect that his labor has upon his material environment. In the products of his labor the bondman thus encounters his objectified self and achieves a degree of self-knowledge denied to the master. Though Emerson did not go so far as to accept this dramatic Hegelian reversal in the spiritual relationship

---

31. Hegel, *Phänomenologie des Geistes*, 146–50.

between master and bondman, he was as convinced as Hegel that work was indispensable to self-realization: "The distinction and end of a soundly constituted man is his labor. Use is inscribed on all his faculties. Use is the end to which he exists" (*W* 11:542).[32]

Emerson also recognized that the importance of human endeavor resides in striving itself rather than in any goal striven for. From the late eighteenth century onward the human's perpetual incompleteness ceased to be regarded as a tragic limitation. The *summum bonum* was no longer a final state of perfection but an endless striving toward an ever-unattainable goal, a *Streben nach dem Unendlichen*. For Hölderlin's *Hyperion*, human excellence and grandeur consist in endless aspiration: "Das ist die Herrlichkeit des Menschen, daß ihm ewig nichts genügt" ("That is the glory of man, that nothing ever satisfies him").[33] The supreme expression of this idea is Goethe's *Faust*, which Emerson considered "the most remarkable literary work of the age" (*W* 10:328). Somewhat earlier Lessing made the famous statement that if God were to offer him a choice between the possession of truth and an insatiable desire for truth, he would choose the latter, even if this meant that he would err forever. Possession of truth, Lessing says, would produce inertia, stagnation, and pride, whereas the search for truth involves a never-ending development of human abilities and powers, which is the only "perfecting" accessible to humans.[34]

For Emerson also, "truth" resides in the effort to attain it, not in the illusion of possessing it. The only way to be "a candidate for truth" is to avoid that illusion and the spiritual "repose" it implies. Emerson makes the value of striving most obvious when he contrasts truth not with untruth, but with repose: "God offers to every mind its choice between truth and repose." Only by *pursuing* truth can we respect "the highest law of [our] being," because only thus can we develop our noblest human faculties (*CW* 2:202). Searching for truth is always a moral obligation, but by stressing that truth is forever unattainable, Emerson puts the focus on striving itself; on account of the moral demands and benefits inherent in striving, he

32. For a detailed discussion of Emerson's "doctrine of use," see Michael Lopez, *Emerson and Power: Creative Antagonism in the Nineteenth Century*, 53–105.

33. Friedrich Hölderlin, *Hyperions Jugend, Sämtliche Werke und Briefe*, 1:524.

34. Gotthold Ephraim Lessing, *Eine Duplik, Werke*, 8:32–33.

rightly considers the search for truth to be an integral part of his self-realizationist ethic.

In addition to harmony, Emerson the metaethical intuitionist perceived a second absolute value inherent in the Self, and therefore also to be pursued by the finite self: universality. As indicated in chapter 2, the concept of universality played a role of the utmost importance in the moral thought of Emerson's day. Kant—for whom universality was an Idea of the Reason since it is not derivable from experience—held that only principles open to universalization are morally valid. The best known among his formulations of the categorical imperative reads: "Act only on that maxim through which you can at the same time will that it should become a universal law." This commitment to universality is reemphasized when Kant, regarding nature as a perfect model of universal lawfulness, reformulates thus: "So act as if the maxim of your action were to become through your will a universal law of nature."[35] If a maxim fails the test of universalizability, or if it self-destructs when universalized, it cannot be a morally valid principle of action. An eighteenth-century planter may have been guided by the maxim that slavery is right. Universalization of this maxim, however, would lead to universal slavery, including the enslavement of the planter aristocracy. Apart from the maxim's not being universalizable on purely logical grounds (if *all* are slaves, nobody would be a slave since there would be no enslavers), there is the obvious fact that no planter could *rationally will* (given the consequences for himself) that his maxim would become a *universal* law. Hence his maxim is incompatible with morality.

Whereas Kant regarded universalizability as primarily a criterion of moral judgment, Hegel considered it a test of the self's capacity for growth, for development beyond the particular so as to encompass the universal. Hegel was not satisfied with a universality that was such only by virtue of its complete indeterminacy and consequent emptiness. He wanted a concrete universality—a universality achieving concreteness in the individual who had risen above mere particularity. The individual is called upon to translate the self-realizationist urge of

---

35. Kant, *Grundlegung zur Metaphysik der Sitten, Gesammelte Schriften*, 4:421; by "maxim" Kant here means "a subjective principle of action"—420*n*.

universal Spirit *(Geist)* into concrete experience and thus to become the means of the Spirit's self-realization. Allen Wood clarifies the intimate interrelationship between individual and universal:

> The human spirit forms different conceptions of itself at different times and places. But Hegel views these conceptions as stages of a single process, a series of attempts to grasp and actualize the nature of spirit. The process is progressive; spirit raises itself from less adequate conceptions of itself to more adequate ones.[36]

The ultimate goal, as we learn from the concluding chapter of the *Phenomenology of Spirit,* is the complete self-realization of universal Spirit, that is, the completion of the process sketched by Wood and the raising of the *entire* process and *all* its stages (the less adequate conceptions never having been discarded: they were *aufgehoben,* i.e., annulled yet preserved in a higher form)[37] to the level of absolute Spiritual self-knowledge.

Emerson's ethics incorporates both the Kantian criterial and the Hegelian self-realizationist conception of universality. There is no evidence that Emerson knew Hegel's work in sufficient detail early enough for it to have had any direct formative influence on him. Nevertheless, one might argue that the Hegelian paradigm is finally more helpful than the Kantian in one's attempts to make sense of Emerson's theory of universality. Unlike Kant, both Emerson and Hegel were committed to a self-realizationist ethic. Unlike Kant, moreover, both Emerson and Hegel were pantheists, and their pantheism enabled them to view universality as something more pervasive and vital than Kant's universality, which was, more strictly, a formal principle in logic.[38] Unlike Kant, finally, both Emerson and Hegel were deeply committed to a view of Spirit, God, Mind, or Reality as evolving and developing, as endlessly involved in process. For all these reasons, Hegel articulated—and he did so with unmatched richness and profundity of argument—a view of universality more in tune with Emerson's Romantic sensibility, and more relevant to Emerson's ethical thinking.

36. Wood, *Hegel's Ethical Thought,* 203.
37. Hegel, *Phänomenologie des Geistes,* 90.
38. Kant, *Kritik der reinen Vernunft* A 70/B 95.

Emerson invariably objects to particularity, or *mere* individuality, as precluding the self's higher development and, therefore, as ethically unacceptable. The human being in his or her particularity cannot help falling into morally unjustifiable egoism:

> All men, in the abstract, are just and good; what hinders them, in the particular, is, the momentary predominance of the finite and individual over the general truth. The condition of our incarnation in a private self, seems to be, a perpetual tendency to prefer the private law, to obey the private impulse, to the exclusion of the law of universal being. (*CW* 1:104)

Particularity leads to egoism and evil, but as Emerson's phrase "in the abstract" indicates, the universality he refers to here is an empty concept, an idea that stands in need of concrete realization (as so often in his prose, Emerson here exploits a key term's etymological implications: "abstract," cf. Latin *abstractus*, drawn away, withdrawn, removed, detached from—specifically in this context, from anything at all corresponding to human experience). As humans we cannot return to the state of "all men, in the abstract" since our "incarnation in a private self" is an inescapable fact of our humanity. The only course open to us is to rise above particularity by attempting to make the universal concrete within our experience. Put differently, universality as conceptual abstraction has to be translated into universality as concrete experience, and this can be accomplished only through the individual who *realizes* in consciousness the universality that we all share "in the abstract":

> There are two facts, the Individual and the Universal. To this belong the finite, the temporal, ignorance, sin, death; to that belong the infinite, the immutable, truth, goodness, life. In Man they both consist. The All is in Man. In Man the perpetual progress is from the Individual to the Universal. (*JMN* 5:229)

The true universal, therefore, is not a concept separate from the individual. The individual contains universality: "All is in Each" (*JMN* 5:136).[39] The individual is, one might say in Hegelian language, a concrete universal: universality is the to-be-realized essence of the

---

39. For the Goethean and pantheist context of this idea, see my *Emerson's Modernity and the Example of Goethe*, 51–54.

individual, who embodies the concept of universality in its dialectical tension with particularity. In the very attempt to make the universal real, the individual rises above particularity: "Man helps himself by larger generalizations. The lesson of life is practically to generalize . . . to resist the usurpation of particulars; to penetrate to their catholic sense." Only by "ascending out of his limits into a catholic existence" can the human escape from the "poor empirical pretensions" that constitute particularity (*CW* 4:104, 20; 3:135). In fact, "the height of culture . . . consists in the identification of the Ego with the universe" (*W* 12:62). Even goodness itself is such only by virtue of its being guided by "universal insights" and its being productive of "results that are of universal application" (*JMN* 8:235).

The claim that "universal insights" are determinative of goodness brings Emerson very close to a Kantian categorical imperative. He expresses himself repeatedly in ways that clearly echo the categorical imperative, and he sometimes explicitly notes his affiliation with Kant, as when he writes: "Morals is the direction of the will on universal ends. He is immoral who is acting to any private end. He is moral,—we say it with Marcus Aurelius and with Kant,—whose aim or motive may become a universal rule, binding on all intelligent beings" (*W* 10:92). Emerson's associating Marcus Aurelius with Kant is careless, for there is nothing in Marcus Aurelius anticipating the categorical-imperative idea expressed in the last-quoted sentence. The first two sentences of the quotation are relatable to the general Stoic notion that one's rational nature demands one to live in accordance with the divine *logos* as one finds it expressed in the rationally ordered universe. Perhaps Emerson had in mind an Aurelian statement such as this:

> This must always be borne in mind, what is the Nature of the whole Universe, and what mine, and how this stands in relation to that, being too what sort of a part of what sort of a whole; and that no one can prevent thee from doing and saying always what is in keeping with the Nature of which thou art a part.[40]

In any case, one should not judge Emerson's confusion too harshly: there are some obvious points of contact between Kant's thought and Stoicism, and a few scholars have even argued for a significant

40. Marcus Aurelius Antoninus, *To Himself,* translated by C. R. Haines (Loeb Classical Library), 2.9.

Kantian debt to the Stoics, although such claims are now generally dismissed.

Emerson is on surer ground elsewhere: "What is *moral?* It is the respecting in action catholic or universal ends. Hear the definition which Kant gives of moral conduct: 'Act always so that the immediate motive of thy will may become a universal rule for all intelligent beings'" (*W* 7:27). As René Wellek pointed out, such explicit acknowledgments of Kant as formulator of the categorical imperative appear rather late in Emerson's career (the passages just quoted date from the 1860s).[41] There are, however, indications that Emerson had been long familiar with the categorical imperative. His first exposure to the idea probably came through Coleridge's *The Friend,* which he was reading "with great interest" as early as December 1829 (*L* 7:188). Coleridge not only provided an excellent statement of the categorical imperative but highlighted it by calling it "the one universal and sufficient principle and guide of morality": "So act that thou mayest be able, without involving any contradiction, to will that the maxim of thy conduct should be the law of all intelligent Beings."[42] It is clearly in the spirit of the categorical imperative that Emerson argues, in an 1831 sermon, against indifference to the Sabbath; the Sabbath-breaker, surely, mindful of "the evils that would ensue," cannot will that "all men should do as he does and so the day be abolished" (*CS* 3:165). The categorical character of moral obligation thus precludes the possibility of exceptions and of merely subjective moral principles. The categorical imperative, after all, makes the moral validity of principles of action *dependent upon* their universalizability. In sum, "Virtue is the adoption of [the] dictate of the Universal mind by the individual Will" (*EL* 2:84).

Needless to say, for the individual the pursuit of universality is what Emerson, in another context, calls "a perpetual inchoation" (*CW* 1:124). As shown above, only in the individual can universality achieve realization. However, no human can escape from the defects and finiteness inherent in individuality. The individual is thus necessarily both the realizer and the obstructer of universality. Since Emerson often stressed the analogy of goodness and beauty, one may illustrate with an example from his aesthetics. Contemplating the

41. Wellek, *Confrontations,* 194.
42. Samuel Taylor Coleridge, *The Friend,* 1:194.

greatest artistic and literary achievements, we should try to see what "man was tending to do in a given period, and was hindered, or, if you will, modified in doing, by the interfering volitions of Phidias, of Dante, of Shakespeare, the organ whereby man at the moment wrought" (*CW* 2:63). "Man" is an abstract, empty universal that achieves concreteness and reality only in the individual—in Phidias, Dante, Shakespeare, or whoever. The literary and artistic potential of universal "man" finds but limited and defective expression in works that bear the marks of their authors' temperamental flaws, stylistic obsessions, errors in judgment, prejudices, and similar limitations inherent in individuality. *Without* individuals such as Phidias, Dante, and Shakespeare, however, the universal would never achieve even partial realization, would never become a concrete universal. Though "obstructing" the universal, the great work of art is at the same time its limited realization. Emerson makes a similar point when he says that Plato's philosophical achievement "stands between the truth and every man's mind" (*CW* 4:26). Platonic philosophy, obviously, is an expression of *Plato's* insights into and interpretations of "the truth." This does not mean, however, that "the truth" would ever have been concretely available *except through* the limited expression of it in the thought of thinkers such as Plato. Plato "obstructs" abstract truth in the very act of expressing it and making it concrete. But such concretization is the only way of giving us (albeit partial) access to truth. Emerson recognizes this when he says that it is "impossible to think on certain levels, except through [Plato]" (*CW* 4:26).

True universality, therefore, is not available to the finite self, but pursuing it remains a self-realizationist imperative and thus a moral obligation. We keep "demand[ing] of men a . . . universality we do not find." Their failure does not, however, absolve us from our own duty ever to "press . . . onward to the impersonal and illimitable" (*CW* 1:122; 2:186).

4

Others

S elf-realization is inconceivable without the existence and involvement of others. The very notion of "self" depends upon the
contrastive notion "other," and one achieves self-identification only
through awareness of the otherness of others. Moreover, as Aristotle
recognized when he made ethics part of politics, one cannot achieve
maturity as a human being without rational participation in the life
of the polis, the larger structured community: "He who is incapable of
living in society, or has no need to because he is self-sufficient, must
be either a beast or a god."[1] The education of the will, the building
of character, intellectual development, and cultural enrichment all
presuppose interactive involvement with one's fellow humans. On
these grounds Michael Lopez is certainly right when claiming that
Emerson views "our social selves as . . . the necessary foundation for
our identity and for our capacities for action."[2] There is, furthermore,
a whole range of human emotions that come fully into play only
in relation to other humans. One can certainly "love" a landscape,
for instance, or "love" one's dog, but such "love" lacks the challenge,
mutuality, and inexhaustibility characteristic of love between two humans at its best. Without positive emotions directed at fellow human
beings—emotions such as love, friendship, affection, and sympathy—
no one can be said to be truly human. Self-realization, in sum, has an
inescapably *relational* dimension.

Involvement in society also means that one inevitably lives much of
one's life in a public space, and as a result one's sense of one's identity
also depends to a high degree on what one is *perceived* to be. Among

1. Aristotle, *Politics* 1.2.
2. Lopez, *Emerson and Power*, 76.

Emerson's older contemporaries it was especially Hegel who stressed the importance of *recognition* to the making of identity. One cannot achieve real self-consciousness, in Hegel's view, without one's being recognized as a true self by others and without one's absorbing that recognition into one's self-reflection; moreover, the value of others as recognizers of one's true self depends upon one's granting them equal recognition as true selves. Such recognition became crucial in the age of Hegel and Emerson because institutions and hierarchies were no longer capable of "granting" identity by virtue of a person's place (class, rank, family) in the social structure. As Stanley Cavell sees it, modern self-directed skepticism is a response to or expression of "the dependence of the human self on society for its definition, but at the same time its transcendence of that definition, its infinite insecurity in maintaining its existence." The post-Enlightenment, post-Revolutionary age was, in Emerson's words, "the age of severance, of dissociation, of freedom, of analysis, of detachment. Every man for himself. . . . There is an universal resistance to ties and ligaments once supposed essential to civil society. The new race . . . are fanatics in freedom" (*W* 10:326–27). In such an atomistic environment, meaningful identity was no longer a social given, but something to be struggled for, something to be acquired and made real to oneself in part by making it accepted as such by others. Hence the modern stress on the need for mutual recognition and for such ethical components of recognition as acknowledgment of the intrinsic dignity of everyone as a human being and respect for everyone as an individual entitled, as fully as oneself, to autonomy and to the pursuit of his or her particular kind of integrity. The concept of "respect for persons" or "dignity of persons," much discussed in modern ethics, received its first authoritative expression in Kant's most moving formulation of the categorical imperative: "So act as to treat humanity, both in your own person and in the person of every other, always at the same time as an end, never simply as a means."[3]

3. Hegel, *Phänomenologie des Geistes*, 141–50. Cavell, *In Quest of the Ordinary*, 174. On the need for recognition, see Charles Taylor, *The Ethics of Authenticity*, 43–53. "Acknowledgment" plays a key role in the thought and literary criticism of Stanley Cavell; see especially *The Claim of Reason: Wittgenstein, Skepticism, Morality, and Tragedy*, 329–496, and *Disowning Knowledge: In Six Plays of Shakespeare*. Kant, *Grundlegung zur Metaphysik der Sitten, Gesammelte Schriften*, 4:429.

Respect for the individuality, independence, and dignity of others is the dominant principle of Emerson's ethics in its other-regarding aspects. Unconditionally committed to the integrity of the self, Emerson quite naturally made concern for the selfhood of every person the criterion by which to judge attitudes and actions toward them. He recognized the inescapable moral implication of one's self in the selfhood of others: preserving the moral integrity of one's self precludes one's violating the integrity of any other self. By thus universalizing the rights of the self and giving them primacy, he attempted to solve what Anders Hallengren identifies as "the central problem . . . to which Emerson the moralist had to find an answer": how can one reconcile the demands of the self with the demands of others? How can one reconcile, in other words, the self's absolute commitment to its own integrity and authenticity with the demands of justice and fairness toward others?[4] Resolving the conflicts implied in such questions necessitated, according to Emerson, a deeper understanding of the true needs of the self and a realization that the moral agent advantages the self of others in the very act of asserting the rights of his or her self.

The Christ of the Divinity School "Address" provides Emerson with an excellent example. By virtue of being true to himself, he was true to the self of others. Though respecting Moses and the prophets, he felt "no unfit tenderness at postponing their initial revelations . . . to the eternal revelation in the heart. Thus was he a true man" (*CW* 1:81). Christ knew, as Emerson puts it elsewhere, that "Heaven deals with us on no representative system. Souls are not saved in bundles" (*W* 6:214). He therefore located the moral law within each of us and stressed individual responsibility: "Having seen that the law in us is commanding, he would not suffer it to be commanded." Any externally imposed command Christ considered incompatible with human dignity, and for this reason he deserves to be regarded as "the only soul in history who has appreciated the worth of a man." Christ, in other words, was as just to others as he was to himself. By obeying the moral law within, he achieved true human dignity; by his example he inspires each of us to "dare, and live after the infinite Law that is

4. Hallengren, *The Code of Concord*, 115.

in [us]." True Christianity—that is, a Christianity faithful to the spirit of Christ's teaching as interpreted by Emerson—does not require us to "subordinate [our] nature to Christ's nature" because that not only would violate our selfhood but by the same token would turn Christ, "the friend of man," into an oppressive "eastern monarch"—a role that would obviously destroy *his* moral integrity (*CW* 1:81–82). True Christianity does not, therefore, demand faith *in* Christ. It does insist that we have "the faith *of* Christ," that is, "a faith like Christ's in the infinitude of man" (*CW* 1:85, 89; emphasis added).

The example of Christ also brings into focus Emerson's entire ethics of influence. The only acceptable kind of influence is one that provokes those subjected to it to resist it, thereby stimulating them to actualize their latent originality. Influence thus conceived provokes them to be all the more emphatically themselves. Nothing valuable can be "given" us, as Goethe's Faust knew so well.[5] In his sermons Emerson inculcated "the everlasting truth that the only good that any man can obtain he must get by the cultivation of himself" (*CS* 4:150). Influence conceived as provocation also shapes Emerson's argument in "The American Scholar." Books should neither instruct nor indoctrinate: "They are for nothing but to inspire." Indeed, "I had better never see a book than to be warped by its attraction clean out of my own orbit, and made a satellite instead of a system" (*CW* 1:56).

Emerson's overriding concern with the integrity of the self ("Nothing is at last sacred but the integrity of your own mind"—*CW* 2:30) thus severely limits the concept of influence as generally understood. Any attempt to shape another's destiny, to prescribe his course, or to make him over in one's own image undermines the integrity of both the influencer and the person influenced: "Whenever I find my dominion over myself not sufficient for me, and undertake the direction of [another] also, I overstep the truth, and come into false relations to him. . . . it is a lie, and hurts like a lie both him and me" (*CW* 3:125). A parent desiring "that his child should repeat his character and fortune" not only fails to respect the child as a human being sui generis but demeans himself by "a low self-love" (*W* 10:137). Emerson himself,

---

5. "Was du ererbt von deinen Vätern hast / Erwirb es, um es zu besitzen" ("What you have inherited from your fathers, you need to make your own, in order to gain possession of it")—*Faust*, pt. 1, 682–83.

as is well known, had no wish to degrade his auditors or readers to
the level of discipleship; he regarded it as evidence of his integrity as
a thinker that his thought had repelled potential disciples:

> I have been writing & speaking what were once called novelties, for
> twenty five or thirty years, & have not now one disciple. Why? Not
> that what I said was not true; not that it has not found intelligent
> receivers but because it did not go from any wish in me to bring
> men to me, but to themselves. I delight in driving them from
> me. . . . This is my boast that I have no school & no follower. I
> should account it a measure of the impurity of insight, if it did
> not create independence. (*JMN* 14:258)

Influence, as conceived by Emerson, liberates men and women by forc-
ing them back upon their own resources of thought and inspiration
and thus challenging them to break out of the prison of conventional
or routine thinking and acting.

True influence, in sum, is a matter of "form" rather than "content."
The influencer is valuable not on account of any ideas he advances,
but because he sets an example of original thinking and acting by
daring to think his own thoughts and to live in accordance with them.
One should not accept his ideas, lest one fail to think one's own,
but his example can stimulate one to do precisely that. Formally,
every example of "mental and moral force is a positive good" because
one "cannot even hear of [it] . . . without fresh resolution" (*CW* 4:8–
9). Emerson's thinking of true influence as formal is also related to
his limited respect for historical factuality. It is only as "form" that
qualities or virtues are perpetually relevant, whereas their realized
"content" is inevitably time-bound—that is, subject to limitations on
phenomenal, cultural, and personal grounds and, in any case, remote
from the concerns of the Now. Hence Emerson's statement: "Although
the commands of the Conscience are *essentially* absolute, they are
historically limitary" (*CW* 1:188). Courage, for instance, is always in
demand, but the specific courage displayed by Martin Luther at the
Diet of Worms is not. Consequently, his influence on us should be
formal only. We should be as courageous as he was, but in ways that
are truly our own and concerning matters of crucial importance to *us*.
Similarly, Kant may inspire us to a self-reliance as uncompromising
as his, but being self-reliant *in the manner* of Kant would involve an

imitation so slavish as to amount to an abdication of the rights of the self and would, therefore, be oxymoronically absurd.

Questions concerning benevolence, charity, and philanthropy constitute another important preoccupation of Emerson's other-regarding ethics. He insists that moral goodness needs to be other-directed. It is inherent in "man's natural goodness . . . to do good to others" (*JMN* 3:174). Paralleling the claims made for the primacy of the practical Reason (see chapter 2), Emerson maintains that the highest kind of wisdom is practical wisdom, moral wisdom, or, in his words, "an operative wisdom, a wisdom of good works" (*CS* 1:131). Striving to attain this wisdom, which "is the end and perfection of the character" (*CS* 1:131), is our highest duty within the purview of other-regarding ethics. True benevolence, true charity ("what is charity but wisdom of good works?"—*CS* 1:132) is an obligation, the fulfillment of which helps us attain our moral destiny as social beings. Emerson's commitment to ethics even during his years of most intense religious involvement emerges in his desire to establish the law of benevolence on a foundation more universal than that of Christian agape. As he puts it in an 1830 sermon: "It is an exaggeration to say that Christianity first taught the law of benevolence. God taught it to the first man, and to every man in the Constitution of his own mind, and in the Constitution of society. . . . It is an universal sentiment" (*CS* 2:196).

The last words ("universal sentiment") in this passage are symptomatic of Emerson's affiliation with what Norman Fiering calls the Shaftesbury-Hutcheson gospel, which made feeling (sentiment, sympathy, the "affections") the chief modality of the moral life and the basis of a benevolism and humanitarianism extended to all living things.[6] Although, as already indicated, the "rational" moral sense of Reid and Stewart was in all probability more attractive to the American Unitarians than the "sentimental" moral sense of Shaftesbury and Hutcheson, the "benevolent affections" nevertheless, as Howe points out, "played a crucial role" in Unitarian thought, and especially Hutcheson's description of them was "greatly admired."[7] Emerson often sounds very much like a Hutchesonian. The art of living consists

6. Fiering, *Jonathan Edwards's Moral Thought*, 356–57.
7. Howe, *The Unitarian Conscience*, 48–49, 58–59.

primarily in being a "man of benevolent affections" (CS 3:46). It is "the glory of the human soul to embrace . . . all men in its affection." The "benevolent man feels" for others; he "sympathizes" with his fellow humans (CS 3:47). Benevolent affection "begins with the nearest relation and reaches to the farthest. It dictates our intercourse at the fireside and it reaches our conduct to our country, to other nations, and to the brute creation" (CS 3:89). Emerson's allegiance to universal benevolism also emerges in his repeated echoing of Hutcheson's anticipation of the central Utilitarian tenet (the greatest happiness of the greatest number). In an 1831 sermon Emerson considers it "our great duty . . . not to live to ourselves but to the greatest good of the greatest number of our fellow beings" (CS 3:200; also CS 2:197; 3:43).

As one might expect, Emerson is deeply concerned about the integrity-as-persons of those made interdependent by the very structure of beneficence, to wit, the benefactor and the beneficiary. As far as the benefactor is concerned, it was a commonplace of eighteenth-century ethics to speak of the necessary balance between self-love and love for others.[8] Although self-love (also called "interest" or "prudence") had to be kept within strict limits and was not in itself considered a basis of virtue, it was regarded as a necessary factor in human personality and as a tendency that could be made to harmonize with or to subserve the duty of benevolence. For eighteenth-century moralists, self-love had thus primarily instrumental value. Toward the end of the century, Kant considered both the intrinsic and the instrumental value of self-love when he pointed out that the maxim that one should completely sacrifice one's happiness or possessions for the benefit of others is proven to be self-contradictory when subjected to the test of universalization (and therefore to be morally unacceptable), but also that this maxim, if acted upon, would preclude a person's continued benefaction.[9]

Emerson built upon such eighteenth-century views. He recognized that "true success in life consists in striking the mean between the love of self and of our neighbor. . . . [A] man has a good deal to do in the world for himself before others . . . which, if he refuses to do for

8. Fiering, *Jonathan Edwards's Moral Thought*, 158.
9. Kant, *Metaphysik der Sitten, Tugendlehre*, "Einleitung" 8.2; §31, *Gesammelte Schriften*, 6:393, 454.

himself, he will not be able to do for any body else" (CS 2:132). He also repeatedly stressed that self-love can be harmonized with benevolence and that the self is often the chief beneficiary of its other-directed goodness. Humans should realize that "Charity . . . is necessary to their own happiness," that "he who withholds his aid from his fellowmen is more a loser than his fellowman from whom he withholds it," and that man advances "the perfection of his being" by imparting "his knowledge, his virtue, his possessions, his goodwill" (CS 2:197). Benevolence can thus easily be construed as a duty one owes to oneself. It is, in fact, "an indispensable part of a finished character to comply with the law of charity" (CS 3:86). A morally advanced person realizes that justice and fairness to others are inspired not by "selfish calculation" or "prudence" but by "a necessity to the soul of the agent" (CW 1:214).

Emerson's concern with the integrity of the agent is even more obvious when he considers that integrity threatened by the demands of others. He cites with approval a saying he attributes to Socrates, that "the gods prefer integrity to charity" (CS 4:174). What provokes him above all are attempts to turn the duty of charity into a tool of moral pressure and social conformity. In the well-known words of "Self-Reliance":

> Do not tell me . . . of my obligation to put all poor men in good situations. Are they *my* poor? I tell thee, thou foolish philanthropist, that I grudge the dollar, the dime, the cent I give to such men as do not belong to me and to whom I do not belong. . . . Though I confess with shame I sometimes succumb and give the dollar, it is a wicked dollar which by and by I shall have the manhood to withhold. (CW 2: 30–31)

It is a wicked dollar because giving it did not result from a sense of duty to "persons to whom by all spiritual affinity I am bought and sold" (CW 2:31). Giving induced by conformity to dictates alien to the self amounts to a violation of self. As Nietzsche pointed out, often the real incentive for almsgiving is not compassion but cowardice.[10]

---

10. Friedrich Nietzsche, *Menschliches, Allzumenschliches* 2.2.239–40, *Sämtliche Werke*, 2:660. For Emerson's significant anticipations of and influence on Nietzsche's other-regarding ethics, see my "Areteic Ethics: Emerson and Nietzsche on Pity,

This argument represents one of several Emersonian attempts to redefine the nature and content of *giving*. He came to regard benevolence as a total commitment of self rather than as a series of good deeds, which are often no more than an excuse for one's failure to truly commit the self to the benefit of others. One has to be totally *engagé:* "Generosity does not consist in giving money or money's worth. These so-called *goods* are only the shadow of good. . . . We owe to man higher succors than food and fire. We owe to man man" (*W* 7:114–15). But in order to make this gift of self as valuable as possible, the giver needs first to "enrich" himself. We can truly serve others only by serving ourselves first, that is, by making ourselves better, nobler human beings. Thus the person who faithfully does his own work "helps society at large with somewhat more of certainty than he who devotes himself to charities" (*W* 7:141). No one, Emerson believes, exemplified this principle more successfully than Goethe. "The true charity of Goethe" did not consist in "his donations and good deeds," but in his having spent a fortune on self-culture, on his lifelong devotion to *Bildung*. It is obvious that Goethe's achievement has done more for humanity than has any "amount of subscription to soup-societies" (*CW* 3:60–61). As Emerson explains in "Uses of Great Men,"

> If you affect to give me bread and fire, I perceive that I pay for it the full price, and at last it leaves me as it found me, neither better nor worse; but all mental and moral force is a positive good. It goes out from you, whether you will or not, and profits me whom you never thought of. (*CW* 4:8–9)

Nietzsche's Zarathustra expresses both the richness of the true self and its higher mode of giving through a beautiful paradox: "I give no alms. For that I am not poor enough."[11]

Emerson's insistence on the benefactor's total commitment of self was also aimed at preventing benevolence from becoming a mere

---

Friendship, and Love." Stanley Cavell provides an important and wide-ranging defense, on grounds different from mine, of Emerson's position as expressed in the passage quoted from "Self-Reliance"; see *Conditions Handsome and Unhandsome: The Constitution of Emersonian Perfectionism*, 134–38; also Cavell, *The Senses of "Walden,"* 153–54, 157.

11. Friedrich Nietzsche, *Also sprach Zarathustra*, "Zarathustra's Vorrede" 2, *Sämtliche Werke*, 4:13.

abstraction and the agent from becoming a merely theoretical bene-factor. Hegel urged that we take seriously the word "neighbour" in the commandment "Thou shalt love thy neighbour as thyself" (Leviticus 19:18; Matthew 22:39). If interpreted as commanding love toward all, the commandment would deny love a real, concrete content; it would turn love into an empty concept *(ein Abstraktum)*. In fact, it would turn "love" into the opposite of real love *(zum Gegenteil der wirklichen Liebe)*.[12] Emerson agreed that such generalized "love" not only would destroy the benefactor's integrity or authenticity but also would invite hypocrisy: the abstraction would become a substitute for concrete realization and a cloak for indifference, selfishness, or even exploitation. No matter how sincere his allegiance to universal benevolism, Emerson also recognized that in practical terms benev-olence was both local and specific: "It is in being good to wife & children & servants that the kingdom of heaven begins" *(JMN* 4:41). He was always skeptical about the sincerity of those committed to a generalized, "faraway" benevolence:

> If malice and vanity wear the coat of philanthropy, shall that pass? If an angry bigot assumes this bountiful cause of Abolition, and comes to me with his last news from Barbadoes, why should I not say to him, "Go love thy infant; love thy wood-chopper: be good-natured and modest: have that grace; and never varnish your hard, uncharitable ambition with this incredible tenderness for black folk a thousand miles off. Thy love afar is spite at home." *(CW* 2:30)

Emerson here points to a moral defect or blind spot to which self-proclaimed humanitarians seem particularly susceptible, in our day as well as in his. Its paradigmatic exemplar is Jean-Jacques Rousseau, who with fervent eloquence advocated love of humankind but who abandoned each of his five children to a foundling home. Charles Dickens, in his inimitable way, labeled this kind of humanitarianism "Telescopic Philanthropy."[13]

12. Georg Wilhelm Friedrich Hegel, *Vorlesungen über die Philosophie der Religion, Werke,* 17:283.

13. For Rousseau's enthusiasm for universal love, see, for instance, *Émile ou de l'éducation,* 62, 266; Dickens, *Bleak House,* ch. 4, title.

The integrity of the beneficiary is, needless to say, as important as that of the benefactor. The proper attitude toward the former is already implied in much of what precedes concerning the latter. Here also, the essential criterion is respect for personhood and individuality. Emerson regards benevolence as not really directed at what is weak and pitiful in others. True benevolence is love rather than pity—love for the human being underneath the misery or poverty. It attempts to remove misery and poverty because they impede the attainment of full humanity. Poverty must be attacked because one of its "greatest evils" is "the privation of many of the best aspects of human nature" (*CS* 2:200). Similarly, "if [a man] is sick, is unable, is mean-spirited and odious, it is because there is so much of his nature which is unlawfully withholden from him." Benevolence should attempt to free him from "this his prison" and restore to him the humanity that is lawfully his (*W* 7:115). This principle informs Emerson's advice to the 1838 graduating class at Harvard Divinity School. Referring to future parishioners, he entreats each graduate: "[L]et their timid aspirations find in you a friend; let their trampled instincts be genially tempted out in your atmosphere; let their doubts know that you have doubted, and their wonder feel that you have wondered" (*CW* 1:90). This kind of "giving" enhances the benefactor without offending the beneficiary.

Emerson's interpretation of giving as restoring to the beneficiary something that is lawfully his or hers is an expression of his acute awareness that giving as traditionally understood undermines the respect owed the beneficiary by virtue of his or her personhood. Such giving is presumptuous and insulting: "It is not the office of a man to receive gifts. How dare you give them?" True giving, by contrast, involves sharing our common humanness: "The gift, to be true, must be the flowing of the giver unto me, correspondent to my flowing unto him." Or stated in a fine paradox, whereas "we do not quite forgive a giver . . . any one who assumes to bestow," we "can receive anything from love, for that is a way of receiving it from ourselves" (*CW* 3:94–95). This concern with the integrity of the beneficiary also emerges in Emerson's insistence that the ideal gift is a *useless* one. His favorite example of such a gift is flowers because they represent, above all, beauty, which is a value sui generis and therefore untranslatable into any other value system. In other words, since the essential role of flowers is to embody beauty and since beauty eclipses utilitarian

values, flowers are *essentially* useless. They express the "proud assertion
that a ray of beauty outvalues all the utilities of the world" (*CW* 3:93).
Their very "uselessness" precludes giver and recipient standing in a
false relation to each other. As already indicated, bestowing benefits
is presumptuous; receiving them violates our deepest wish "to be self-
sustained." Hence, "the fitness of beautiful, not useful things for gifts"
(*CW* 3:94–95).

Another important aspect of Emerson's other-regarding ethics concerns the individual's attitudes and relations to others as members of
organized society and its various component structures—for instance,
as citizens of a state, supporters of a political party, adherents of a
reform movement. Since Emerson holds that commitment to a group
and to what it stands for involves abdication of individuality, he
regards the state, a political party, or a social movement as a homog-
enizing entity that the individual actually or spiritually has to remain
separate from if he or she wishes to safeguard his or her integrity.
Emerson finds it difficult to give substance to humans as *part of* a
larger societal structure. He thinks in terms of the individual (concrete,
true, real) *versus* the state, organization, or movement (abstract, unau-
thentic, only phenomenal), and he measures the individual's worth
by the degree of his or her opposition to the group. On this point
Emerson is in full agreement with his admired Montaigne, to whom,
as Hugo Friedrich said, "the best thing about man is the part that strives
against seizure by society."[14] Embracing the group and its values is
fatal to personhood, as Emerson indicates when he considers Wendell
Phillips to have "only a *platform*-existence, & no personality." People
like Phillips are "mere mouthpieces of a party, take away the party &
they shrivel & vanish" (*JMN* 13:281–82). Even Emerson's theory of the
family does not envision a unity involving the partial submergence of
individuality; instead it advocates "proximities" of absolute individuals (*CW* 2:41–42). But since one's self-definition and worth depend
upon one's opposition to societal structures, Emerson cannot treat
the individual in isolation from them. As a result, abstractions such as
"the state" and "society" play a significant part in his other-regarding
ethics.

14. Hugo Friedrich, *Montaigne*, 249.

The value distinction inherent in this argument—the superiority of the individual to society—expresses a fundamental Emersonian conviction. What Lockridge says about the British Romantics is true also of Emerson. Like them, he "insist[ed] on the ontological priority of the moral to the social."[15] He took this position as soon as he began to formulate his reflections on ethical, social, and political matters. Mary Kupiec Cayton reminds us that as a Harvard student Emerson had already resolved to "survey the political condition of the world as ethics[;] discover the Lex legum [law of laws] on which legislation is to proceed" (*JMN* 1:254).[16] And since morality is available only through individual consciousness and conscience, the individual has the duty to evaluate and delimit the claims of society in the light of his or her moral insights. Politically, this is a potentially anarchical tenet: society and the state have legitimacy only to the degree that they express values that accord with *my* moral convictions; as a moral being I have the duty to undermine institutions or contravene laws that do not answer to the demands of *my* conscience; indeed, the only acceptable social system is one re-created in *my* image as a moral being. Every reader of Emerson (and Thoreau) is familiar with such claims, both explicit and implicit. Their informing principle is the absolute supremacy of the moral sentiment: "Wherever the sentiment of right comes in, it takes precedence of everything else" (*CW* 4:53).

The individual does have some constructive obligations to society. Since only the individual can be ethical, since only he or she can enact the commands of the moral sentiment, no societal system or structure—which, as indicated above, is inconceivable without the members' abdication of true individuality—has any lasting moral validity. In Emerson's words, "the permanent good is for the soul only & cannot be retained in any society or system" (*JMN* 10:328). As David Robinson points out, Emerson holds that "it is individuals and their particular lives that finally constitute the texture of social life, and the only sphere of moral action."[17] Whatever good is to be found in a society results from the degree to which true individuals have been able to make their moral insights momentarily

15. Lockridge, *The Ethics of Romanticism*, 108.

16. Mary Kupiec Cayton, *Emerson's Emergence: Self and Society in the Transformation of New England, 1800–1845*, 40.

17. Robinson, *Emerson and the Conduct of Life*, 73.

prevail—momentarily, because society's inherent anti-individualism and predilection for expediency will soon render the moral influence ineffectual. The individual's duty, therefore, is to *keep* confronting and challenging society with his or her moral insights. Each of us has the obligation to pay his or her "debt of thought to mankind," to shake society out of the "repose" that is fatal to truth, and to "introduce moral truths into the general mind" (*CW* 2:187, 202; 4:12). This is the duty of "Man Thinking," as described in "The American Scholar," and of the ideal clergyman Emerson calls for in the Divinity School "Address." It will also be the duty of the true reformers whom Emerson envisions, the "men and women who shall renovate life and our social state" (*CW* 2:43).

Emerson was less enthusiastic, to be sure, about the actual reformers and the numerous reform movements he observed around him. He found that most reformers had become the fanatic slaves of their own ideology and as a result had lost the human dignity inherent in spiritual independence. They are "narrow, self-pleasing, conceited men, and affect us as the insane do." Instead of appealing to "the sentiment of man," the conscience, or the individual's innate sense of decency, they rely on "personal and party heats . . . measureless exaggerations, and the blindness that prefers some darling measure to justice and truth" (*CW* 1:176). Moreover, by its very nature a reform movement, like a political party or the state, sacrifices the independence of its members to its cause or platform. It can mobilize its forces only by "degrad[ing] . . . man to a measure" (*CW* 1:177). It is thus in obvious violation of the respect-for-persons principle expressed in the formulation of the categorical imperative quoted near the beginning of this chapter. Not surprisingly, Emerson concludes, perhaps somewhat smugly, that "the superior mind will find itself equally at odds with the evils of society, and with the projects that are offered to relieve them" (*CW* 4:97).

The only kind of reformers Emerson can accept at all are those whom, in the first of his "Lectures on the Times," he refers to as "the students" (*CW* 1:172, 179), that is, the contemplators of the ideal, whose inaction results from "a scorn of inadequate action" (*CW* 1:180). Emerson's preferring "the students" to "the actors" (*CW* 1:172) is in line with his general tendency to privilege principle over action, as discussed in the preceding chapter. The students look "with faith to a fair Future" and do not profane their vision "by rash and unequal attempts to realize it." In the midst of "the dwarfish Actual," they represent "the exorbitant Idea." But the "new modes of thinking" they inspire cannot fail of their ultimately renewing effect upon society (*CW* 1:180–81). The students thus represent Emerson's conviction that thought is the most powerful agent in history and that truly creative thought will both remove the oppressive weight of the past and initiate "new and higher modes of living and action" (*CW* 1:181). Such thought is not translatable, however, into a collective ideology, and it does not inspire mass movements. On the contrary, the students' approach to reform reflects their trust in the power of the moral sentiment, a trust, needless to say, that is Emerson's own: "I think *that* the soul of reform . . . reliance on the sentiment of man, which will work best the more it is trusted; not reliance on numbers, but, contrariwise, distrust of numbers, and the feeling that then we are strongest, when most private and alone" (*CW* 1:176). The students' idealism, in other words, has to be actualized by everyone individually. The moral sentiment is not available "externally," and obedience to it is not possible by deputy or en masse. Put simply, the heart of reform is the moral regeneration of the individual.

Emerson's overall view of society is not as negative, however, as this argument might suggest. His general optimism, his meliorism, his belief in the ultimate moral governance of the universe (see the questionable status of evil, discussed in chapter 2) inevitably also colored his view of society. In its actual state, society may be evil, but its "tendencies" point to a better future; even its current evil is a necessary antithesis in a dialectical progress toward good. Throughout his intellectual career, Emerson believed deeply in the power and ultimate prevalence of the affirmative, the positive, the constructive. These he considered the factors that keep the universe in existence. He never seriously doubted that "the law after which the Universe was made" implies "a force always at work to make the best better and the worst good" (*W* 11:486). What is negative and disruptive is defeated, absorbed, or transcended by nature and by the deepest tendencies in human nature (*W* 7:306–8; 12:61–62). The genius of human language ultimately negates negation. Wittgenstein said that the limits of our language are the limits of our world;[18] and through its regularity and

18. Ludwig Wittgenstein, *Tractatus Logico-Philosophicus* 5.6.

inner logic, language gives us a world that has structure and coherence. And as we saw in the preceding chapter, the negative and the disruptive also run counter to our deep emotional and psychological yearning for unity and harmony. It is not surprising, therefore, that Emerson treats even society and the state as dimensions of a transcendent whole. His "wise skepticism," while relentlessly questioning and criticizing actual institutions and social attitudes, nevertheless recognizes their ultimate relatedness to a deeper reality. Appearances notwithstanding, such institutions and attitudes are "reverend . . . in their tendency and spirit" (*CW* 4:89, 97). Emerson illustrates his complex position perhaps most clearly in an 1837 lecture on "Politics":

> [W]e find in all times and countries every great man does in all his nature point at and imply the existence and well-being of all the orders and institutions of a state. He is full of reverence. He is by inclination, (how far soever in position) the defender of . . . the church, the priest, the judge, the legislator, the executive arm. Throughout his being is he loyal, even when by circumstance arrayed in opposition to the actual order of things. Such was Socrates, St. Paul, Luther, Milton, Burke. (*EL* 2:78)

However indirectly, society and the state do serve moral ends and thus contribute to an all-encompassing moral order. Their very conventions and routines, although in most cases fatal to originality and authenticity, provoke some individuals to intellectual and moral self-assertion. Part of the problem with social and political institutions and conventions is that they are objects of common knowledge. Our very familiarity with them stands in the way of our fully, consciously, critically knowing them. Their very *Alltäglichkeit* ("everydayness"), as Wittgenstein said, makes them "invisible" to us. Or as Whitehead put it, "Familiar things happen, and mankind does not bother about them. It requires a very unusual mind to undertake the analysis of the obvious."[19] Such analysis presupposes our destroying our familiarity with the object of thought so that we are prepared to encounter it in its essential nature, in its fundamental *otherness*—and then achieve real knowledge of it by overcoming that otherness. Only through defamiliarization can we fulfill our moral obligation to achieve *awareness*

---

19. Ludwig Wittgenstein, *Philosophische Untersuchungen*, 1.129; Alfred North Whitehead, *Science and the Modern World*, 4.

of what surrounds us and in the process extend the domain of our conscious life. In Emerson's words, "the interrogation of custom at all points is an inevitable stage in the growth of every superior mind" (*CW* 4:97). Put differently, the only way we can escape spiritual emptiness and alienation as members of society is by raising our social existence to the level of moral awareness. In practice this means that each of us must "call the institutions of society to account, and examine their fitness to him" (*CW* 1:153). As citizens, we should never "let the conscience sleep, but . . . keep it irritated by the presence & reiterated action of reforms & ideas" (*JMN* 8:134). In this spirit Emerson insists that we adhere to the reality of virtue rather than to what in society is reputed to be such ("Is the name of Virtue to be a barrier to that which is Virtue?"—*CW* 4:101); that we "not be hindered by the name of goodness, but . . . explore if it be goodness"—*CW* 2:29–30); that before we urge patriotism we make sure what it stands for (*JMN* 5:87); and that we stop living in illusions about ourselves and our political freedom (our timidity has turned us into "slaves . . . crowing about liberty"—*W* 6:23).

Society presents other provocations advancing the cause of ethics. Its very resistance to new ideas urges their proponents to clarify and purify them. Evil itself, Emerson insists, plays a positive ethical role. Wicked politicians have an eventually beneficial effect through the moral resistance they provoke. Oppression rouses the spirit of liberty. Slavery recoils on the enslaver (*EL* 2:154; *W* 11:125). The forces of evil provide the antagonism that the good needs in order to assert itself: "without enemies, no hero" (*W* 6:255). Emerson's cosmic optimism maintains that "Nature turns all malfeasance to good" and that "the first lesson of history is the good of evil" (*W* 6:252–53). Ultimately every society tilts to the good, not necessarily as a result of deliberate moral choice but because contravening the moral order of things turns out to be ruinous: "The laws of nature are in harmony with each other: that which the head and the heart demand is found to be, in the long run, for what the grossest calculator calls his advantage. The moral sense is always supported by the permanent interest of the parties" (*W* 11:125). That "permanent interest" is not always a matter of political or economic advantage. Emerson seems to extend the principle of mutual recognition examined above when, discussing emancipation in the British West Indies, he says that "the civility of no race can be perfect whilst another race is degraded" (*W* 11:145). The abolition of slavery is thus not only a response to the claims of interracial justice but also an advantage, moral and psychological, to the slaveholding race.

The best evidence, Emerson suggests, of the fundamental moral decency of society is that those who aspire to lead it invariably present the causes they argue for in a morally attractive light, irrespective of whether these causes are intrinsically good or evil. Daniel O'Connell provides Emerson with a clear illustration:

> As soon as one acts for large masses, the moral element will & must be allowed for, will & must work. Daniel O'Connell is no saint, yet at this vast meeting on the hill of Tara 18 miles from Dublin, of 500 000 persons, he almost preaches; he goes for temperance, for law & order, & suggests every reconciling, gentilizing, humanizing consideration. There is little difference between him & Father Matthew, when the audience is thus enormously swelled. (*JMN* 9:21)

Even more striking than the example of O'Connell is that of tyrants. Tyranny always attempts to justify itself by presenting its wickedness as, in fact, a higher good. "It is remarkable," Emerson writes, "how rare in the history of tyrants is an immoral law. Some color, some indirection was always used" (*W* 11:187). In our century we know all too well that wiping out entire populations can be presented as the rightful acquisition of *Lebensraum,* or that genocide can be perpetrated in obedience to laws enacted to ensure racial "purity." To Emerson, the nadir of legal immorality was the Fugitive Slave Law; but those who supported that law, like Daniel Webster, paid tribute to the moral sense of the nation at large by presenting it as "a pacification . . . a measure of conciliation" (*W* 11:198).

Emerson's other-regarding ethics finds its most rarefied expression in his treatment of friendship and love. The interpersonal relationships denoted by these terms are, in his view, ethically the most fragile but also potentially the most enhancing. Indeed, "he will have learned the lesson of life who is skilful in the ethics of friendship" (*W* 7:129). Similarly, "love is a name for almost all virtue" (*CS* 2:136), a statement stressing both the ethical primacy of love and the difficulty of living up to its ethical demands. Friendship and love are ethically "vulnerable" for three reasons: first, the relationships are often perceived as a means of escape from individual inadequacy (loneliness, need of sympathy, sense of incompleteness) and thus are in danger of becoming a refuge for weakness rather than a basis for the joint pursuit of human excellence; second, the reciprocal nature of the relationships involves a precarious balance between selfishness and altruism; and third, our human craving for stability and certitude induces us to ignore that the health of the relationships requires their being ever-evolving. Friendship and love, Emerson suggests, can succeed in their ethicizing role only if they build on strength rather than weakness, encompass the clearly defined rights of self and other, and involve self and other in an unending dialectic.

Rather than being a refuge for the weak, friendship and love should be made instrumental to the attainment of human excellence. Emerson is aware that the instrumental value of these relationships depends upon each person bringing to them the highest possible degree of individual excellence. "Let us feel," he says in "Friendship," "the absolute insulation of man. We are sure that we have all in us." Only when we have made ourselves "finished men" will we be in a position to "grasp heroic hands in heroic hands" (*CW* 2:125). Put differently, "we must be our own, before we can be another's," and only because "we are more our own," can we become "more each other's" (*CW* 2:124, 126). Each individual must contribute his or her "completed" self: "There must be very two, before there can be very one." Or stated in a sublime paradox, "The condition which high friendship demands, is, ability to do without it" (*CW* 2:123).

Emerson recognizes that there is an inevitably selfish or possessive element in friendship and love. Unlike benevolence, friendship and love demand reciprocity. Neither relationship is satisfactory unless the love or friendship one feels for a person is returned in some degree. And the deeper one's feelings, the more intense one's longing that they be reciprocated. Deep love, as Dante's Francesca da Rimini said in self-justification, does not permit the person loved not to love in return ("Amor, ch'a nullo amato amar perdona").[20] This characteristic

20. Dante, *Inferno* 5.103.

of the relationship can easily endanger the individuality or integrity of the persons involved in it. Emerson counters this danger in two ways. He advocates a friendship and love based on distance rather than closeness; and he redirects the possessive instinct to values and ideals that turn possessiveness into a morally enhancing rather than diminishing trait.

In Emerson's treatment of friendship and love, the empirically grounded affinitive emotions play a less important part than the emotion of respect commanded by the moral law. Whatever Emerson's temperamental limitations may have been on the emotional plane, ethically he was justified in deemphasizing the affinitive emotions. He is in emphatic agreement with a central Kantian tenet when he insists that "Reverence is a great part of [friendship]" (*CW* 2:123).[21] As he sees it, emotional closeness undermines respect; as already indicated, respect for the dignity of persons is of paramount moral importance to him as well as to Kant. Emerson safeguards the integrity of everyone involved by treating respect for others as the natural counterpart to self-respect: "Selfreliance applied to another person is reverence, that is, only the selfrespecting will be reverent" (*JMN* 7:371). Put simply, "the complement of . . . self-respect . . . is deference" (*CW* 3:80). Everyone gains morally when our reverence is such that we "seek our friend . . . sacredly" and do not try to "appropriate him to ourselves." Friendship, in a word, "demands a religious treatment," and "no degree of affection need invade this religion." In all relationships we should keep "the island of a man inviolate"; indeed, "lovers should guard their strangeness" (*CW* 2:117, 123; 3:80–81). Our attempts to overcome this strangeness would be a violation of the respect we owe to the mystery that is the other. Emerson, obviously, sees nothing valuable in romantically idealized or sentimental notions of friendship and love. Any relationship involving abdication of self he regards as pernicious.

The strength of Emerson's conviction on this point may be gauged from his stressing repeatedly that in friendship and love opposition is preferable to surrender. It is far better to be "a nettle in the side of your friend than his echo" (*CW* 2:122–23). Although those who love us are dear to us and "enlarge our life," dearer still "are those

---

21. Kant, *Metaphysik der Sitten, Tugendlehre* §46, *Gesammelte Schriften*, 6:469–71.

who reject us as unworthy, for they add another life" (*CW* 3:162). Perhaps most telling is the statement: "Let [thy friend] be to thee forever a sort of beautiful enemy, untamable, devoutly revered" (*CW* 2:124). George Kateb has commented learnedly on possible ancient or modern sources of and parallels to Emerson's concept of the friend as a "beautiful enemy," but he finds none of them quite satisfactory. The most likely source for the term, it seems to me, is Goethe's *Elective Affinities (Die Wahlverwandtschaften,* 1809), which Emerson read (in German) as early as 1832 (*JMN* 6:106). In a short story inserted in his novel, Goethe refers twice to the heroine as the "schöne Feindin" (beautiful enemy) of the man she loves. It should be noted, however, that in Emerson's theory of friendship, "beautiful enemy" has implications far beyond the rather straightforward meaning the term has in Goethe's story.[22]

Emerson's conception of friendship was not always so agonistic. In some sermon paragraphs blending (unattributed) statements on the excellences of friendship from Aristotle and Montaigne (*CS* 4:50), he claims, among other things, that "a true friend is another self"—by which he means, another oneself, a second myself—thus adopting a central Aristotelian definition of "friend." Montaigne had also adopted this view. Actually, as John Michael points out, "Montaigne exceeds Aristotle's idea of the identity between friends." He is even more emphatic, as we learn from his essay "Of Friendship," that the friend "is not another person: he is me." On occasion, Emerson found himself in agreement with such sentiments. "In the friendship I speak of," Montaigne wrote, "they [our souls] mix and blend so thoroughly that they efface the seam that joined them and cannot find it again."[23]

---

22. Johann Wolfgang Goethe, *Die Wahlverwandtschaften* 2.10, *Gedenkausgabe,* 9:220–21; George Kateb, *Emerson and Self-Reliance,* 110–12. Kateb states that Emerson's thought of the friend as beautiful enemy "seems to exceed even Nietzsche in its daring" (110), and by way of comparison he points to a (somewhat distant) parallel in *The Gay Science* (§279). He overlooks, however, the passage in *Thus Spoke Zarathustra* where Nietzsche not only equals Emerson in "daring" but also seems to echo him: "In one's friend one should still honor the enemy. . . . In one's friend one should have one's best enemy" *(Also sprach Zarathustra,* pt. 1, "Vom Freunde," *Sämtliche Werke,* 4:71). The only scholar, so far as I know, to have claimed that the "schöne Feindin" of *Die Wahlverwandtschaften* is "the probable immediate source of Emerson's term" is Erik Thurin *(Emerson as Priest of Pan,* 182).

23. Aristotle, *Nicomachean Ethics* 9.4.5; 9.9.1; *Magna Moralia* 2.15. Michael, *Emerson and Skepticism,* 115. Michel de Montaigne, *Les Essais,* 191, 188.

With apparent approval, Emerson copied this passage (in Cotton's translation) on a loose sheet of paper filed with his lecture "The Heart" (*EL* 2:466). Emerson also knew that Montaigne's great essay was inspired by the latter's friendship with Étienne de la Boétie. He states in "The Heart" that "there is no more remarkable example in modern times of a thorough and noble friendship than that of Montaigne and Stephen de Boece" (*EL* 2:290). It is all the more remarkable, therefore, that he chose to make his poem "Étienne de la Boéce" (*W* 9:82) the means of expressing a strikingly different, an agonistic view of friendship:

> I serve you not, if you I follow,
> Shadowlike, o'er hill and hollow;
> And bend my fancy to your leading,
> All too nimble for my treading.
> When the pilgrimage is done,
> And we've the landscape overrun,
> I am bitter, vacant, thwarted,
> And your heart is unsupported.
> Vainly valiant, you have missed
> The manhood that should yours resist . . .

The germ of Emerson's conception of friendship as contest is in all probability traceable to another emphasis in Aristotle's complex ethic of friendship. (Aristotle, as Anders Hallengren has usefully reminded us, affected Emerson's ideas more significantly than the usual view of Emerson the Platonist or Neoplatonist suggests.)[24] Aristotelian friendship involves emulation and mutual correction. Aristotle concludes his long and detailed discussion of friendship in the *Nicomachean Ethics* with the statement that good humans "seem actually to become better by putting their friendship into practice, and because they correct each other's faults, for each takes the impress from the other of those traits in him that give him pleasure—whence the saying: Noble deeds from noble men."[25] Emerson, as he did so often, showed his genius by creatively engaging such ideas and developing them into insights that can only be called Emersonian.

24. Hallengren, *The Code of Concord*, 347–48.
25. Aristotle, *Nicomachean Ethics* 9.12.3, H. Rackham's translation (Loeb Classical Library). For discussion of Aristotle's view, see Nussbaum, *The Fragility of Goodness*, 362–63.

Much of what precedes makes it abundantly clear that, according to Emerson, the possessive element in friendship and love cannot possibly have the other person for its object. In a *perfect* friendship, friends would be, in Thucydides' words as quoted by Emerson, "a possession for all time" (*CW* 2:115).[26] But as Kant remarked, such perfect friendships are nothing more than "the hobbyhorse of novelists" (*das Steckenpferd der Romanenschreiber*).[27] Emerson agreed: "Friends, such as we desire, are dreams and fables" (*CW* 2:125). As will be obvious from the rest of this chapter, Emerson's reinterpretation of "possessiveness" is rife with conceptual echoes of the theory of love that Socrates attributes to Diotima in Plato's *Symposium*. What friends can "possess," Emerson asserts, is a shared ideal or aspiration, a joint commitment to the pursuit of virtue or excellence. What truly binds friends and lovers is not "the low and proprietary sense of *Do you love me*," but "the divine affinity of virtue with itself" (*CW* 4:72; 2:115). To those who find this kind of love or friendship rather too ethereal, Emerson replies that it is "foolish to be afraid of making our ties too spiritual, as if so we could lose any genuine love" (*CW* 2:125).

A love or friendship based on the common pursuit of spiritual values is of necessity processual rather than static. Not only are values such as truth, goodness, virtue, and excellence unattainable in their absoluteness (and thus invite to endless pursuit), but they also invalidate all attempts to confine them to the qualities embodied in the loved person: "It is not me, but the worth [in me], that fixes [your] love: and that worth is a drop of the ocean of worth that is beyond me" (*CW* 4:72–73). Considerations like these led Emerson to rethink the question of reciprocity in friendship and love. As he puts it in the concluding paragraph of his essay on "Friendship,"

---

26. Emerson owned a copy of Thucydides' *History of the Peloponnesian War* (Walter Harding, *Emerson's Library*, 272), and he repeatedly referred to or quoted from it. As a teacher of moral lessons, the Greek historian ranked among the very best, in Emerson's view: "The charm of Plutarch & Plato & Thucydides for me I believe, is that there I get ethics without cant" (*JMN* 5:353). Thucydides made the famous claim that his work was intended not as a prize-essay to be heard and forgotten, but as "a possession for all time" (*ktēma es aei—Historiai* 1.22.4)—a possession for those through the ages who truly "hear" and understand it. Freely applying this idea to friendship, Emerson writes: "Who hears me, who understands me, becomes mine,—a possession for all time" (*CW* 2:114–15). He also quoted the phrase in Greek in *English Traits* (*CW* 5:12; see 5:199 n.12.8).

27. Kant, *Metaphysik der Sitten, Tugendlehre* §46, *Gesammelte Schriften*, 6:470.

> It has seemed to me lately more possible than I knew, to carry a friendship greatly, on one side, without due correspondence on the other. . . . It is thought a disgrace to love unrequited. But . . . true love cannot be unrequited. True love transcends the unworthy object, and dwells and broods on the eternal. (*CW* 2:127)

Instead of being based on personal reciprocity, true love and friendship consist in an endless dialectical process involving as opposites the infinitude of spiritual values and their finite realization in the persons of lovers and friends. Consequently,

> Of progressive souls, all loves and friendships are momentary. *Do you love me?* means, Do you see the same truth? If you do, we are happy with the same happiness: but presently one of us passes into the perception of new truth; we are divorced, and no tension in nature can hold us to each other. (*CW* 4:72)

Such "divorce," however, is a necessary antithesis in the dialectical progress to a higher synthesis: "It is only when you leave and lose me by casting yourself on a sentiment which is higher than both of us, that I draw near and find myself at your side" (*CW* 4:72). In short, as Emerson puts it in "Friendship," "we part only to meet again on a higher platform" (*CW* 2:126).

In the course of their dialectical progress, love and friendship thus increasingly transcend the personal. What Gregory Vlastos says about Plato's theory in the *Symposium* is perfectly applicable to Emerson's position: "The individual, in the uniqueness and integrity of his or her individuality, will never be the object of . . . love. . . . Plato's theory . . . does not provide for love of whole persons, but only for love of that abstract version of persons which consists of the complex of their best qualities." In his review of the Emerson-Carlyle correspondence, Henry James stated the matter more simply: "Emerson speaks of his friends too much as if they were disembodied spirits."[28] Emerson urges commitment to the spiritual, moral, or intellectual ideal itself rather than to its temporary and imperfect incarnations. Instead of "loving [the virtues] in one," we should "lov[e] them in all"—which amounts to transcending the personal element altogether and loving the virtues

---

28. Gregory Vlastos, *Platonic Studies*, 31; Henry James, *The American Essays*, 47.

for their own sake. Our affections "are but tents of a night" that should not distract us from contemplating the "overarching vault, bright with galaxies of immutable lights" (*CW* 2:106, 109–10). Emerson concedes that the heart resists such abstractions, that its natural tendency is to idealize the person loved, to see perfection in the imperfect. But, he insists, "even love, which is the deification of persons, must become more impersonal every day" (*CW* 2:107). For Emerson, it appears, love and friendship are but stages in the unending progress of the soul: beautiful though these human relations now often are, they "must be succeeded and supplanted . . . by what is more beautiful, and so on for ever" (*CW* 2:110).

5

Everyday Life

*E*thics is concerned not only with one's duties to oneself and to others, but also, more generally, with the quality of human life. Questions about the nature of the good life and the means of attaining it have been with us ever since Socrates decided that the unexamined life was not worth living. In premodern times the good life was held to consist in one's dedication to, for instance, the search for the highest knowledge (Socrates, Plato), the contemplation of philosophical truth (Aristotle), absolute rational self-mastery (the Stoics), sainthood (the medieval Church), the chivalric ideal (the later Middle Ages), or heroic virtue (French neoclassicism). Although none of these pursuits has lost its idealistic attraction and several of them may continue to define the good life for some individuals, they are too "exceptional" to have wide appeal in an egalitarian world. With the coming of the modern age, Charles Taylor points out, "the previous 'higher' forms of life were dethroned" and "ordinary life," the "sense of the importance of the everyday in human life," became "the very center of the good life." Or as Agnes Heller puts it, "in our modern world the human condition resides in everyday life," and, consequently, the good of the human condition depends on the quality of everyday life.[1] What gives value and meaning to our existence, what makes our lives fulfilling and worth living, has to be looked for in the everyday.

As a source of meaning and value, everyday life poses two problems. First, its very ordinariness, repetitiveness, and routines seem both to frustrate the conscious, aware, authentic living that alone can render

---

1. Plato, *Apology* 38A. Johan Huizinga, *Herfsttij der Middeleeuwen;* Paul Bénichou, *Morales du grand siècle.* C. Taylor, *Sources of the Self,* 13–14. Agnes Heller, *Can Modernity Survive?* 45.

human experience meaningful and to preclude the generation of any values likely to appear worth pursuing. Formerly, the "higher" ideals had their locus outside and "above" everyday life and thus could inspire those living everyday lives. Nothing, in theory at least, prevented a medieval peasant from aspiring to sainthood or a slave from becoming a Stoic philosopher (as the case of Epictetus proves). In the modern age, inspiration has to come from within everyday life, and everyday life is, almost by definition, uninspiring. The second problem arises from the fact that we live our everyday lives in the modern world—a world experienced by many as emptied of value and meaning. The "devaluation" of our world was already keenly felt by Emerson and his contemporaries. Laurence Lockridge has described Romantic ethics as "a crisis ethics brought about by the impoverishment and imminent collapse of collective value structures" and as an assertion of value "against a backdrop of negation." The Romantics considered meaning or meaningfulness to be as much threatened as value: they experienced firsthand what Max Weber famously called *die Entzauberung der Welt* ("the disenchantment of the world")—a world where the dominance of rationalism, intellectualism, and scientism had led to imaginative and symbolic impoverishment. One important Romantic task was to reendow life with a richer meaning, with depth, dignity, and purpose. In Lockridge's words, "the good life is one that generates as it goes a continuously enhanced significance."[2] Emerson, characteristically, spends little time analyzing the problems that threaten everyday life—both intrinsically and in its relation to the modern world—as a source of value and meaning. But since so many of his assertions and affirmations appear to be responses to those problems, there can be no doubt about his troubled awareness of them. His prescriptions for the good life can be grouped under three headings: Imagination, Beauty, and Experience.

I

Emerson recognized the banality of the everyday as a central fact of modern life that had to be confronted head-on. He had little

2. Lockridge, *The Ethics of Romanticism*, 145–46. Max Weber, "Wissenschaft als Beruf," *Gesammelte Aufsätze zur Wissenschaftslehre*, 536.

respect for such oblique solutions, or pseudo-solutions, to the modern malaise as joining utopian communities, pursuing the remote or the exotic, and embracing an ancient faith ("This running into the Catholic Church is disgusting," he wrote, a statement no doubt based on the "disgust" he experienced when his friend Anna Barker Ward converted to Catholicism—*JMN* 15:336; 14:330–31). Not even Romantic Hellenism, which to many was culturally the most inspiring solution, held any appeal for him. As Barbara Packer says, "Romantic Hellenism bored Emerson."[3] Instead of indulging in vain attempts to escape from our modern condition, we should face it and try to redeem it. The chosen instrument of such redemption Emerson believed to be an enhanced imagination that would enable us to apprehend the inexhaustible symbolic richness of our everyday world and thus, in effect, to bring about a "re-enchantment" of that world:

> The invariable mark of wisdom is to see the miraculous in the common. What is a day? What is a year? What is summer? What is woman? What is a child? What is sleep? To our blindness, these things seem unaffecting. We make fables to hide the baldness of the fact. . . . [But] to the wise . . . a fact is true poetry, and the most beautiful of fables. (*CW* 1:44)

Emerson insisted repeatedly that an ability to take the ordinary as a cause for wonder marks "the difference between the wise and the unwise: the latter wonders at what is unusual, the wise man wonders at the usual" (*CW* 3:167). We therefore must rediscover the wonder in the everyday, the magic in the plainest fact. Indeed, *"in the common things, is always the field of the most splendid discoveries."* Unfortunately, we fail to see the splendor in the grass (Wordsworth obviously fits into this argument) because of our foolish preoccupation with "inscrutable mysteries or obscure controversies or distant countries" (*CS* 4:79). This whole argument makes it clear that Emerson's famous advocacy, in "The American Scholar," of literature exploring "the near, the low, the common" (*CW* 1:67) was inspired as much by ethical as by aesthetic considerations: he was pleading for recognition of the *worth* of the ordinary and commonplace. As Nicolai Hartmann emphasizes, the

---

3. Packer, *Emerson's Fall*, 40.

very appreciation of the everyday, the affirmation of its overriding significance, is in itself a crucial ethical stance.[4]

The imaginative restoration of our world is contingent upon our commitment to simplicity, our avoidance of routine, and our reverence for symbol. Simplicity requires our removing or transcending the obstacles, both within and without, that prevent our direct confrontation with the essential facts. Among such obstacles are respect for tradition ("Reverence for the deeds of our ancestors is a treacherous sentiment"—W 7:177; see also the Divinity School "Address" and the opening lines of *Nature*); our tendency to glamorize what is distant in time and space ("The first step of worthiness will be to disabuse us of our superstitious associations with places and times"—CW 2:152); the attractions of escapism which prevent our realizing that "fact is better than fiction" (W 7:107); and society's insistence on conformity and our consequent victimization by "this Gorgon of Convention and Fashion" (W 7:133). What matters is the here and now, "the quality of the moment . . . the depth at which we live" (W 7:183). The moment truly lived amounts to an experience of eternity (W 7:178, 183); to inspired perception there are no dull, despised, prosaic facts, but "the day of facts is a rock of diamonds, [and] a fact is an Epiphany of God" (EL 3:47). What we need is not an escape into some romanticized past or utopian future, but "insight into today," "the theory of this particular Wednesday" (CW 1:67; W 7:179).[5]

Simplicity is "the perfectness of man" because it embodies unqualified "trust in the Soul itself" (EL 3:171, 302). Since the Soul always *is*, its only valid incarnation is the ever-present Now. The human must, therefore, embrace the Now and endeavor to become aware of the Soul-in-the-Now. The Soul does not fade in the light of common day but appears to those knowing how to read it by that light. "I at least fully believe," Emerson wrote in 1836, "that God is in every place, & that, if the mind is excited, it may see him, & in him an infinite wisdom in every object that passes before us" (JMN 5:150). Two years earlier he noted that "to a soul alive to God every moment is a new world" (JMN 4:266). From "The Over-Soul" we learn that a person attuned to the

---

4. Hartmann, *Ethik*, 7–16.
5. See further Robinson, "A Theory of Wednesdays," *Emerson and the Conduct of Life*, 174–80.

Soul encounters it—or, pantheistically speaking, the One and thus his or her true Self—"in the hour that now is, in the earnest experience of the common day" (*CW* 2:172). Once awakened to this cardinal fact, we shall no longer regard our everyday lives and the modern world as hopelessly banal and expend our spirit in nostalgic longing for the grandeur of an imagined past. Our present lives are "needlessly mean" because we fail to remember that the source of true splendor is simplicity: "by the depth of our living [we] should deck [our lives] with more than regal or national splendor" (*CW* 2:152–53).

A major impediment to deep, aware, imaginatively enriched living is routine in its various forms. "Repetition," Emerson writes, "is anti-spiritual," and "the coarse mattings of custom" prevent "all wonder" (*CW* 4:154; 3:167). He agrees with Carlyle that mysteries and miracles confront us every day, but that custom has made us insensible of them.[6] The banality of our daily lives seems to more than justify all the ennui and *taedium vitae* we sometimes experience, and yet one's very existence as a human being is a fact "of such bewildering astonishment that it seems as if it were the part of reason to spend one's lifetime in a trance of wonder" (*CS* 4:230). This trance of wonder recalls Pascal's astonishment, when he considered the immensity of space and time, at being "here, now."[7]

Emerson also devotes much of his eloquence in prose and verse to awakening us to a sense of the miraculous in the everyday aspects and processes of nature. In his autobiography Goethe tells the story of a man of great distinction who every spring was exasperated at the earth's inveterate habit of turning *green*—as if one's familiarity with that occurrence in any way diminished its miraculousness.[8] As Carlyle says, of all the tricks that custom plays upon us, "perhaps the cleverest is her knack of persuading us that the Miraculous, by simple repetition, ceases to be Miraculous."[9] Or in the words of the Divinity School "Address," "the mystery of nature . . . has not yielded yet one word of explanation," and the *real* miracles are such things as "the blowing clover and the falling rain" (*CW* 1:76, 81). Nature is dull

6. Carlyle, *Sartor Resartus*, 259–60.
7. Blaise Pascal, *Pensées*, 125.
8. Johann Wolfgang Goethe, *Dichtung und Wahrheit*, bk. 13, *Gedenkausgabe*, 10:632.
9. Carlyle, *Sartor Resartus*, 259.

and repetitive only to the atrophied imagination. To imaginatively empowered perception, every glimpse of nature "hath a grandeur" (CW 1:39). Such perception sees no repetition whatever in nature: "To the attentive eye, each moment of the year has its own beauty, and in the same field, it beholds, every hour, a picture which was never seen before, and which shall never be seen again" (CW 1:14).

Emerson's chief antidote to routine, to the "anti-spiritual" repetitiveness to which humans are liable, is spontaneity, which he calls "the essence of genius, of virtue, and of life" (CW 2:37). He preaches "the soul active," the ever-creative, ever-renewed and renewing self, as "the sound estate of every man" (CW 1:56–57). Newness, freshness, and surprise are hallmarks of the Soul's self-revelations. In fact, even "the moral sentiment is well called 'the newness,' for it is never other" (CW 3:40). Emerson, therefore, prefers thinking to thought, speculation to doctrine, action to its results, creativity to its products. His defense of inconsistency is a further expression of this outlook (CW 2:33).

Nothing hinders the imaginative experience of everyday life more than the routine of our daily work, and nothing is more responsible for the instrumentalization of human beings. Indeed, "the laborer [is] sacrificed to the splendid result," and "the tools run away with the workman" (CW 1:121, 129). The worker should not be "bereaved of that nobility which comes from the superiority to his work," and he should remember that his work has no value "except so far as it embodies his spiritual prerogatives" (CW 1:121). Edward Waldo Emerson noted that a statement like this anticipates some of William Morris's ideas about restoring joy and beauty to labor (W 1:435).[10] The fundamental ethical problem here is the violation of personhood inherent in reducing what should be an end (the human being and his or her spiritual self-realization) to a means (the human-as-machine in the service of productivity). Only to the degree that the products of labor objectify the human spirit do they attain moral value and thus transcend the purely economic category of price. The human spirit, needless to say, cannot express itself through something as antispiritual as routine. Only an authentic, truly creative act can embody an

10. For additional commentary, see Robinson, Emerson and the Conduct of Life, 160; also 217n156, for Emerson's influence on the founders of the arts and crafts movement.

aspect of one's spirit. Optimally, one's every act should be so true an expression of one's ever-evolving spirit as to be unique. Unique acts are the only ones that completely escape from the taint of routine. Therefore, "I do not wish to do one thing but once" (*CW* 1:212).

Like simplicity, and unlike routine, symbolic awareness and reverence for symbol are positive factors in the imaginative enrichment of our lives. Emerson was as convinced as Ernst Cassirer that the human is *animal symbolicum*.[11] We live in a *human* world—a world shaped by human creativity (language, art) and efforts at interpretation (myth, religion, science). The symbolic universe resulting from these activities has become our "natural" home to the point that generally we are no longer aware of its symbolic dimension. The imaginative enrichment of our lives involves our being reawakened to the fact that "we are symbols, and inhabit symbols" (*CW* 3:12). Symbolic awareness will enable us to apprehend the spirit of which the events or facts of everyday life are expressions; it will help us perceive the deeper meanings of common things and occurrences. Thus it will transform our everyday world into "a temple, whose walls are covered with emblems" (*CW* 3:10). We simply "must have symbols," and the imagination is "the great awakening power" that makes us realize that we live indeed in a world of symbols (*W* 7:212). The importance of this realization is apparent from Emerson's claim that "the imagination is not a talent of some men but is the health of every man" (*W* 8:56).

Emerson heightens the ethical significance of his argument by treating the imagination as a source of joy: "There is a joy in perceiving the representative or symbolic character of a fact, which no bare fact or event can ever give" (*W* 6: 304). Or as he put it elsewhere, "the deepest pleasure comes I think from the occult belief that an unknown meaning & consequence lurk in the common every day facts" (*JMN* 5:212). Joy and pleasure, needless to say, enhance the quality of everyday life. Moreover, since hedonism is itself an ethical orientation of ancient and distinguished pedigree, Emerson's concern with joy and pleasure locates his treatment of the imagination all the more firmly within ethics.

Our reverence for symbol should be *enacted* in our daily lives. Our common everyday acts should acquire sacramental significance. From

11. Ernst Cassirer, *An Essay on Man*, 26.

the poet, the philosopher, and the saint, for whom "all things are . . . sacred . . . all days holy, all men divine," we should learn that "any thing man can do, may be divinely done" (*CW* 2:8, 83). The most honorable ambition is not "to win laurels in the state or the army . . . but to be a master of living well, and to administer the offices of master or servant, of husband, father and friend." This ambition we can realize only if we hold ourselves and others "sacred" (*W* 7:122). In his essay "Friendship," Emerson urges that we "dignify to each other the daily needs and offices of man's life" (*CW* 2:121). He had no patience with empty rituals, but ritual at its best, that is, as an expression in action of spiritual truth, he valued highly. As he put it in "Manners," "The compliments and ceremonies of our breeding should recall, however remotely, the grandeur of our destiny" (*CW* 3:81). Every act "becomes an act of religion" when the person acting is guided by spiritual law. Religion should "cease to be occasional" so that "the consecration of Sunday" will no longer "confess the desecration of the entire week," nor "the consecration of the church confess the profanation of the house" (*W* 7:132–33). Every day and every act, in sum, should embody the Spirit striving for self-realization in the lives of all of us.

II

Emerson considered a craving for beauty to be a fundamental trait of humanity. The desire for beauty, "extend[ed] . . . to the uttermost," is as much "an ultimate end" of the human spirit as the yearning for truth or for goodness. Beauty is an aspiration so essentially defining our humanity that "no reason can be asked or given why the soul seeks beauty" (*CW* 1:17). Although beauty as such defies analysis (*EL* 1:101; *W* 6:289, 303), its manifestations have a "pictorial" or symbolic quality that makes them more concretely accessible to the perceiver than the conceptualizations of truth or the actualizations of goodness. For this reason, beauty "is the form under which the intellect prefers to study the world"; it is the form that leads us to "thinking of the foundations of things" (*W* 6:287–88). Similarly, beauty "is the mark God sets upon virtue" (*CW* 1:15). Truth and goodness, in other words, are most readily *apprehensible* as beauty: they *appear* as intellectual or moral beauty. This giving an aesthetic dimension to conceptual and ethical categories should come as no surprise from a man who wrote: "I am in all my theory, ethics, and politics a poet" (*L* 3:18).

Beauty thus plays an indispensable role in the good life. It is "needful to man" (*CW* 1:13) not only because it educates the senses and the feelings—thus fulfilling its purely "aesthetic" function (the Greek term *aisthēsis* means "sensation," "perception," "feeling")—but also because of its educative role in the moral and intellectual spheres. The search for beauty is not only human but also humanizing precisely because beauty educates all of our highest faculties: it appeals to us aesthetically (the beauty "of general nature, of the human face and form, of manners"), intellectually (the beauty "of brain or method"), and ethically ("moral beauty or beauty of the soul"—*W* 6:287). Most relevant to my subject, of course, is the role of beauty in everyday life and everyday ethics.

Arguing against his audience's assumption that beauty occupies a realm far removed from the routine and banality of everyday life, Emerson assured them that, on the contrary, daily life is "embosomed in beauty" (*CW* 2:77). He attempted to convince them of the validity of this claim, first, by reawakening them to a sense of the inexhaustible beauty of nature, and, second, by presenting art not as something exceptional and set apart from common experience but as something "natural." The beauty of art, in other words, is as "democratically" available as the beauty of nature, if only we are capable of perceiving it. As far as nature is concerned, its beauty is so often attested to and invoked in Emerson's prose and poetry as to make superfluous a discussion of the importance he attached to it. Suffice it to say that Emerson held that in order to appreciate nature fully we need to shed our adult insensitivity and rediscover our childhood's sense of wonder: "The lover of nature is he . . . who has retained the spirit of infancy even into the era of manhood" (*CW* 1:9). Although this argument has a strongly Wordsworthian (and Coleridgean) flavor, Emerson is more optimistic than the poet of "Ode: Intimations of Immortality" about the possibility of one's retaining "the spirit of infancy." To be sure, it is "the bane of life that natural effects are continually crowded out, and artificial arrangements substituted." But the experiences of "early youth [when] the earth spoke and the heavens glowed" need not be lost as we grow older, as Emerson emphasizes in explicit contradiction to a passage he quotes from Wordsworth's "Ode" (*W* 7:297, 299). "In the woods," Emerson says synecdochically, "a man . . . at what period soever of life, is always a child" (*CW* 1:10).

As for art, why should we think of it as confined to ancient cities and modern museums when it is all around us? Every day the aesthetically sensitive eye can appreciate

> the eternal picture which nature paints in the street with mov-
> ing men and children, beggars, and fine ladies, draped in red,
> and green, and blue, and gray; long-haired, grizzled, white-faced,
> black-faced, wrinkled, giant, dwarf, expanded, elfish,—capped
> and based by heaven, earth, and sea. (*CW* 2:212)

Even when speaking of the visual arts as more traditionally conceived, Emerson argues against their "separate and contrasted existence." He insists that "beauty must come back to the useful arts, and the distinction between the fine and the useful arts be forgotten" (*CW* 2:217–18). Having adopted German and Coleridgean organicism, which, in M. H. Abrams's words, "may be defined as the philosophy whose major categories are derived metaphorically from the attributes of living and growing things,"[12] Emerson found it easy to interpret great works of art as "natural" expressions of the human mind. Both Greek and Gothic art illustrate the fact that "all beauty [is] organic," that it grows from within outward, that "outside embellishment is deformity" (*W* 6:290). In truth, it is the soul that "created the arts wherever they have flourished"; York Minster and St. Peter's in Rome are but "copies of an invisible archetype" inhering in the human mind (*CW* 2:47; 1:40).

Once this idea is accepted, American artists will stop imitating European models and create art that authentically expresses the soul of modern America, that is, art "called out by the necessity of the people" (*JMN* 5:210–11). "Necessity" not only stimulated the demand for socially responsible art, but it was also an essential criterion of beauty itself, as Emerson had learned from Goethe as early as 1836 (*JMN* 5:129). In fact, "whatever is beautiful rests on the foundation of the necessary" (*W* 7:52). Clearly, Emerson was groping toward a theory of function-based beauty that anticipated the philosophy of

---

12. M. H. Abrams, *The Mirror and the Lamp: Romantic Theory and the Critical Tradition*, 168.

functional beauty that Horatio Greenough explained to him in 1852 (*JMN* 13:86) and that reached its maturity in the functionalism of the early twentieth century. Organicism and "necessity" taken together led to a "democratization" of the concept of art and, potentially, to a general availability of beauty in everyday life.

Experiencing beauty is an important part of the good life not just on aesthetic grounds, but also because of other emotions evoked by the experience. In language reminiscent of *King Lear,* Emerson says that without a sense of beauty a human seems "a poor, naked, shivering creature" trapped in a cold, indifferent universe (*W* 7:213). Beauty, by contrast, "warms the heart"; it "delights" and "emancipates"; it brings cheerfulness and inspires enthusiasm; and it thus enables us momentarily "to forget ourselves," to escape from the burden of identity, thought, and memory (*W* 7:306; *CW* 2:190). Such momentary disindividualization is a precondition of spiritual health; it also gives us a sense of belonging to a transindividual reality. Emerson appropriately alludes to the root meaning of enthusiasm (Greek *enthousiasmos,* ultimately from *entheos:* having the god within, possessed by the god [thus, inspired]) when he says: "Enthusiasm . . . is the passing from the human to the divine" (*W* 10:171). Such states of mind not only are necessary for exceptional achievement ("Nothing great was ever achieved without enthusiasm"—*CW* 2:190), but they obviously also enhance the spiritual quality of everyday life.

The role of beauty in such enhancement is given additional emphasis by Emerson's tendency to rank beauty higher than usefulness. A person who "only lives to the useful" is "a beggar." Such a person merely serves "as a pin or rivet in the social machine" and never fulfills the higher demands of humanness. In fact, "the most useful man in the most useful world . . . would remain unsatisfied." As soon as one develops a sense of beauty, however, "life acquires a very high value." Beauty constitutes life's "most ascending quality" (*W* 6:159, 289). This hierarchy of values demonstrates how strongly the aesthetic view of life appealed to Emerson. Making oneself useful is, to be sure, a matter of obligation. Usefulness is something we owe to the world we live in. Living a useless life is despicable, Emerson claimed, pertinently, in an essay on "Aristocracy": "To live without duties is obscene" (*W* 10:52). Nevertheless, the flower of humanness is the ability to transcend the obligation attendant upon usefulness and to attain the freedom inherent in aesthetic experience, which, as Kant said in the *Critique of Judgment*, is purely "disinterested" *(ohne alles Interesse)* and therefore does not involve moral assent *(Beifall)*.[13] Such "useless" freedom is the finest achievement of human culture. Nicolai Hartmann regarded it as the real vindication of human existence: it is, in Hartmann's apt coinage, our "anthropodicy" *(Anthropodizee)*.[14] Clearly, Emerson was sometimes tempted to embrace this view.

Emerson's predilection for an aesthetic view of life is additionally underscored by his tending to aestheticize ethics itself. He holds that the moral law should attract through its charm and beauty, not oblige through commands. Rightly apprehended, the moral law does not command in any dogmatic fashion; instead it evokes love and veneration on account of its transcendent beauty. As Emerson puts it in "The Sovereignty of Ethics," "the inspirations we catch of this law are . . . joyful sparkles, and are recorded for their beauty, for the delight they give, not for their obligation; and that is their priceless good to men, that they charm and uplift, not that they are imposed" (*W* 10:209). Elsewhere he says that "poetry . . . the love of beauty, lead [us] to the adoration of the moral sentiment," but that the New Testament has lost "the charm of poetry" through its "inadmissible claim of positive authority," its imposing "an external command, where command cannot be" (*W* 10:115–17). The Christ of the Divinity School "Address," not surprisingly, escapes from the distortions imposed on him by the New Testament and exemplifies Emersonian aestheticism. In what Joel Porte calls Emerson's "startlingly heretical portrait" of Christ, the dominant traits are Beauty and Joy. Christ, Porte says, "is offered to us as a kind of first-century aesthete, replete with 'locks of beauty,' who was 'ravished' by the 'supreme Beauty' of the soul's mystery and went out in a 'jubilee of sublime emotion' to tell us all 'that God incarnates himself in man.' "[15]

The relevance of this argument to everyday life is obvious when we consider that a moral law that inspires on account of its beauty will lead to actions that are themselves beautiful. In *The Conduct of Life*,

---

13. Immanuel Kant, *Kritik der Urteilskraft* §§ 2, 5, *Gesammelte Schriften*, 5:204, 210.
14. Hartmann, *Ethik*, 462.
15. Joel Porte, *Representative Man: Ralph Waldo Emerson in His Time*, 115. The passages Porte quotes are from *CW* 1:81, 83.

Emerson complains of the dearth of such actions: "I suffer every day from the want of perception of beauty in people. They do not know the charm with which all moments and objects can be embellished, the charm of manners, of self-command, of benevolence" (*W* 6:159). Self-command and benevolence are obvious enactments of the moral law; as for manners, politeness, courtesy, they have "benevolence as [their] foundation" (*CW* 3:83). What matters to Emerson here is the charm, the beauty, the attractiveness of actions that are morally right. Ethics is thus potentially a major source of beauty in everyday life. Indeed, the virtues "must be practised for their elegance. The virtuous man must be a poet & not a drudge of his virtues" (*JMN* 4:385). The identification of the good with the beautiful is as old as Plato (*Symposium* and elsewhere) and became a commonplace in Platonizing Western thought—although Irving Babbitt complained rather peevishly that the identification was disproved as far back as the Trojan War ("Helen was beautiful, but was neither good nor true")![16] For Emerson, it is a "truth, that perfect beauty and perfect goodness are One," that goodness is "Beauty in its highest form," and that "in the impression beauty makes upon us what is finest is moral" (*EL* 1:100, 110; 2:275). Through this subtle interweave of morality and beauty Emerson avoided Nietzsche's ultimate reduction of ethics to aesthetics (*Reduktion der Moral auf Aesthetik*).[17] Nevertheless, Emerson did claim an important role for beauty in actual moral life. Ethics was not just a matter of doing one's duty (as discussed in chapters 3 and 4): doing one's duty could itself become an experience of beauty that enhanced one's everyday life.

III

Emerson's concern with the quality of everyday life was also motivated by a fear that he shared with many of his contemporaries and many moderns—the fear of not having really lived, of not having truly confronted the experience called life. Like many of us, he was haunted by a sense that life is both elusive and illusive, that it is too impalpable

16. Irving Babbitt, *Rousseau and Romanticism*, 271.
17. Friedrich Nietzsche, Manuscript note (1881), *Sämtliche Werke*, 9:471.

and unreal to admit of true confrontation. How deeply he was affected by this problem appears from Robert D. Richardson's biography, where Emerson's "powerful craving for direct, personal, unmediated experience" becomes virtually an interpretational leitmotiv.[18] Emerson was heir to an intellectual outlook that had thoroughly problematized experience. Hume had been unable to make up his mind about the relationship of experience to thought, or about whether experience is primarily one's own individually or ours by virtue of our being part of humankind. A major question confronting Kant in the *Critique of Pure Reason* was, "How is experience possible?" What appeared to Emerson to be threatened was the possibility of experience itself. Was the self reduced to some form or other of epistemological solipsism so that it could not apprehend anything but the content of its own inner consciousness? Was the self, in other words, deprived of any meaningful experience of a reality (however defined) outside itself? What David Robinson calls Emerson's "passion for reality" was an anxious response to such questions.[19]

That these questions had at least as much existential as philosophical urgency for Emerson is also evidenced by some well-known sentences from the essay "Experience":

> There are moods in which we court suffering, in the hope that here, at least, we shall find reality, sharp peaks and edges of truth. But it turns out to be scene-painting and counterfeit. The only thing grief has taught me, is to know how shallow it is. That, like all the rest, plays about the surface, and never introduces me into the reality, for contact with which, we would even pay the costly price of sons and lovers. . . . [Our] souls never touch their objects. An innavigable sea washes with silent waves between us and the things we aim at and converse with. . . . I take this evanescence and lubricity of all objects, which lets them slip through our fingers then when we clutch hardest, to be the most unhandsome part of our condition. (*CW* 3:29)

The good life obviously demands that we endeavor to overcome this "most unhandsome part of our condition." Emerson's contribution

---

18. Richardson, *Emerson: The Mind on Fire*, 3 (source of quotation), 27, 46, 67–68, 116, 139, 438, 446.

19. Robinson, *Emerson and the Conduct of Life*, 83.

to the endeavor is to remind himself and us of the need to achieve a deeper sense of the unrealized experiential possibilities of everyday life.

The first step on the road to genuine experience is to become better acquainted with the stranger that each of us is to himself or herself. We should learn to "open [our] eyes . . . to the wonders of [our] constitution," "to contemplate with delight and reverence [our] own faculties," and to take "pleasure . . . in the right use of our powers" (CS 4:147; 2:188). We should also become aware that in our own proper person we reexperience and make concrete the moral and intellectual struggles that constitute the course of human history and thereby achieve a deeper insight into what it truly means to be a human being. "Habits of reflexion and solitude" will further our awareness of "depth in human nature" and thus give us a sense of the inexhaustible richness and complexity of our humanness (CS 4:215–16). The fact that no one can sound the depth nor fully articulate the richness and complexity of his or her being makes the individual's experience all the more interesting and challenging: "Know thyself," it appears, does not refer to a command capable of fulfillment but to an endless quest. Since, as already indicated, human individuality is not an *objective* given but is largely constituted by self-conception and self-articulation, the *awareness* of depth and richness within makes for an individual who *is* deep and rich and who continues to reach for a deeper and richer himself or herself.

Given the Emersonian principle that we can see only what we are (CW 1:45; 2:86; 3:46), such a person experiences not only a rich inner life but also the world as a place full of interest, complexity, and depth. He or she does not "glid[e] ghostlike through the world" nor experience the world as itself "slight and unreal" (CW 3:161). Most of us "swim, day by day, on a river of delusions." Such persons, by contrast, suggest that "life is a sincerity." Their example demonstrates that reality *is* accessible, that there are indeed "sane men who enjoy . . . a rich and related existence" (CW 4:12). Emerson wants us to regain, in Stanley Cavell's words, "an intimacy with existence." To him, "the everyday, the ordinary, is not a given but a task"; that is, each of us must recover a sense of the uniqueness, meaning, and depth of everyday life.[20]

---

20. Cavell, *In Quest of the Ordinary*, 6, 171.

A favorite Emersonian way of stressing the value of everyday experience is to assert its equivalence with the experiences of the great. The richness and fullness of life are available to everyone attuned to the immense possibilities of the everyday. Indeed, "life is always rich, and spontaneous graces and forces elevate it in every domestic circle, which are overlooked while we are reading something less excellent in old authors" (W 10:198). Even the simplest life truly lived contains all the essential human experiences and thus enables the man or woman in question to "taste the real quality of existence" (W 6:323). This fact explains why great historical figures do not impress us unduly. Indeed, "in their grandest strokes we feel most at home. All that Shakspeare says of the king, yonder slip of a boy that reads in the corner, feels to be true of himself" (CW 2:5). The circumstances and manifestations may be different, but the content and structure of success and failure, of desire and disappointment, of virtue and vice, of regret and remorse are experienced similarly by king and commoner, prince and pauper. Riches and poverty are but "a thick or thin costume"; fundamentally, "the life of all of us [is] identical," that is, the same depth of human experience is available to each of us (W 6:323). Emerson's claims exemplify what Stanley Cavell calls the Romantic "discovery that the everyday is an exceptional achievement . . . the achievement of the human."[21]

Emerson's appreciation of the value of everyday experience makes him reject any form of *contemptus mundi*. In his early sermons he already spoke against the notion that the Christian faith "puts . . . contempt on outward things" or "teaches us . . . to despise the world" (CS 2:244). The exemplary pastor "does not affect to hate the good and the glory of this world" (CS 1:239). The goods of this world may be inferior to the goods of the spirit, but the former should not be suppressed to make way for the latter; instead, we should experience the goods of this world as embodiments of spiritual laws. Metaphysically speaking, the world's ontological status may be questionable, but experience can be humanly enriching only on the assumption that the world—this *"other me"* (CW 1:59)—is real. Experience is the process through which the other loses part of its otherness and contributes to the enlargement and deepening of the experiencer's being. Experience

---

21. Cavell, *The Claim of Reason*, 463.

makes us more than what we were: "So much only of life as I know by experience, so much of the wilderness have I vanquished and planted, or so far have I extended my being, my dominion" (*CW* 1:59). Experience is thus an obvious ingredient of the good life, and the more challenging the otherness to be overcome and absorbed, the richer the potential benefits for the self of the experiencer. For those able to overcome their otherness, such challenges as "drudgery, calamity, exasperation, want, are instructers in eloquence and wisdom" (*CW* 1:59).

6

Nature

*E*merson's ethics of nature is inseparable from questions concerning the ontological status of nature, or, put differently, concerning the nature of reality. Such questions gave rise to Western philosophy, and they have proved inescapable ever since. The Presocratics were preoccupied, in W. K. C. Guthrie's words, "with the nature of reality and its relation to sensible phenomena . . . the relation between reality and appearance." Determinations concerning the status of the phenomenal world, debates about the degree to which it was "real," not only shaped the different Presocratic philosophies but also, according to Guthrie, lost none of their significance in subsequent Greek thought: "In one form or another [they] constitute[d] the fundamental difference between rival philosophies."[1] One need think only of Aristotelian empiricism versus Platonic idealism, or of the supernaturalism of Plotinus versus the materialism of the Epicureans.

As already suggested in the preceding chapter, questions concerning the nature of reality and the reality of the extra-mental world were of the utmost importance also to Emerson. He was, at times, categorical in his answers, as in his introduction to the lecture series on "Human Culture": "Ideal is not opposed to Real, but to Actual. The Ideal is the Real" (*EL* 2:217). But a dialectical thinker such as Emerson could not long remain satisfied with such absolute, and therefore abstract and ultimately empty, definitions. "The Ideal is the Real" is the kind of speculative sentence whose subject continues to defy conceptualization because, as Hegel pointed out, the predicate absorbs the subject and becomes itself the subject in our thinking. Put differently, the subject dissolves into its predicate so that the latter

1. W. K. C. Guthrie, *The Sophists*, 4.

ceases to be predicative of the original subject and instead becomes predicative of itself.[2] Emerson's statement thus amounts to little more than saying that "the Real is the Real." Rather than pursuing such definitional blind alleys, Emerson searched for "a *theory* of nature" (*CW* 1:8; emphasis added), thus resorting to a term whose fundamental meaning (Greek *theōria:* a looking at, a viewing) not only reverberates throughout his book *Nature* but also involves a perspectivism suggesting intellectual openness. It is not surprising, therefore, that although in *Nature* Emerson propounds an idealistic interpretation, he stresses its provisional character: it is "merely . . . a useful introductory hypothesis" (*CW* 1:38). An interpretation granting nature *nothing more* than phenomenal status ultimately satisfies the human spirit as little as it does the human heart (*CW* 1:37–38). Indeed, idealism is as likely as materialism to cause man's alienation from nature: it "makes nature foreign to me" (*CW* 1:38).

Emerson's ambivalent relationship to philosophical idealism, much discussed during the past couple of decades,[3] emerges not only in his ontology and epistemology but also in his ethics. In other words, the ontological status of nature and the degree and modes of our knowledge of nature prove inseparable from Emerson's ethical arguments concerning nature. As will become apparent, those arguments involve assumptions traceable to Emerson's varying degrees of commitment to philosophical idealism.

Emerson ethicizes the individual's relation to nature by making such morally relevant concepts as striving and desire part of his ideal theory. He was able to do so in a philosophically meaningful way because, as such scholars as Stanley Cavell, David Van Leer, and Russel B. Goodman have shown, of all the strains of idealism that affected Emerson, the most important by far was the Kantian. Kant rejected

---

2. Hegel, *Phänomenologie des Geistes,* 51–52.

3. Two helpful surveys are Lawrence Buell, "The Emerson Industry in the 1980's," especially section 3, "The De-Transcendentalization of the Emerson Image"; and Michael Lopez, "De-Transcendentalizing Emerson." Lopez himself has argued repeatedly for a reconception of Emerson as a post-idealist thinker and has done so most impressively in *Emerson and Power.* Arguments for Emerson as (pre-)pragmatist are found in, among others, Richard Poirier, *The Renewal of Literature: Emersonian Reflections;* West, *The American Evasion of Philosophy;* Robinson, *Emerson and the Conduct of Life;* and Jacobson, *Emerson's Pragmatic Vision.* See also my *Emerson's Modernity and the Example of Goethe,* chapter 3, "The Critique of Idealism."

what he considered to be the guiding principle of "all genuine idealists, from the Eleatic School to Bishop Berkeley," to wit, "All cognition through the senses and experience is nothing but sheer illusion
(Schein), and only in the ideas of the pure understanding and reason
is there truth." He condemned such influential expressions of this
view as Plato's "visionary *(schwärmerische)*" idealism, the "sceptical"
idealism of Descartes, and the "dogmatic" idealism of Berkeley. Kant's
critical idealism, by contrast, *involves* empirical realism. Kant did not
doubt the reality of the sensible world: it is part of our experience
and not a mere figment of our imagination; in fact, he pointed out,
even Descartes's supposedly indubitable *"inner* experience . . . is possible only on the assumption of *outer* experience." What Kant, as an
idealist, did insist on was the primacy of the mind in shaping our
knowledge of the external world: the mind inevitably structures the
data of the senses—what Kant calls the "manifold of sensation" *(ein
Mannigfaltiges der Sinnlichkeit)*—in accordance with its own laws. As
a result, "the order and regularity in the appearances we call nature
we ourselves introduce, and we would never be able to find them
there had not we, or *the nature of our mind,* originally put them there."
The only external world we have access to is the world as we know
it, that is, the world as structured by the categories and rules of the
understanding. Emerson fully accepted this view, as is evidenced by
his untiring assertions of the correspondence of nature to the mind.
But like Kant's, Emerson's idealism also involved empirical realism.
As Goodman puts it, "Emerson wants both to assert the vast powers of
the human mind in forming our experience and to acknowledge the
objectivity or substantiality of the world that this mind encounters."[4]

This duality within Kantian and Emersonian idealism creates a
space for ethical engagement. On the face of it, the idealism of both
Kant and Emerson seems to preclude any human responsibility for or
in relation to nature. The laws of the mind are what they are, and the

---

4. On striving as a moral concept, see Hartmann, *Ethik,* 236–42; for its moral significance in relation to self-culture, see chapter 3 above. Cavell, "Thinking of Emerson," *The
Senses of "Walden,"* 123–38, and "Emerson, Coleridge, Kant," *In Quest of the Ordinary,*
27–49. Van Leer, *Emerson's Epistemology;* Russell B. Goodman, *American Philosophy and
the Romantic Tradition,* 41–51. Immanuel Kant, *Prolegomena zu einer jeden künftigen
Metaphysik,* "Anhang," *Gesammelte Schriften,* 4:374–75. Kant, *Kritik der reinen Vernunft*
B 275, A 76/B 102, A 125 (emphasis added).

mind therefore inevitably "produces" in accordance with its laws the structure or system we call nature. Does such a deterministic view leave any room for human effort? Answering this question requires us to remember that it is the transcendental subject (Kant's "transcendental unity of apperception"), not the empirical "I" (Kant's "empirical apperception" or "subjective unity of consciousness") that is the ultimate source of the laws to which nature conforms. This distinction is clearly in Emerson's mind when he describes the world as "the perpetual creation of the powers of thought, of those that are dependent and of those that are independent of your will" (CW 1:204). The powers of thought independent of the will constitute, to use Kant's phrase, "the nature of our mind" *(die Natur unseres Gemüths)*; they create a world "not . . . now subjected to the human will" (CW 1:38). The empirical "I," on the other hand, is the locus of self-conscious experience; it is the individual self thinking, willing, and acting, a self dependent for its very existence on the world acknowledged by empirical realism. In the argument with Descartes referred to above, Kant insists that "empirically determined consciousness of my own existence" depends on my "immediate consciousness of the existence of other things outside me." Ernst Cassirer clarifies Kant's position thus: "Empirical self-consciousness does not precede the empirical consciousness of objects temporally and concretely; rather, in one and the same process of objectification and determination the whole of experience is divided for us into the field of the inner and the outer, the self and the world."[5] Enmeshed in the world of sensibilia, the empirical self becomes at one and the same time aware of itself and of the world's otherness. That otherness challenges the self, and it is in the self's various attempts to come to terms with that otherness that moral questions arise.

Its very recognition of nature-*as-other* imbues the self with an awareness of its own limits and of the limitations nature imposes upon its freedom. As Schelling pointed out, our granting objective status to anything amounts to accepting a restriction on our freedom.[6] Hence the self's attempts to transcend its limits, to reassert its freedom. It

5. Kant, *Kritik der reinen Vernunft* A 125, A 107/B 139, B 275–76. Ernst Cassirer, *Kant's Life and Thought,* 195.

6. Friedrich Wilhelm Joseph Schelling, *Philosophische Briefe über Dogmatismus und Kriticismus,* letter 10, *Werke,* 1:264.

can do so by striving to overcome nature's otherness, by extending its dominion at the expense of nature's. One important road toward this goal is the study of nature. Knowledge of nature, Emerson suggests, helps us overcome our alienation from nature because such knowledge makes us increasingly recognize nature as an *"other me"* (*CW* 1:59). At the very outset of his career as a lecturer, Emerson announced that it was "the greatest office of natural science (and one which as yet is only begun to be discharged) to explain man to himself" (*EL* 1:23). Through studying nature and discovering its laws, the individual gains insight into nature-as-structured-by-the-mind and thereby insight into that mind itself. The fact that nature is a product of the human mind is not, however, an immediate datum of individual consciousness, but deeper insight into nature helps the individual become aware of "the identity of nature's mind, and man's" (*EL* 2:34).

The role played by understanding and knowledge in the gradual identification of self with nature, and thus in overcoming the alienation of self from nature, illustrates the principle that "all knowledge is assimilation to the object of knowledge" (*CW* 1:131–32), a principle clarified by Hegel's ampler definition: "Every form of understanding is indeed an identification of the I and the object, a reconciliation of entities that remain separate outside this understanding; what I do not understand, what I do not know, remains to me something alien and other."[7] Emerson did not believe, however, that as far as the individual mind and nature were concerned, this identification could ever be complete. The meaning of nature is inexhaustible; not even "the wisest man [can] extort all her secret" (*CW* 1:9). This means, ipso facto, that not even "the wisest man" will ever sound the depths of the human mind: "so much of nature as [man] is ignorant of, so much of his own mind does he not yet possess" (*CW* 1:55). Realizing this lack of self-knowledge is, of course, a provocation to endless striving to extort nature's secret or, if you will, to subjugate nature through knowledge of its laws and thereby achieve deeper insight into the mind. Nature is indeed "the work of a perfect mind but of one which [the individual] can follow and evermore become" (*EL* 2:33).

M. H. Abrams has drawn attention to "the role of political-power metaphors in Romantic treatments of the relation between subject

---

7. Georg Wilhelm Friedrich Hegel, *Vorlesungen über die Ästhetik, Werke,* 13:433.

and object, mind and nature."[8] He quotes a passage from Fichte that illustrates both the use of such metaphors and the fact that power over nature is ultimately unattainable:

> To subjugate all non-rational nature to himself, to rule over it freely and according to his own law, is the ultimate goal of man—an ultimate goal which is utterly unattainable. . . . His way to it must be endless . . . and therefore his true vocation as *man*, that is as a rational but finite and as a sensuous but free being, is to approximate this goal unto infinity.[9]

Political-power metaphors were often in Emerson's mind when he discussed the individual's relation to nature. He often conceived of man's role as exerting "dominion" over nature, "extort[ing] from nature its sceptre," or "subduing" nature by thought (*CW* 1:25, 152, 106). In the Divinity School "Address" Emerson inveighed against "this eastern monarchy of a Christianity" (*CW* 1:82), but when expressing man's power over nature, he had no objection to orientally despotic imagery: religion and ethics "put nature under foot"; indeed, man "is to put Nature under his feet" (*CW* 1:35; *JMN* 5:146). Emerson, to be sure, knew as well as Fichte that though man may win battles in his conflict with nature, he will never win the war. But endless struggle is to be welcomed as a warrant of power, since "power ceases in the instant of repose" (*CW* 2:40). Michael Lopez has demonstrated in great detail the importance in Emerson's thought of "the belief that conflict is necessary and, ultimately, creative." Emerson, as Lopez puts it, "conceived of the universe as a system of antagonisms, a discipline for the strengthening . . . of the self."[10]

Emerson further ethicizes the individual's relation to nature by characterizing that relation as informed by desire: "The advantage of the ideal theory . . . is . . . that it presents the world in precisely that view which is most *desirable* to the mind" (*CW* 1:36; emphasis added). Desire *(Begierde)* was a momentous term in German idealism. Kant

8. M. H. Abrams, *Natural Supernaturalism: Tradition and Revolution in Romantic Literature,* 357.

9. Johann Gottlieb Fichte, *Einige Vorlesungen über die Bestimmung des Gelehrten,* lecture 1, *Sämmtliche Werke,* 6:299–300; quoted in Abrams, *Natural Supernaturalism,* 359 (I have adopted Abrams's translation).

10. Lopez, *Emerson and Power,* 190.

defined "the faculty of desire" *(das Begehrungsvermögen)* as "the faculty . . . to cause, through one's representations *(Vorstellungen* ["ideas" in the phenomenal, non-Kantian sense of "ideas," i.e., "mental *images"])*, the reality of the objects of these representations." Desire thus implies the ability or, at any rate, the intent to actualize the content of one's ideas. Or as J. N. Findlay puts it in reference to Hegel's concept of *Begierde,* desire is "the attitude which seeks to *make* external things conform to our requirements." The idealist thinker offering the most fruitful parallel to Emerson's ethics of nature is Schiller, in *On Naive and Sentimental Poetry (Über naive und sentimentalische Dichtung,* 1795–96). Schiller describes the modern condition as one of desire—desire for a lost unity, a lost harmony with nature, which has its counterpart in a lost inner harmony, a loss of integration of thought and sensation. No longer being real for us moderns, such unity and harmony have become ideal *(idealisch)*—something we can no longer experience but only strive to attain. As an object of striving, Schiller says, unity becomes a "moral unity" *(moralische Einheit).* As moderns we cannot escape from the condition of desire, not only because we cannot help yearning for a state we have lost, but also because that state is forever lost: we cannot possibly reachieve "naive" unity with nature and "naive" integration of self. However, our endless pursuit of an unattainable ideal puts us morally on a much higher plane than those who "possessed" nature and thus were exempt from desire and striving. "Naive" humans enjoyed a natural, hence limited perfection; moderns strive endlessly to attain an ideal perfection. There is "no question," Schiller says, that it is the latter who enact the highest purpose of humanity.[11]

I find no convincing evidence that Emerson had any detailed knowledge of Schiller's great treatise. I am using it only as an enlightening parallel to Emerson's ethics of nature. The similarities are both structural and thematic—structural, because both authors use the paradigm original perfection-loss-attempted restoration; thematic, because both authors give each member of their triadic structure a similar content. Emerson also presents the modern condition as one in which the

---

11. Kant, *Kritik der praktischen Vernunft,* "Vorrede," *Gesammelte Schriften,* 5:9n. J. N. Findlay, *Hegel: A Re-examination,* 96. Friedrich Schiller, *Über naive und sentimentalische Dichtung, Werke,* 4:307–10.

human suffers from a loss of original harmony with nature and of harmonious integration of self. Our present condition is one of inward and outward disharmony: "The ruin or the blank, that we see when we look at nature, is in our own eye. . . . The reason why the world lacks unity, and lies broken and in heaps, is, because man is disunited with himself" (*CW* 1:43). Emerson's primordial man, by contrast, represented a state of perfect integration with nature. His emanative powers had a reach recalling that of the Adam Kadmon of the Kabbalah: "He was permeated and dissolved by spirit. He filled nature with his overflowing currents. Out from him sprang the sun and moon. . . . The laws of his mind, the periods of his actions externized themselves into day and night, into the year and the seasons" (*CW* 1:42). Like Schiller, Emerson holds that the original state confronts us moderns as an ideal that is no longer attainable but that by eliciting our endless striving makes our pursuit of it a *moral* pursuit, thereby lifting us *morally* to a higher plane than those enjoying the original state. Emerson uses such traditional religious terms as "purification of [the] soul" and "redemption of the soul" (*CW* 1:38, 43) to emphasize the inescapably moral character of our quest for a vision of nature that would restore our harmonious union with it. As Lee Rust Brown rightly says, Emerson's concern with opaqueness and transparency ("The axis of vision is not coincident with the axis of things, and so they appear not transparent but opake."—*CW* 1:43) was not "merely epistemological," but "also practical and ethical."[12]

There are two sides, however, to our current problem of alienation: not only are we as humans alienated from nature, but nature is also alienated from us. The redemption of the soul involves a corresponding redemption of nature. Although, as Barbara Packer has reminded us, Emerson holds that nature is akin to man by virtue of its having, like man, its foundations in spirit,[13] nature is, in words of Emerson already quoted, "a remoter and inferior incarnation of God, a projection of

---

12. This general resemblance between Schiller and Emerson may arise from both authors' expressing one of the central preoccupations of the Romantic imagination—what M. H. Abrams calls "The Circuitous Journey: Through Alienation to Reintegration" (*Natural Supernaturalism*, 197–252). On Adam Kadmon, see Gershom Scholem, *Kabbalah*, 130–31, 137–42; also Thurin, *Emerson as Priest of Pan*, 189, 217. Lee Rust Brown, *The Emerson Museum: Practical Romanticism and the Pursuit of the Whole*, 47.

13. Packer, *Emerson's Fall*, 65.

God in the unconscious" (*CW* 1:38). Or as Hegel put it so strikingly, nature is "der *Abfall* der Idee von sich selbst," "the *defection* of the Idea from itself."[14] Emerson believes that as humans we have the duty to "redeem" nature by imbuing it with mind and thereby making it more like us.

Emerson's position is all the more interesting in the light of Kant's insistence that one cannot have any *duties* to nature, that since nature has instrumental value only (it exists for human benefit), all so-called duties to nature are actually indirect duties to humankind. Destruction of natural beauty is immoral, Kant says, not because it violates any duty to nature but because we destroy things that others may find some use for: one owes no consideration to things, but one ought to "consider [one's] neighbor" (*in Ansehung anderer Menschen*). Emerson disagrees because for him nature has also intrinsic, not just instrumental, value. Like Coleridge, he is committed to the "dignity" of nature; he urges "reverence" for nature (*CW* 1:9). Terms like "dignity" and "reverence" are meaningless to Kant unless used in relation to the moral law and to persons as bearers of the moral law. For him, nature can never be an object of reverence (*Achtung*). As he makes clear in the *Critique of Judgment*, even the feeling of the sublime in nature is actually "respect (*Achtung*) for our own vocation (*Bestimmung*) which we direct to an object of nature through a certain subreption (confusing respect for the idea of humanity in our own subject with respect for the object)." Emerson, by contrast, is to be ranked among the thinkers who grant nature, in Stephen Toulmin's words, "honorary . . . citizenship in Kant's Kingdom of Ends, together with the dignity and respect appropriate to that citizenship."[15] In sum, Emerson accepts that humans have responsibilities toward nature.

14. Georg Wilhelm Friedrich Hegel, *Enzyklopädie der philosophischen Wissenschaften im Grundrisse*, *Werke*, 9:28.

15. Immanuel Kant, *Vorlesungen über Moralphilosophie*, *Gesammelte Schriften*, 27:460. For Coleridge, see McFarland, *Coleridge and the Pantheist Tradition*, 222. Kant, *Kritik der Urteilskraft* §27, *Gesammelte Schriften*, 5:257. Stephen Toulmin, *The Return to Cosmology: Postmodern Science and the Theology of Nature*, 271. By "Kingdom of Ends" (*Reich der Zwecke*) Kant means the ideal moral commonwealth humans should aspire to create. Every rational being has the obligation to act "as if he were always, through his maxims, a legislating member in the universal Kingdom of Ends" (*Grundlegung zur Metaphysik der Sitten*, *Gesammelte Schriften*, 4:438).

These responsibilities do not, on Emerson's interpretation, include modern ecological concerns. In *The Environmental Imagination*, Lawrence Buell's richly informative contribution to ecocriticism (defined by Buell as "study of the relation between literature and environment conducted in a spirit of commitment to environmentalist praxis"), we are urged not to underrate Emerson's "environmentalist achievement" —his having taken, in *Nature*, "a great stride toward . . . [a] naturalism" that called forth "a nature more substantialized than the neoclassic cosmic abstraction called Nature." But Buell admits that Emerson's "naturalism" remained a "religiophilosophical mode of reflecting on nature" that "sacralized nature as humankind's mystic counterpart." When all is said and done, Emerson is peripheral, if not irrelevant, to Buell's concerns. According to Buell himself, "the key figure" of the American Renaissance "in [his] book's scheme of things" is not Emerson but Thoreau. It was the latter who "enlisted . . . in the service of a sacred environmentalist cause that [radicalized] the ruralist nostalgia widespread in England and New England . . . by demanding that it be taken seriously as a criterion for regulating social action."[16] Emerson's sense of responsibility for nature and the environment took a different form: it emerged not as environmentalist activism but as pleas for an appreciation and enhancement of their ideal and mind-like potential.

Emerson starts with the premise that nature is not just an incarnation of thought (of Spirit, Idea, or God), but that for us humans it *is* a thought. On account of its complexity and universality, nature cannot fall within the scope of perception but can only be an object of thought. We perceive a few details or a small corner of nature and make them "ideal" by integrating them with a larger whole that is accessible only to thought. And not only is that larger whole inaccessible except through thought, but as a concept it *depends* on thought, on a mind thinking it. The individual may thus be said to create his or her world by thinking it. This epistemological idealism has moral implications since one is responsible for the quality of the world one creates. Accordingly, the "best" world will be one raised to the level of our "best" thought.

16. Lawrence Buell, *The Environmental Imagination: Thoreau, Nature Writing, and the Formation of American Culture*, 430n20, 117–18, 6, 211.

One way of accomplishing the enhancement of nature is through moral action itself. Since ethics is "the practice of ideas, or the introduction of ideas into life" (*CW* 1:35), it inevitably affects the phenomenal world, in which moral action (like all action) of necessity takes place. The moral actor enhances the world not only by his or her transformative effect upon phenomena (which involves imprinting them with mind), but also by changing the quality, and hence the content, of others' perceptions of the world. "Every heroic act," Emerson says, "causes the place and the bystanders to shine" (*CW* 1:15). A righteous, noble, or heroic action adds a moral dimension to our perception of the environment in which it occurred. Our very enthusiasm for remarkable achievements transfigures the natural settings associated with them. In spite of the dilapidation and squalor of Iona, Dr. Johnson, remembering the island's illustrious past, felt that he was treading on "ground . . . dignified by wisdom, bravery, [and] virtue."[17] Emerson was in full agreement with such sentiments. As he saw it, after the heroic self-sacrifice of Leonidas and his three hundred Spartans the defile of Thermopylae is not just any pass in Thessaly but one sacred to the moral imagination. The same can be said, mutatis mutandis, of Tower Hill after the executions of Sir Harry Vane and Lord William Russell (*CW* 1:15).

Another way of overcoming the world's alienation from spirit is by bringing it within the purview of our aesthetic sensibility. Our very perception of beauty involves our making the world of appearances conform to human values and ideals. Emerson emphasizes the predominant role of the human spirit in aesthetic experience and the comparatively minor contribution of sensibilia, as when he says that "the perception of Beauty is an office of the Reason" (*EL* 2:267). Beauty, in order to be perceived as such, must of course *appear* and is thus dependent upon sense experience, but what matters to Emerson is the spirit's transformative effect upon the data of the senses: beauty "is the incessant creation of the spirit of man . . . places and materials are indifferent to [the spirit] and subject to it . . . a beautiful soul dwells always in a beautiful world" (*EL* 2:271). Such an aesthetic theory stresses the harmonizing of self and world on the self's terms, or, put

17. Samuel Johnson, *Journey to the Western Islands of Scotland*, 135.

differently, the remolding of the world to make it fit the demands of spirit. Perceiving the world as beautiful amounts to turning the realm of sensibilia into raw material for the spirit's self-objectification. By imbuing the world with spirit, the perception of beauty makes it more akin to us, more human.

What is true of the perception of beauty is a fortiori true of the creation of art. Hegel said that art arose out of the spirit's need to reproduce itself in the outside world. By exteriorizing itself in art, the spirit imposes its vision upon matter and thus creates an image of itself-in-the-other, thereby not only attaining greater self-knowledge but also raising the other to a higher level. In a world transformed by art the spirit recognizes the "external reality of itself" *(äußere Realität seiner selbst)*.[18] Emerson's style may be less philosophical than Hegel's, but he held identical views. For him also, artistic creation amounts to the individual transforming part of nature into his or her self-image. Art is indeed "nature passed through the alembic of man." Nature is the artist's means of objectifying his or her spirit, and this objectification not only deepens the spirit's self-knowledge ("the production of a work of art throws a light upon the mystery of humanity") but also enhances nature by informing it with spirit (*CW* 1:16–17). Nature transfigured by artistic creation ranks higher than nature perceived as beauty precisely because the former is imbued with a higher degree of human consciousness. Since "Nature is good, but Intellect is better," it follows that "the beauty of things . . . becomes a new, and higher beauty, when expressed" (*CW* 4:36; 3:8). The ultimate aim is to transform as much as possible of nature into this "higher beauty" so as to make nature the truest possible image of the human spirit.

This aim is not as unattainable as might at first appear. Emerson's already mentioned refusal to distinguish between the fine and the useful arts (*CW* 2:218) is symptomatic of the high value he puts on the humanization of nature by whatever means. Although not unaware of some of the horrors attendant upon industrialization (*L* 3:442), Emerson stressed the positive results of human intervention in nature: "See what a skilful and beneficent hand [man] has laid upon the globe. Not finding the world in its original state sufficiently commodious,

---

18. Hegel, *Vorlesungen über die Ästhetik, Werke,* 13:51–52.

he has undertaken to alter and amend it. He may be said to keep the world in repair" (*EL* 1:43). While environmentalists might worry about railroads and factories defacing the landscape, Emerson tried to justify them aesthetically by emphasizing that they were adaptations of natural forces and hence recognizable, by a person of "deeper insight," as parts of "the Whole" (*CW* 3:11).[19] Such views help explain a remarkable fact about Emerson: as Leonard Neufeldt has pointed out, Emerson "was virtually alone" among the literary figures of his time "in his endorsement of the possibilities of technology and science for the individual and the culture."[20] He applauded man's physical transformation of the nonhuman world as an expression of the un-ending human effort to "tame the chaos" (*CW* 4:20), to make the forces of nature more responsive to the human will. By the invention of the steamship, for instance, the human is no longer at the mercy of capricious winds but has turned natural forces into reliable aids (*CW* 1:11–12). By means of the useful arts, *homo faber* has indeed re-created the world in his own image: "By the aggregate of these aids, how is the face of the world changed, from the era of Noah to that of Napoleon!" (*CW* 1:12).

What ultimately informs this argument is Emerson's pantheistic or secularized reinterpretation of the old Christian idea that humans were called upon to be God's coworkers in completing the creation, an idea found in such early authorities as Origen, Basil the Great, Gregory of Nyssa, and Ambrose, and which Emerson himself repeatedly expressed in his sermons.[21] He says, for instance, that a grateful man "serves [God's] purposes in the Universe. . . . A grateful man is a fellow-worker with God" (*CS* 1:135). Or elsewhere: "We are to be fellow workers with God and every moment of life and every power we have is to be spent in the effort to add to the vast amount of well being of the whole" (*CS* 1:302). Completing God's creation also means, of course,

19. For a fuller discussion of Emerson's aesthetic argument, see Leo Marx, *The Machine in the Garden: Technology and the Pastoral Ideal in America*, 240–42, and Thomas Krusche, *R. W. Emersons Naturauffassung und ihre philosophischen Ursprünge*, 176–78.

20. Leonard Neufeldt, *The House of Emerson*, 78–79.

21. C. Taylor, *Sources of the Self*, 547n3. For the Judeo-Christian legitimization of this idea, see Luigi Zoja, *Crescita e colpa: Psicologia e limiti dello sviluppo*, 35. Further detail is provided by Clarence J. Glacken, *Traces on the Rhodian Shore: Nature and Culture in Western Thought from Ancient Times to the End of the Eighteenth Century*, 293–302.

completing oneself. The virtuous man, Emerson says, is not satisfied with his mind as he finds it, but devotes himself to "making it what it should be, [thus] recommending himself to the Supreme Being by finishing his work after his design" (*CS* 4:132).

These ideas were absorbed into Emerson's later thought. In his version of pantheism, Nature *is* God striving toward self-awareness, a condition that Nature achieves (though still incompletely) in humanity. Nature remains unconscious of its own striving until it reaches the point of human self-awareness. The human, in other words, *is* Nature having risen to consciousness. This ascent to consciousness is the supreme fact in the cosmos, and Emerson resorts to a Hebraistic superlative to state it: "The fact of facts is the termination of the world in a man." This is indeed "the last victory of intelligence" (*CW* 1:127). In man and woman, nature's unconscious purposiveness becomes consciously purposive: unlike nature, unlike the worm in the verse motto of *Nature* (*CW* 1:7), the human has the ability to *conceive* of purposes and deliberately to select the means necessary to advance their accomplishment. This ability entails the obligation to enhance nature's striving, not only by perfecting oneself, but also by making nature conform to human purposiveness. As Nicolai Hartmann said, it is part of our moral vocation to influence nature's destiny, to become, in fact, "co-creators of the world" *(Mitschöpfer der Welt)*.[22]

Stephen Whicher was, I believe, the first scholar to point out that Emerson's moral position was at times akin to soft determinism.[23] Unlike hard determinists, who trace all human decisions and actions to causally necessary chains of antecedents, soft determinists, while acknowledging the individual's inescapable involvement in a deterministic universe, insist that the individual nevertheless maintains the power to act freely in and upon that universe. As a soft determinist Emerson recognized, on the one hand, that in relation to nature the individual's freedom does not enable him or her to contravene causal necessity, and on the other, that the individual can (and therefore ought to) further and enhance nature's tendencies. This distinction explains the moral dimension of Emersonian meliorism. As he sees it, meliorism is an incontrovertible fact of nature: "To meliorate is the law

22. Hartmann, *Ethik*, 440–41.
23. Whicher, *Freedom and Fate*, 172.

of nature." There is room, however, for moral agency: "Men are valued precisely as they exert onward or meliorating force" (*W* 6:140). Or stated in greater detail: "The destiny of organized nature is amelioration. . . . It is for man to tame the chaos . . . to scatter the seeds of science and of song, that climate, corn, animals, men, may be milder, and the germs of love and benefit may be multiplied" (*CW* 4:20). A world thus "redeemed" would no longer be alienated from us. It would be a world recognizably akin to us, and thereby it would satisfy important demands of the spirit and the heart. Feeling at home in one's world is obviously a major constituent of the good life.

7

Literature

M. H. Abrams's well-known classification of traditional critical approaches is helpful toward defining Emerson's general attitude to literature.[1] Emerson showed little or no interest in works of literature as autonomous, self-sufficient entities (the critical orientation Abrams labels "objective") and comparatively little interest in works of literature as representations of observable reality (Abrams's "mimetic" approach). He usually regarded literature as a means of achieving certain effects on an audience and as an expression of an authorial self (Abrams's "pragmatic" and "expressive" orientations). Although ethical considerations seem most obviously involved in the perception of literature as "pragmatic," Emerson was also very much concerned with the ethics of self-expression. In addition, the very lifeblood of literature—language itself—seemed to him to involve important ethical questions, and it is these questions that demand our attention first.

I

As the sine qua non of our humanity, language is inevitably affected by and implicated in ethics. Language is as necessary to our self-awareness as to our socialization. It mediates thought and articulates feeling, and it enables us to share in and to contribute to human society and culture. Language, in sum, is so central to self-realization and relations with others as to be continually verging upon important areas of ethics. Moreover, given his Spirit-Nature hierarchy and his

---

1. Abrams, *The Mirror and the Lamp*, 3–29.

recognition that language has its being in the world of space and time, Emerson cannot but regard language as an inadequate, limited, flawed instrument of spiritual expression. Nature, to be sure, "is the symbol of spirit" (*CW* 1:17)—but only the symbol. That which is symbolized transcends the symbol. This is all the more true when nature is articulated as language and thus loses its universality. Every language is culturally and historically specific, and every human using it imposes upon it the additional limitations of his or her individuality. The ways in which we as limited, imperfect individuals cope with the inadequacies of language also fall within the purview of ethics.

Emerson urges that we try to approximate the universality of nature in the language we use. Since "it is the universal nature which gives worth to particular . . . things" (*CW* 2:4), we should strive for a language that, though incapable of attaining universality, at least suggests it. Only such a language will enable us to do some justice to spirit when we attempt to express it. As Emerson sees it, one can approach linguistic universality by fully accepting and putting into practice the principle of the "immediate dependence of language upon nature" (*CW* 1:20), that is to say, by using a language that is concrete and picturesque, a language that is *symbolic*. Emerson knew as well as Goethe and Coleridge that the symbol is rooted in concrete, objective reality, and that consequently the symbolic potential of language depends upon its also being rooted in such reality. He praised Goethe's writing because in it "you shall find no word that does not stand for a thing" (*JMN* 5:133). The thing in its turn suggests meanings not available except through the thing, which thus becomes symbol. True poetry, Emerson says, "is the perpetual endeavor to express the spirit of the thing, to pass the brute body and search the life and reason which causes it to exist" (*W* 8:17). But while endlessly suggestive of meaning, the symbol maintains its concrete identity. The figures in Goethe's "Helena" (an episode of *Faust*, Part Two, published separately) affect the mind as "eternal entities, as real to-day as in the first Olympiad," but they owe that effect to Goethe's "desire that every word should be a thing" (*CW* 2:19).

Such "natural"—concrete, picturesque, symbolic—language is "universal" because it alone can give us glimpses of universal spirit. For this reason, Emerson calls it "the first language . . . [and] the last" (*CW* 1:20), at once the most elemental and the supreme language, and the only language shareable by all humans: "The same symbols are found to make the original elements of all languages . . . [and] the idioms of all languages approach each other in passages of the greatest eloquence and power" (*CW* 1:19–20). The enemy of universality and expressive integrity is abstract language. Exploiting once again the original meaning of the term, Emerson regarded linguistic *abstractness* (from Latin *abstrahere:* to pull away, to remove, to detach) as language *detached* from its roots in nature and hence susceptible to artifice and manipulation. His fear of abstraction led him to define "the education of the mind" as "a continual substitution of facts for words" (*JMN* 4:327). He regarded concrete, picturesque language as "a commanding certificate that he who employs it, is a man in alliance with truth and God" because "a man's power to connect his thought with its proper symbol . . . depends on the simplicity of his character, that is, upon his love of truth and his desire to communicate it without loss." By contrast, abstract language—"this rotten diction"—evidences "the corruption of man," a corruption prevalent "in every long-civilized nation" and consisting in the displacement of "simplicity and truth" by "duplicity and falsehood" (*CW* 1:20).

There is obviously an element of primitivism in Emerson's argument. In words reminiscent of Hamann's "Poesie ist die Muttersprache des menschlichen Geschlechts" ("poetry is the mother tongue of the human race"), Emerson says that "as we go back in history, language becomes more picturesque, until its infancy, when it is all poetry; or, all spiritual facts are represented by natural symbols" (*CW* 1:19). Language tends to lose its symbolic creativity and truthfulness in "long-civilized nation[s]": "new imagery ceases to be created, and old words are perverted to stand for things which are not" (*CW* 1:20). Emerson here deepens the moral significance of his argument by linking it with Plato's *The Sophist:* "things which are not" literally translates "*ta mē onta*," which Plato uses repeatedly to refer to falsehood in thought or speech. Emerson further emphasizes the fraudulent nature of abstract language by echoing a passage from Goethe's brief essay "Symbolik," where the value of words is discussed in monetary terms. Goethe distinguishes between coins made of precious metals and "paper money" *(Papiergeld),* and points out that whereas the former have inherent value *(Realität),* the latter's value is purely conventional *(nur Konvention).* In Emerson's version, "a paper currency is employed when there is no bullion in the vaults. In due time, the fraud is manifest, and words lose all power to stimulate the understanding or the affections" (*CW* 1:20).[2]

Abstract language corrupts by shielding both speaker and hearer from reality. Language is an instrument of self-knowledge, but it can function as such only if it concretely and authentically articulates our experience. The prelinguistic self is chaotic and formless; language attempts to structure, grasp, and reveal it. Language is not only "the finest tool of all"; it is also the tool "nearest to the mind" (*W* 7:163). Although language, rooted as it is in nature, is "material," it is "material only on one side. It is a demi-god," and thus capable, to some degree, of grasping and giving voice to one's spiritual self. The self "struggles to the birth," and its release from chaos brings the joy of self-realization. That is why speech "is a great pleasure . . . [that] cannot be foreborne" (*W* 7:43, 38). Abstract, generalized language, however, masks us from ourselves and thus causes alienation. In a sense, this problem results from the very nature of language. Language, after all, is something we inherit from our culture, and we cannot achieve full human status without initiation into the language of our culture—a process charmingly described by St. Augustine in his *Confessions*.[3] This also means, however, that no language truly expresses any person's unique self: there simply is no language that is entirely one's own, or to put it in Wittgensteinian terms, there is no "private language."[4] The self experiences self-separation or alienation because in its attempts to realize its subjectivity it of necessity objectifies itself: in the very act of expressing itself, the self necessarily exteriorizes itself into an objective system not of its own creation. As Emerson points out, developing an idea of Coleridge, "The very language we speak, thinks for us, by the subtle distinctions which already are marked for us by its words, and every one of these is the contribution of the wit of one and another sagacious man, in all the centuries of time" (*EL* 1:229–30; *JMN* 5:9).

2. Johann Georg Hamann, *Kreuzzüge des Philologen, Sämtliche Werke*, 2:197. Plato, *Sophistēs* 238B, 240D–241A, 260C. Johann Wolfgang Goethe, "Symbolik," *Gedenkausgabe*, 16:855. For a useful introduction to the entire problematic of language versus truth, see Harald Weinrich, *Linguistik der Lüge*.

3. St. Augustine, *Confessions* 1.8 (13).

4. Wittgenstein, *Philosophische Untersuchungen* 1.199, 243, 269, 275. For a subtle discussion of Wittgenstein's argument, see Cavell, *The Claim of Reason*, 343–54.

This statement points both to the problem and to its partial solution. We have to personalize our language by contributing and putting into practice our own "subtle distinctions." One way of achieving this creative appropriation of language is to engage in what Coleridge called "desynonymizing." Coleridge claimed that "all Languages perfect themselves by a gradual process of desynonymizing words originally equivalent."[5] Emerson applauded Coleridge's efforts at desynonymization because he grasped its significance for ethics:

> Is not this the history of all advancement? We look at good & ill which grows together as indissolubly connected: if an improvement takes place in our own mind we get a glimpse of an almost imperceptible line that separates the nature of the thing from the evil admixture. By a more diligent inspection that division will farther appear, till it peals off like dead bark. This is the sense of Coleridge's urged distinction between the similar & the same. . . . this is the progress of every soul. What it joined before it now severs. . . . All our knowledge comes in this way. (*JMN* 3:209)

Abstract language not only shields the user from essential reality but also corrupts those hearing or reading it. Generalizations, euphemisms, clichés, and vagueness relieve the speaker or writer from the obligation to think clearly about the subject under consideration (thus concealing its real meaning even from him or herself, as Orwell famously pointed out in "Politics and the English Language"), but they also prevent the audience from facing realities that demand ethically informed decisions and actions. Even after his infamous Seventh of March (1850) speech in support of the Fugitive Slave Bill, Daniel Webster kept assuring the nation that it was enjoying the fruits of liberty. Emerson reacted sharply to Webster's abuse of the language:

> I opened a paper today in which he pounds on the old strings in a letter to the Washington Birth Day feasters at N.Y. "Liberty! liberty!" Pho! Let Mr. Webster for decency's sake shut his lips once & forever on this word. The word *liberty* in the mouth of Mr Webster sounds like the word *love* in the mouth of a courtezan. (*JMN* 11:345–46)

5. Samuel Taylor Coleridge, *The Notebooks*, 3:4397; see also *Biographia Literaria*, 1:82–83, and Thomas McFarland, *Originality and Imagination*, 148–49. For Coleridge's desynonymization of ethical terms, see Lockridge, *The Ethics of Romanticism*, 68–69.

"Liberty!" is a slogan whose very emptiness assures its anodynic effect. Emerson found "nothing . . . more disgusting than this crowing about liberty by slaves, as most men are" (*W* 6:23). Wesley T. Mott has drawn attention to Emerson's deep awareness that the corrupting effect of language involves a shift from concreteness ("words that are things") to abstractness ("the word-as-artifact").[6] Words-as-artifacts are "abstracted" from any moral *reality* and therefore can be made to signify almost anything. Emerson comments most caustically on such immoral use of language in a speech delivered in 1856:

> Language has lost its meaning in the universal cant. *Representative Government* is really misrepresentative; *Union* is a conspiracy against the Northern States which the Northern States are to have the privilege of paying for; the *adding of Cuba and Central America to the slave marts* is *enlarging the area of Freedom. Manifest Destiny, Democracy, Freedom,* fine names for an ugly thing. . . . They call it Chivalry and Freedom; I call it the stealing all the earnings of a poor man and the earnings of his little girl and boy. . . . But this is Union, and this is Democracy; and our poor people, led by the nose by these fine words, dance and sing, ring bells and fire cannon, with every new link of the chain which is forged for their limbs by the plotters in the Capitol. (*W* 11:259–60)

These remarks of Emerson's on the troubled American 1850s echo those of his admired Thucydides on even more troubled late-fifth-century (BCE) Greece. Like Emerson, Thucydides witnessed "moral degradation in time of stress," and a salient feature of such degradation was "the slippage and corruption of an entire moral language."[7]

Apart from expressing his disgust at such flagrant violations of ethico-linguistic integrity, Emerson also confronts the lack of "truth" in language as such. As already indicated, he associated truth with simplicity and simplicity with unity (*CW* 1:20; *CS* 2:175), thereby recalling the Latin meaning of *simplex* (one, uncompounded). Language, on the other hand, he perceived to be inherently *duplex* (twofold, double) and therefore incapable of doing justice to something as "simple" as truth. The "law [of] Ethics," we remember, "cannot yet be stated, it is so simple" (*EL* 1:370). Statement involves analysis, separation,

6. Wesley T. Mott, *"The Strains of Eloquence": Emerson and His Sermons*, 111–12.
7. Thucydides, *Historiai* 3.82.4–8; Nussbaum, *The Fragility of Goodness*, 404.

differentiation, and hence destruction of unity and simplicity. Words "break, chop, and impoverish [truth]" (*CW* 1:28). Put differently, what remains undifferentiated, one, *simplex* is inaccessible to the selectivity, distinctions, and emphases inherent in statement. "The thought we *express*" is, therefore, always "partial & finite" (*JMN* 5:30; emphasis added). Emerson would have relished Schiller's paradox: "*Spricht* die Seele so spricht ach! schon die *Seele* nicht mehr" ("When the soul *speaks*, then it is, alas, no longer the *soul* that speaks").[8] Defection from simplicity, unity, and truth is inherent in even the highest modes of expression: "Art expresses the one or the same by the different. Thought seeks to know unity in unity; poetry to show it by variety, that is, always by an object or symbol" (*CW* 4:32).

Confronted with the inadequacy of language, Emerson sometimes urges silence. As he states in his essay "Intellect," "There is somewhat more blessed and great in hearing than in speaking. . . . If I speak, I define, I confine, and am less. . . . Silence is a solvent that destroys personality, and gives us leave to be great and universal" (*CW* 2:202–3). At other times he counsels patience and acceptance of the fact that one's expressive power will fail to do justice to the "Things of the heavenly mind" ("Merops," *W* 9:127–28). Most interestingly, he advocates the use of as transparent as possible a language because such a language he feels to be least likely to distort spiritual truth. The ideal of linguistic transparency is not necessarily incompatible with Emerson's commitment to symbolism. In his theory, the symbol is far less opaque than it is in the interpretations and literary practice of, say, Goethe, Coleridge, or Melville—authors whose symbolizing seems to be an unending *reaching for* meanings. Goethe's sense of the opaqueness of the symbol is evident from a statement such as "Symbolism transforms . . . the idea into an image in such a way that the idea always remains infinitely active and unattainable in the image, and would remain inexpressible even though expressed in all languages."[9] Emerson, by contrast, stresses transparency: "A happy symbol is a sort of evidence that your thought is just" (*W* 8:13). Moreover, he implies that the very radiance of thought blinds us to

8. Friedrich Schiller, "Tabulae votivae," *Werke*, 3:145.
9. Johan Wolfgang Goethe, *Maximen und Reflexionen* [no. 1113], *Gedenkausgabe*, 9:639.

the symbol: "As the eyes of Lyncaeus were said to see through the earth, so the poet turns the world to glass" (*CW* 3:12). As Vivian C. Hopkins has pointed out, "in Emerson's theory, the most successful symbol would leave with the observer a dominant impression of spirit, independent of material shape, color, or sound."[10] In other words, what Emerson values in poetry is the thought rather than the artistry. Poets, he says, "live . . . to the beauty of the symbol," but "wise men . . . live above the beauty of the symbol, to the beauty of the thing signified." The latter have "spiritual perception," whereas the former have merely "taste" (*JMN* 5:326). Although language cannot possibly convey the purity of "spiritual perception," the best language, it seems clear, is the one most capable of "giving a spiritual, that is, an ethico-intellectual expansion to every truth" (*CW* 4:49). Such a language provides scope ("expansion") for the articulation of *thought* and permits the highest degree of expressive *truthfulness:* it is thus indeed "ethico-intellectual."

II

The literary expression of truth is, in Emerson's view, inseparable from literary self-expression. Only the self can conceptualize and give voice to truth, and the highest attainable self-expression, which is the prerogative of genius, is also the highest expression of truth. Hence Emerson's oft-repeated insistence that genius is always moral. There is, he writes in 1827, "between virtue & genius a natural an eternal affinity" (*JMN* 3:71). Years later his uncertainties about Goethe's moral standing induced him to doubt whether Goethe had indeed "ascended to the highest grounds from which genius has spoken" (*CW* 4:163). Genius involves a "sharpness of moral perception" that Emerson found lacking in Goethe (*JMN* 7:367). As a result, Goethe was a "lawgiver of art" rather than a true artist (*CW* 4:165). Anyone familiar with Goethe's works is likely to quarrel with Emerson's judgments, but Emerson's attitude reveals the depth of his conviction that, as he was still insisting in the late 1860s, "genius [is] always on the side of morals" (*JMN* 16:84). In fact, "every work of pure genius . . . is

10. Vivian C. Hopkins, "The Influence of Goethe on Emerson's Aesthetic Theory," 333.

charged" not only with beauty, but also with "goodness, and truth" (*EL* 3:81).

This moral dimension of genius also guarantees that genius will remain true to itself. The enemy of genius is convention. Genius requires authenticity and sincerity, and these involve the abandonment of one's conventional self and fidelity to one's intuitional, inspired self. Genius comes into its own only "when all limits are taken away; which only can happen in the case of morality." It is morality that gives genius its foundation in the noumenal world, and therefore morality is truly "the only ground on which genius can build" (*JMN* 12:400). Emerson's approach to literature, needless to say, is never purely aesthetic. Although he praises the imagination as "the great awakening power," as the perceiver and creator of beauty, he insists that it is "the Morals" that are "creative of genius" (*W* 6:302–3; 7:212). In an early lecture called "Literature," he makes exactly the same claim, though in different words: "It is in the nature of things that the highest originality must be moral" (*EL* 3:205). In view of such claims, it is not surprising that Emerson regarded originality more as a moral obligation than as a literary desideratum. Any literary production "not entirely & peculiarly" your own work, Emerson wrote in 1834, addressing himself, "is so much lost time to you. . . . It is a parenthesis in your genuine life. You are your own dupe" (*JMN* 4:335). Obviously, in literature, as in life, "integrity . . . dwarfs talent" (*W* 6:277).

Obedience to one's genius has implications for one's attitude toward one's culture or society. The "poet" or "scholar" cannot "become acquainted with his thoughts" unless he maintains his spiritual independence (*CW* 1:109). Inspired by Goethe's example, Emerson notes in 1836: "In the scholar's Ethics, I would put down Beharre wo du stehst. Stick by yourself" (*JMN* 5:187–88).[11] This independence of spirit, which Emerson often metaphorizes as solitude or silence, is also a major theme of what he called his "little poem on poetical ethics called Saadi" (*L* 3:88). Though Saadi "loved the race of men," he "sit[s] aloof" and "dwells alone" (*W* 9:130). Spiritual independence, the kind of self-trust to which Emerson in "The American Scholar" ascribes "all the virtues," makes it possible for the poet or scholar

11. Goethe, *Maximen und Reflexionen* [no. 549], *Gedenkausgabe*, 9:570.

to exercise "the highest functions of human nature"—to fulfill his duties as *"Man Thinking,"* instead of allowing himself to be reduced to the level of "a mere thinker, or, still worse, the parrot of other men's thinking" (*CW* 1:62–63, 53). In a book produced by Man Thinking one encounters an authentic human being rather than the embarrassed mouthpiece of common, unoriginal thoughts. In great works of literature, the human being and the writer show themselves to be "one & not diverse" (*JMN* 5:425). Talent and literary skill "cannot make a writer. There must be a man behind the book" (*CW* 4:162).

This conviction helps explain Emerson's tireless insistence that literature be rooted in personal experience. One may recall his eloquent critique of the luckless Barzillai Frost, the preacher who, as far as one could tell from his sermons,

> had lived in vain. He had no one word intimating that he had laughed or wept, was married or in love, had been commended, or cheated, or chagrined. . . . This man had ploughed, and planted, and talked, and bought, and sold; he had read books; he had eaten and drunken; his head aches; his heart throbs; he smiles and suffers; yet was there not a surmise, a hint, in all the discourse, that he had ever lived at all. (*CW* 1:86)

Not rooted in his life, Frost's preaching was, literally, lifeless. He had never learned the truth that, as Emerson puts it in "Literary Ethics," "human life . . . is . . . the richest material for [the scholar's] creations" (*CW* 1:111). Or as we are told in his most famous address on the subject of literature, "the scholar loses no hour which the man lives" (*CW* 1:61). Only true, sincere encounters with oneself and one's life experience can produce the moral and emotional depth and richness required for the creation of great literature. Unfortunately, most poets would rather not encounter their true self or confront what is deeply and perhaps disturbingly human in their experience. They prefer the self-unawareness guaranteed by "a civil and conformed manner of living," and they write poems "from the fancy, at a safe distance from their own experience" (*CW* 3:3). And yet, only he that truly and sincerely "writes to himself, writes to an eternal public" (*CW* 2:89). When one dares to confront and honestly express one's deepest humanity, one speaks for all humans. All great literature is, therefore, essentially autobiographical, and it is so in a dual sense: it is the autobiography of the author and the autobiography of humankind. As Emerson says about one of his heroes, "Dante's praise is, that he dared to write his autobiography in colossal cipher, or into universality" (*CW* 3:21).

Emerson's concern with the ethical dimension of literature is equally apparent from the fact that in his own authorial practice he was primarily committed to what one might loosely call "wisdom literature." At the age of twenty-one he expressed his admiration for books that "embody the wisdom of their times & so mark the stages of human improvement." As examples he mentioned "the Proverbs of Solomon, the Essays of Montaigne, & eminently the Essays of Bacon," and he gave voice to an ambition that more than any other shaped the course of his career as a writer: "I should like to add another volume to this valuable work" (*JMN* 2:265). One might argue that Emerson's entire oeuvre embodies his endeavor to add such a volume to the world's literature. The primary role of wisdom, as he saw it, was an ethical one. Wisdom helps us answer correctly the fundamental questions of ethics: "What must I do?" and "How shall I live?" It was thus natural for him to claim that the highest kind of literature is that which teaches moral wisdom. He invariably insisted that "the very highest class of books are those which express the moral element," which deal with "what ought to be" (*EL* 3:202–3). The greatest poetry is oriented toward ethics, and the supreme poets are invariably moral lawgivers (*JMN* 5:476; *W* 8:64–65).

The Shakespeare of *Representative Men* obviously fails on this point, but Emerson was too sincere an admirer of Shakespeare's genius to fully adopt any ethico-poetical criterion that would exclude the Bard from the ranks of the supremely great. Emerson's "ethical poetry," in other words, is a rich and flexible concept (though, as already indicated, not flexible enough to allow a wholehearted appreciation of Goethe's work). As he puts it in "The Sovereignty of Ethics," "in the voice of Genius I hear invariably the moral tone, even when it is disowned in words" (*W* 10:185). Such a statement also contains an element of Emersonian self-justification. The iconoclast of the Divinity School "Address" and the moral antinomian of "Self-Reliance" preached a deeper, *Reason*-sanctioned morality that was inaudible to those who listened with the ears of the *Understanding* and who consequently took offense at his words. To Emerson's delight, Bronson Alcott perceived a similar dichotomy between the words and the real message of Emerson's *Poems* (1846): "Alcott, among many fine things he said of my volume of Poems, said, the sentiment was moral and the expression seemed the reverse" (*JMN* 9:464).

Emerson considered his desire to excel as a moral writer to be a sign of his literary modernity. Although "from the beginning" the highest literature had been ethical, all past attempts to translate essential ethics into statement had but produced works that were partial and fragmentary. Humanity still craves "the true poetry," the real "Moral Poem" of which even Jesus "chanted . . . only stanzas"; it is "the tendency of the ripe modern mind to produce it" (*JMN* 5:476). Emerson clearly considered himself a representative of that modern tendency. His stressing the superiority of ethical to imaginative literature aligned him with those among his contemporaries who claimed that art (including literary art) could no longer adequately express the needs of the modern spirit and that only "philosophy" (comprehensively conceived: ethics, criticism, sociology, etc.) could do so. One need think only of Macaulay's claim, in his essay on Milton (1825), that "as civilisation advances, poetry almost necessarily declines"; of Hegel's insistence that for us moderns art has ceased to be the highest mode of the Spirit's self-realization; of Carlyle's "mean opinion of creative literature"; or of Matthew Arnold's conviction that what his age needed most was "criticism," that is, "the endeavour, in all branches of knowledge . . . to see the object as in itself it really is." As was the case in England, so also in nineteenth-century America, Lawrence Buell points out, some of the most disconcerting detractions of the literary arts came from the artists themselves. Buell cites as examples Bryant, who "at the moment he was being heralded as a symptom of American poetic emergence, suggested that poetry was obsolete," and Lowell, whose enthusiasm for the nation's poetic aspirations may be judged from the statement that "we can . . . borrow a great poet when we want one."[12]

Like these important nineteenth-century figures, Emerson accepted the dethronement of imaginative literature: "The very highest class of books are those which express the moral element, the next, works of

---

12. Thomas Babington Macaulay, *Critical and Historical Essays*, 1:153; Hegel, *Vorlesungen über die Ästhetik, Werke*, 13:141–42; for Carlyle, see Walter E. Houghton, *The Victorian Frame of Mind, 1830–1870*, 130; Matthew Arnold, *On Translating Homer*, lecture 2, and "The Function of Criticism at the Present Time," *The Complete Prose Works of Matthew Arnold*, 1:140; 3:258–85; Lawrence Buell, *New England Literary Culture: From Revolution through Renaissance*, 64.

imagination, and the next, works of sciences." Works of science rank lowest because their conclusions are always provisional, that is, always subject to revision as a result of new evidence, new "facts," new interpretations; works of science, in other words, deal with "what appears." Works of imagination rank higher because, when rightly conceived, they deal with "what really is." At their best, works of imagination represent the Spirit and its ideas (Latin *imago* translates Greek *idea):* they "ascend to that power of thought that the writer sees Nature as subordinate to the soul and uses it as his language" (*EL* 3:202–3, 207). When falling short of this achievement, works of imagination are merely works "of costume or of circumstance" (*W* 12:375). One remembers in this context Emerson's lack of enthusiasm for almost all works of fiction. But even the greatest works of imagination, which deal with "what really is," are inferior to moral works, whose subject is "what ought to be" (*EL* 3:203). This ranking constitutes an interesting literary parallel to Emerson's Kantian privileging of the pure practical over the theoretical reason (discussed in chapter 2).

Emerson is unKantian, however, in his manner of treating ethics: he approaches this subject, like every other, undogmatically and without any pretensions to systemic completeness. He belongs with those modern thinkers whom Richard Rorty has characterized as "edifying" rather than "systematic." Edifying thinkers are less concerned with "truth" or with "getting the facts right" than with "finding new, better, more interesting, more fruitful ways" of expressing ourselves, and "thus of coping with the world." Edifying discourse is "abnormal": it aims "to take us out of our old selves by the power of strangeness, to aid us in becoming new beings." Rorty places the "edifying" thinkers in their appropriate historical context:

> On the periphery of the history of modern philosophy, one finds figures who, without forming a 'tradition,' resemble each other in their distrust of the notion that man's essence is to be a knower of essences. Goethe, Kierkegaard, Santayana, William James, Dewey, the later Wittgenstein, the later Heidegger, are figures of this sort.[13]

Emerson has been repeatedly associated with each of these figures, and with Nietzsche, whom Rorty also includes among the edifying

13. Richard Rorty, *Philosophy and the Mirror of Nature,* 366, 359–60, 367.

thinkers.[14] Indeed, much of what Rorty says concerning edifying thinkers almost reads like a characterization of Emerson's aims and methods as a thinker.

The most obvious literary result of Emerson's being an "edifying" thinker is the fact that he wrote not moral treatises, but moral *essays*. He turned to the essay because its generic characteristics made it an ideal vehicle for the disruption of dogmatic, traditional, or conventional patterns of thought. The essay, after all, is by definition experimental, antisystematic, open-ended, and skeptical; it is, as Joel Porte aptly calls it, "that tentative and fragmentary record of the mind in search of its meaning."[15] All of these characteristics Emerson saw amply displayed in the work of one of his intellectual heroes, who also happened to be the creator of the modern essay—Montaigne. And it seems clear in Emerson's as well as in Montaigne's case that the generic requirements of the essay substantively affected the ethic that both authors propound. As Gustave Lanson put it in a classic study of Montaigne's ethics, "from start to finish, the *Essais* exorcise the phantom of absoluteness"; the morality they present "is not a doctrine, but an art . . . a creative activity."[16]

Equally important, however, is the fact that choosing the essay as a vehicle for self-expression has moral implications of its own. Foremost among these is the writers' duty to maintain their intellectual independence vis-à-vis their own utterances. One should accept one's own statements or texts as always tentative, inchoate, provisional. Every statement has instrumental rather than intrinsic value: its function is not to say anything final but to provoke a new utterance. True essayists maintain their authorial integrity by avoiding dogmatism and embracing instead a "position of perpetual inquiry" (*CW* 1:115). Their words should always suggest "undiscovered regions of thought" (*CW* 1:41). Principles like these led Emerson to claim that "in composition the *What* is of no importance compared with the *How*" (*JMN* 5:304–5). The author must subject the "What" to the free play of his or her mind, to an endlessly dynamic dialectic, in order to maintain the

14. Ibid., 369.

15. Porte, *Representative Man*, xii.

16. Gustave Lanson, "La Vie morale selon les *Essais* de Montaigne," *Essais de méthode, de critique et d'histoire littéraire*, 176–77.

spiritual and intellectual creativeness that is the unceasing duty of Man Thinking.

III

A way of expressing oneself that does justice to moral thought is of the utmost importance not only to the writer but also to his or her audience. Like every other moralist, Emerson understood that having moral insights brought with it the duty to communicate them. Moralists believe that nothing concerns humans more centrally, more deeply, or more universally than ethics. Obviously, moralists who kept their insights to themselves would be acting unethically by depriving others of those insights. Moralists recognize that whatever benefits they themselves may derive from the communication of their insights (benefits such as deepening or clarifying their thought in the process of articulating it), their real duty consists in making their insights available to others.[17] What his age truly needs, Emerson says, is "a moral Education." The writer should become the teacher of the age, occupying "himself in the study & explanation of the moral constitution of man more than in the elucidation of difficult texts." Such a writer-teacher will not be concerned with "conciliating [his] audience"; his real aim will be "to edify them" (*JMN* 4:327, 93–94, 335).

Emerson shared with his fellow Romantics the conviction that "the moral improvement of audience [is] a primary end" of literature.[18] Although neither in thought nor in method an exponent of conventional didacticism, he strongly believed that "the whole use in literature is the moral" (*JMN* 10:22). To the right reader, true literature is indeed "a decalogue" (*W* 10:273). Such convictions help explain Emerson's frequently resorting to imperatives or to a generally "legislative" rhetoric. Though his voice was less dithyrambically or thunderously assertive than that of such "prophets" as Blake, Shelley, or Carlyle, his favorite rhetorical stance toward his audience, nevertheless, was that of a teacher urging, recommending, advising, or cautioning. As

---

17. In this argument I follow Hösle, *Die Krise der Gegenwart und die Verantwortung der Philosophie*, 244.

18. Lockridge, *The Ethics of Romanticism*, 16.

a clergyman addressing sermons to his congregation, he adopted this stance as a matter of course; but one need only think of such key works as "The American Scholar," "Man the Reformer," "Self-Reliance," and *The Conduct of Life* to realize how strongly "legislative" Emerson remained. Cicero said that the best kind of speaker informs, pleases, and persuades his audience ("Optimus est enim orator, qui dicendo animos audientium et docet et delectat et permovet").[19] As a moral legislator, Emerson is interested only in the third of the three oratorical functions identified by Cicero. For Emerson, "speech is power: speech is to persuade, to convert, to compel. It is to bring another out of his bad sense into your good sense" (*W* 8:92).

The true teacher—that is, the "poet" or "scholar" in Emerson's sense of these terms—derives his authority from the fact that he is an exponent of the Absolute, which he has the duty to interpret for the benefit of others. As we learn from "Literary Ethics,"

> The man of genius should occupy the whole space between God or pure mind, and the multitude of uneducated men. He must draw from the infinite Reason, on one side; and he must penetrate into the heart and sense of the crowd, on the other. From one, he must draw his strength; to the other, he must owe his aim. . . . At one pole, is Reason; at the other, Common Sense. If he be defective at either extreme of the scale, his philosophy will seem low and utilitarian; or it will appear too vague and indefinite for the uses of life. (*CW* 1:113)

Emerson often stresses this mediating function of the writer of genius. Although it is true that for his integrity's sake a person of genius cannot afford to "travel . . . with the souls of other men . . . in the daily, time-worn yoke of their opinions," it is equally true that from time to time he must "descend" into the crowd as a benefactor (*W* 6:156). This "descending," this making one's thought available to others, requires talent. Emerson often disparaged talent in comparison with genius, but he also recognized that no person of genius can fulfill his or her "edifying" function without talents, which are "the feet and hands of genius." He repeatedly confronted the tragedy of genius failing "for want . . . of a little talent," most notably perhaps in the person of his

---

19. Cicero, *De optimo genere oratorum* 1.3.

friend Bronson Alcott (*W* 10:276). Pure genius dwells in the realm of the Reason; communication with others requires skills on the level of the Understanding; hence, the more talent one has, the more effective one's communication. As Coleridge put it in a book with which Emerson was familiar, "Genius must have talent as its complement and implement."[20] Cultivating one's talents is consequently a moral obligation not only for reasons of self-realization, but also in order to enable one to become effective as a spokesperson for higher values.

The writer has the further duty of helping us overcome our alienation, our "not-feeling-at-home" in our world. By conceptualizing, interpreting, and expressing our environment, the poet deepens our awareness of it and helps us to see it as a reflection of our own being, thus showing us how pervasively "human" our world is and thereby attenuating our estrangement from it. One of Goethe's greatest merits consisted in his having developed a theory of nature in which "poetry and humanity remain to us" (*CW* 4:158). The need for humanization is not confined to nature, however. In "The Poet," Emerson complains that as Americans we have not yet addressed ourselves "with sufficient plainness, or sufficient profoundness . . . to life . . . [to] our own times and social circumstance." No poet has yet arisen who "knew the value of our incomparable materials" and recognized "the barbarism and materialism of the times" as a necessary stage in the dialectic of human self-realization (*CW* 3:21).

Emerson was always keenly aware of the contradiction at the heart of American cultural experience and the alienation resulting from it. He put our problem most sharply in "The Young American": "Our people have their intellectual culture from one country, and their duties from another. Our books are European. . . . We are sent to a feudal school to learn democracy. . . . [Our] institutions . . . [are] not consecrated to [our] imagination nor interpreted to [our] understanding" (*CW* 1:222). A major responsibility of American literature is to help us overcome our alienation by articulating, through content and form, *our* experience and thus satisfy our need for national self-expression, without which there can be no real national self-definition

20. Samuel Taylor Coleridge, *Specimens of the Table Talk of the Late Samuel Taylor Coleridge*, 2:244. Emerson annotated his copy of this work (Harding, *Emerson's Library*, 64). See also *JMN* 5:52 and *n162*.

and self-knowledge. Foreign or foreign-inspired literature cannot possibly satisfy these needs of the American soul: such literature provides us with voices and models that do not fit our experience. As Emerson warns in "The American Scholar," "The millions that around us are rushing into life, cannot always be fed on the sere remains of foreign harvests" (*CW* 1:52). As the prophetic voice of his people, the poet has the duty to deepen their consciousness of what it really means to be human in their time and place, and he can do so by expressing for them America and American experience in an American idiom. Whitman, more than anyone else, came close to being that much-expected American poet, as Emerson intermittently recognized. "One must thank Walt Whitman," he wrote in 1863, "for service to American literature in the Appalachian enlargement of his outline & treatment" (*JMN* 15:379).

The writer's most important other-directed duty, however, is suggested by Emerson's statement, in an 1841 essay in *The Dial*, that "literature is the effort of man to indemnify himself for the wrongs of his condition" (*W* 12:341). Emphatically and repeatedly, Emerson insists that the poet or scholar should bring hope, consolation, and joy, that, in the words of "The American Scholar," "the office of the scholar" is not only "to guide men," but also "to cheer, to raise" them (*CW* 1:62). "Saadi" (*W* 9:129–35) teaches the same duty. Saadi was "The cheerer of men's hearts," a "joy-giver" who was himself an "enjoyer": "Sunshine in his heart transferred / Lighted each transparent word." By contrast, those who "Never in the blaze of light / Lose the shudder of midnight" were as anathema to Emerson as they were to Dante, who consigned to hell people guilty of "having been dejected in the sweet air that is gladdened by the sun" (" . . . Tristi fummo / nell'aere dolce che dal sol s'allegra").[21] Such gloom, Emerson says, is "least of all . . . to be pardoned in the literary and speculative class," who are called upon to be "professors of the Joyous Science," or as he puts it elsewhere— adopting a term applied to fourteenth-century Provençal poetry (*gai saber* or *gaia sciensa*)—of "the *gai science*" (*EL* 3:368; *W* 8:37).

In addition to communicating affirmation and joy, the poet must also make one's reading his or her work an experience of aesthetic

21. Dante, *Inferno* 7.121–22.

pleasure. Great literature, Emerson claims, invites us to "enter into a region of the purest pleasure accessible to human nature" (W 12:341). Since hedonism is itself an important ethical orientation, the conception of literature as intended to give pleasure in no way undermines the ethical character of literature. This ethical character is all the more emphasized, however, when Emerson interprets aesthetic pleasure as a means of uplifting the reader's heart and spirit, and thus making him or her more receptive to the positive message the poet or scholar attempts to convey. Emerson's position closely resembles that of Coleridge, who states in *Biographia Literaria* that "the communication of pleasure is the introductory means by which alone the poet must expect to moralize his readers."[22] For Emerson also, poetry plays its part in the ethical education of humanity *by means of* its aesthetic power, its ability to charm and give pleasure.[23]

Emerson does not regard the reader as the passive recipient of the joy and hope that literature brings. Only those books are valuable, he says repeatedly, that put us "in a working mood" (W 7:188; 8:296; 9:331). This principle has profound implications for the ethics of both writing and reading. Barbara Packer has shown how thoroughly Emerson's unsystematic, discontinuous, reticent, and assertively uncompromising style reflects not only his belief that language is inadequate as a conveyor of truth but also his conviction that prose and poetry should test and provoke the reader, thus challenging him or her to intellectual activity.[24] Emerson applauded Goethe's "practice to publish his book without preface & let it lie unexplained" as an expression of "the scholar's Ethics"; he credited Walter Savage Landor with "the merit of not explaining" (JMN 5:187–88; 7:54). For Emerson books have value only if they "awaken" us to our own creativity, if they stimulate us to thoughts and actions that are truly our own. By imparting "sympathetic activity to the moral power" (W 7:190), good books enable us to rise above them. Rightly conceived, "the one end" of books is "to inspire" (CW 1:56)—to liberate us from our routine thinking, and

---

22. Coleridge, *Biographia Literaria*, 2:131.

23. Questions concerning the relation of pleasure to instruction in poetry are as old as Hellenistic criticism. Their prominence in later literary discussion is due primarily to the influence of Horace's *Ars poetica*. Coleridge and Emerson but restate positions that have been debated since antiquity.

24. Packer, *Emerson's Fall*, 1–21.

from themselves. Only by provoking us into novel thought can poets be for us "liberating gods" (*CW* 3:17–18).

Emerson, therefore, praised writers of "tonic books," such as Goethe and Coleridge (*JMN* 10:167). The abuse of books begins when readers, out of misplaced respect for them, cease to read skeptically and proudly. No matter what the text, we ought "always [to] read as superior beings" (*CW* 2:4–5), ever mindful that each of us is called upon to *be* an original thinker rather than to copy or imitate one. Emerson has scant respect for those he considers guilty of bibliolatry ("the restorers of readings, the emendators, the bibliomaniacs of all degrees"—*CW* 1:56). But even approaching books on a higher level, through receptivity to its thought and art, has its dangers since "genius is always sufficiently the enemy of genius by over-influence" (*CW* 1:57). Hence Emerson's caution to Charles Woodbury: "Reading long at one time anything, no matter how it fascinates, destroys thought. . . . Do not permit this. Stop if you find yourself becoming absorbed, at even the first paragraph. Keep yourself out and watch for your own impressions."[25]

Nevertheless, books, when rightly written—when they open "a foreground, and like the breath of morning-landscapes invite . . . us onward"—and read reservedly and confrontationally, "are the best of things" (*CW* 4:80; 1:56). No invention of civilization has proved a more potent factor in human edification. As a reader and a writer, Emerson put his principles into practice. He was nobody's disciple, and he discouraged discipleship in others. Yet his achievement as a scholar (in his sense of the term) has made him a uniquely powerful moral force in our world. In view of what he accomplished as a scholar, Emerson may certainly be forgiven these rhapsodic words from "Literary Ethics": "A scholar is the favorite of Heaven and earth, the excellency of his country, the happiest of men" (*CW* 1:99).

25. Charles J. Woodbury, *Talks with Ralph Waldo Emerson*, 29.

Works Cited

This list does not include ancient or modern texts (e.g., Plato; *The Divine Comedy*), my references to which in the notes follow universally accepted practice (e.g., *Republic* 444D–E; *Inferno* 7.121–22) and which thus do not require more specific bibliographical identification.

Abrams, M. H. *The Mirror and the Lamp: Romantic Theory and the Critical Tradition*. 1953. Reprint, New York: W. W. Norton and Co., 1958.

———. *Natural Supernaturalism: Tradition and Revolution in Romantic Literature*. New York: W. W. Norton and Co., 1971.

Anselm of Canterbury. *Opera omnia*. Edited by Franciscus Salesius Schmitt. 6 vols. Edinburgh: Thomas Nelson and Sons, 1946–1961.

Aristophanes. *Clouds*. Edited by K. J. Dover. Oxford: Clarendon Press, 1968.

Arnold, Matthew. *The Complete Prose Works of Matthew Arnold*. Edited by R. H. Super. 11 vols. Ann Arbor: University of Michigan Press, 1960–1977.

Babbitt, Irving. *Rousseau and Romanticism*. 1919. Reprint, Cleveland: World Publishing Co., 1968.

Bacon, Francis. *Novum Organum*. Edited by Thomas Fowler. Oxford: Clarendon Press, 1889.

Baker, Herschel. *The Image of Man*. 1947. (Original title: *The Dignity of Man*). Reprint, New York: Harper and Row, 1961.

Barish, Evelyn. *Emerson: The Roots of Prophecy*. Princeton: Princeton University Press, 1989.

Beck, Lewis White. *A Commentary on Kant's "Critique of Practical Reason."* Chicago: University of Chicago Press, 1960.

Bénichou, Paul. *Morales du grand siècle*. Paris: Gallimard, 1948.

Blake, William. *Poetry and Prose.* Edited by Geoffrey Keynes. London: Nonesuch Library, 1956.

Brown, Lee Rust. *The Emerson Museum: Practical Romanticism and the Pursuit of the Whole.* Cambridge, Mass.: Harvard University Press, 1997.

Browne, Thomas. *The Works of Sir Thomas Browne.* Edited by Geoffrey Keynes. 4 vols. London: Faber and Faber [1964].

Buell, Lawrence. "The Emerson Industry in the 1980's: A Survey of Trends and Achievements." *ESQ* 30 (1984): 117–36.

———. *The Environmental Imagination: Thoreau, Nature Writing, and the Formation of American Culture.* Cambridge, Mass.: Harvard University Press, 1995.

———. *New England Literary Culture: From Revolution through Renaissance.* Cambridge: Cambridge University Press, 1986.

Burkholder, Robert E. Review of *The Topical Notebooks of Ralph Waldo Emerson.* Vol. 2. Edited by Ronald A. Bosco. *Nineteenth-Century Prose* 21 (1994): 115–19.

Bush, Douglas. *English Literature in the Earlier Seventeenth Century.* 2d ed. Oxford: Clarendon Press, 1962.

Carlyle, Thomas. *Sartor Resartus.* Edited by Charles Frederick Harrold. Indianapolis: Bobbs-Merrill Co., 1937.

Cassirer, Ernst. *An Essay on Man.* New Haven: Yale University Press, 1944.

———. *Kant's Life and Thought.* Translated by James Haden. New Haven: Yale University Press, 1981.

———. *The Myth of the State.* New Haven: Yale University Press, 1946.

Cavell, Stanley. *The Claim of Reason: Wittgenstein, Skepticism, Morality, and Tragedy.* New York: Oxford University Press, 1979.

———. *Conditions Handsome and Unhandsome: The Constitution of Emersonian Perfectionism.* Chicago: University of Chicago Press, 1990.

———. *Disowning Knowledge: In Six Plays of Shakespeare.* Cambridge: Cambridge University Press, 1987.

———. *In Quest of the Ordinary: Lines of Skepticism and Romanticism.* Chicago: University of Chicago Press, 1988.

———. *The Senses of "Walden."* Expanded ed. San Francisco: North Point Press, 1981.

Cayton, Mary Kupiec. *Emerson's Emergence: Self and Society in the Transformation of New England, 1800–1845.* Chapel Hill: University of North Carolina Press, 1989.

Coleridge, Samuel Taylor. *Biographia Literaria.* Edited by James Engell and W. Jackson Bate. 2 vols. Princeton: Princeton University Press, 1983.

———. *The Friend.* Edited by Barbara E. Rooke. 2 vols. Princeton: Princeton University Press, 1969.

———. *The Notebooks of Samuel Taylor Coleridge.* Edited by Kathleen Coburn. 4 vols. to date. London: Routledge and Kegan Paul, 1957–.

———. *Specimens of the Table Talk of the Late Samuel Taylor Coleridge.* 2 vols. London: John Murray, 1835.

Copleston, Frederick. *A History of Philosophy.* 9 vols. Garden City, N.Y.: Doubleday and Co., 1962–1977.

Cragg, G. R. *From Puritanism to the Age of Reason.* Cambridge: Cambridge University Press, 1966.

Curtius, Ernst Robert. *European Literature and the Latin Middle Ages.* Translated by Willard R. Trask. 1953. Reprint, New York: Harper and Row, 1963.

Davis, Merrell R. "Emerson's 'Reason' and the Scottish Philosophers." *New England Quarterly* 17 (June 1944): 209–28.

Doppler, Alfred. *Der Abgrund des Ichs.* Graz: Hermann Böhlaus Nachf., 1985.

Edelstein, Ludwig. *The Meaning of Stoicism.* Cambridge, Mass.: Harvard University Press, 1966.

Fichte, Johann Gottlieb. *Sämmtliche Werke.* Edited by J. H. Fichte. 8 vols. 1845–1846. Reprint, Berlin: Walter de Gruyter and Co., 1965.

Fiering, Norman. *Jonathan Edwards's Moral Thought and Its British Context.* Chapel Hill: University of North Carolina Press, 1981.

Findlay, J. N. *Hegel: A Re-examination.* New York: Oxford University Press, 1958.

Friedrich, Hugo. *Montaigne.* Translated by Dawn Eng. Berkeley: University of California Press, 1991.

Frye, Northrop. *Anatomy of Criticism.* Princeton: Princeton University Press, 1957.

Glacken, Clarence J. *Traces on the Rhodian Shore: Nature and Culture in Western Thought from Ancient Times to the End of the Eighteenth Century.* Berkeley: University of California Press, 1967.

Goethe, Johann Wolfgang. *Gedenkausgabe der Werke, Briefe und Gespräche.* Edited by Ernst Beutler. 27 vols. Zurich: Artemis Verlag, 1948–1971.

Goodman, Russell B. *American Philosophy and the Romantic Tradition.* Cambridge: Cambridge University Press, 1990.

Grotius, Hugo. *The Law of War and Peace.* Translated by Francis W. Kelsey et al. 1925. Reprint, Indianapolis: Bobbs-Merrill Co., n.d.

Guthrie, W. K. C. *The Sophists.* Cambridge: Cambridge University Press, 1971.

Hallengren, Anders. *The Code of Concord: Emerson's Search for Universal Laws.* Stockholm: Almqvist and Wiksell International, 1994.

Hamann, Johann Georg. *Sämtliche Werke.* Edited by Josef Nadler. 6 vols. Vienna: Verlag Herder, 1949–1957.

Harding, Walter. *Emerson's Library.* Charlottesville: University Press of Virginia, 1967.

Harpham, Geoffrey Galt. *Getting It Right: Language, Literature, and Ethics.* Chicago: University of Chicago Press, 1992.

Hartmann, Nicolai. *Ethik.* Berlin: Walter de Gruyter and Co., 1926.

Hedge, Frederic Henry. ["Coleridge"]. *The Christian Examiner* 14 (March 1833): 108–29.

Hegel, Georg Wilhelm Friedrich. *Phänomenologie des Geistes.* Edited by Johannes Hoffmeister. Hamburg: Verlag von Felix Meiner, 1952.

———. *Werke.* Edited by Eva Moldenhauer and Karl Markus Michel. 21 vols. Frankfurt am Main: Suhrkamp Verlag, 1967–1971.

Heine, Heinrich. *Sämtliche Schriften.* Edited by Klaus Briegleb et al. 6 vols. Darmstadt: Wissenschaftliche Buchgesellschaft, 1968–1976.

Heller, Agnes. *Can Modernity Survive?* Cambridge: Polity Press, 1990.

Hölderlin, Friedrich. *Sämtliche Werke und Briefe.* Edited by Günter Mieth et al. 2 vols. Munich: Carl Hanser Verlag, 1970.

Hopkins, Vivian C. "The Influence of Goethe on Emerson's Aesthetic Theory." *Philological Quarterly* 27 (1948): 325–44.

Hösle, Vittorio. *Die Krise der Gegenwart und die Verantwortung der Philosophie.* Munich: Verlag C. H. Beck, 1990.

Houghton, Walter E. *The Victorian Frame of Mind, 1830–1870.* New Haven: Yale University Press, 1957.

Howe, Daniel Walker. *The Unitarian Conscience: Harvard Moral Philosophy, 1805–1861.* 1970. Reprint, Middletown, Conn.: Wesleyan University Press, 1988.

Huizinga, Johan. *Herfsttij der Middeleeuwen.* Haarlem: H. D. Tjeenk Willink, 1950.

Hume, David. *A Treatise of Human Nature.* Edited by L. A. Selby-Bigge. 2d rev. ed. by P. H. Nidditch. Oxford: Clarendon Press, 1978.

Jacobson, David. *Emerson's Pragmatic Vision: The Dance of the Eye.* University Park: Pennsylvania State University Press, 1993.

James, Henry. *The American Essays.* Edited by Leon Edel. New York: Vintage Books, 1956.

Johnson, Samuel, and James Boswell. *Johnson's Journey to the Western Islands of Scotland and Boswell's Journal of a Tour to the Hebrides.* Edited by R. W. Chapman. London: Oxford University Press, 1930.

Jonsen, Albert R., and Stephen Toulmin. *The Abuse of Casuistry: A History of Moral Reasoning.* Berkeley: University of California Press, 1988.

Kant, Immanuel. *Gesammelte Schriften.* Critical Edition Sponsored by the Royal Prussian (later by the Prussian, then by the German, and currently by the Göttingen) Academy of Sciences. 27 vols. to date (vols. 1–24, 27–29). Berlin: Verlag von Georg Reimer; continued by Walter de Gruyter and Co., 1902–.

Kateb, George. *Emerson and Self-Reliance.* Thousand Oaks, Calif.: Sage Publications, 1995.

Krusche, Thomas. *R. W. Emersons Naturauffassung und ihre philosophischen Ursprünge.* Tübingen: Gunter Narr Verlag, 1987.

Kuhn, Dorothea. *Empirische und ideelle Wirklichkeit: Studien über Goethes Kritik des französischen Akademiestreites.* Graz: Hermann Böhlaus Nachf., 1967.

Lacoue-Labarthe, Philippe, and Jean-Luc Nancy. *The Literary Absolute: The Theory of Literature in German Romanticism.* Translated by Philip Barnard and Cheryl Lester. Albany: State University of New York Press, 1988.

Lanson, Gustave. *Essais de méthode, de critique et d'histoire littéraire.* Introduction by Henri Peyre. Paris: Librairie Hachette, 1965.

Lessing, Gotthold Ephraim. *Werke.* Edited by Herbert G. Göpfert et al. 8 vols. Munich: Carl Hanser Verlag, 1970–1979.

Locke, John. *The Second Treatise of Government.* In *Two Treatises of Government.* Edited by Peter Laslett. 2d ed. Cambridge: Cambridge University Press, 1967.

Lockridge, Laurence S. *The Ethics of Romanticism.* Cambridge: Cambridge University Press, 1989.

Lopez, Michael. "De-Transcendentalizing Emerson." *ESQ* 34 (1988): 77–139.

———. *Emerson and Power: Creative Antagonism in the Nineteenth Century.* DeKalb: Northern Illinois University Press, 1996.

Macaulay, Thomas Babington. *Critical and Historical Essays.* 2 vols. London: J. M. Dent and Sons, 1961.

McFarland, Thomas. *Coleridge and the Pantheist Tradition.* Oxford: Clarendon Press, 1969.

———. *Originality and Imagination.* Baltimore: Johns Hopkins University Press, 1985.

MacIntyre, Alasdair, ed. *Hegel: A Collection of Critical Essays.* Garden City, N.Y.: Doubleday and Co., 1972.

Marx, Leo. *The Machine in the Garden: Technology and the Pastoral Ideal in America.* New York: Oxford University Press, 1964.

Mather, Cotton. *The Christian Philosopher.* Edited by Winton U. Solberg. Urbana: University of Illinois Press, 1994.

Michael, John. *Emerson and Skepticism: The Cipher of the World.* Baltimore: Johns Hopkins University Press, 1988.

Milton, John. *Complete Prose Works.* Edited by Don M. Wolfe et al. 8 vols. New Haven: Yale University Press, 1953–1982.

Montaigne, Michel Eyquem de. *Les Essais de Michel de Montaigne.* Edited by Pierre Villey. Paris: Presses Universitaires de France, 1965.

Mott, Wesley T. *"The Strains of Eloquence": Emerson and His Sermons.* University Park: Pennsylvania State University Press, 1989.

Murdoch, Iris. *Metaphysics as a Guide to Morals.* London: Penguin Books, 1993.

Mure, G. R. G. *The Philosophy of Hegel.* London: Oxford University Press, 1965.

Neufeldt, Leonard. *The House of Emerson.* Lincoln: University of Nebraska Press, 1982.

Nietzsche, Friedrich. *Sämtliche Werke.* Kritische Studienausgabe. Edited by Giorgio Colli and Mazzino Montinari. 15 vols. 2d ed. Berlin: Walter de Gruyter and Co.; Munich: Deutscher Taschenbuch Verlag, 1988.

Nussbaum, Martha C. *The Fragility of Goodness: Luck and Ethics in Greek Tragedy and Philosophy.* Cambridge: Cambridge University Press, 1986.

Otto, Rudolf. *The Idea of the Holy.* Translated by John W. Harvey. London: Oxford University Press, 1958.

Packer, B. L. *Emerson's Fall: A New Interpretation of the Major Essays.* New York: Continuum Publishing Co., 1982.

Pascal, Blaise. *Pensées.* Edited by Léon Brunschvicg and Ch.-M. des Granges. Paris: Garnier Frères, 1964.

Paton, H. J. *The Categorical Imperative: A Study in Kant's Moral Philosophy.* 1947. Reprint, Philadelphia: University of Pennsylvania Press, 1971.

Pochmann, Henry. *German Culture in America: Philosophical and Literary Influences, 1600–1900.* Madison: University of Wisconsin Press, 1957.

Poirier, Richard. *The Renewal of Literature: Emersonian Reflections.* New York: Random House, 1987.

Porte, Joel. *Emerson and Thoreau: Transcendentalists in Conflict.* Middletown, Conn.: Wesleyan University Press, 1966.

———. *Representative Man: Ralph Waldo Emerson in His Time.* New York: Oxford University Press, 1979.

Raphael, D. Daiches. *The Moral Sense.* London: Oxford University Press, 1947.

———, ed. *British Moralists 1650–1800.* 2 vols. Oxford: Clarendon Press, 1969.

Richardson, Robert D., Jr. *Emerson: The Mind on Fire. A Biography.* Berkeley: University of California Press, 1995.

Robinson, David M. *Apostle of Culture: Emerson as Preacher and Lecturer.* Philadelphia: University of Pennsylvania Press, 1982.

———. *Emerson and the Conduct of Life: Pragmatism and Ethical Purpose in the Later Work.* Cambridge: Cambridge University Press, 1993.

———. "Emerson, Thoreau, Fuller, and Transcendentalism." In *American Literary Scholarship: An Annual, 1993.* Edited by Gary Scharnhorst. Durham: Duke University Press, 1995. Pp. 3–21.

————. "The Sermons of Ralph Waldo Emerson: An Introductory Historical Essay." *CS* 1:1–32.

Rorty, Richard. *Philosophy and the Mirror of Nature.* Princeton: Princeton University Press, 1980.

Rousseau, Jean-Jacques. *Émile ou de l'éducation.* Edited by François and Pierre Richard. Paris: Garnier Frères, 1964.

Schamberger, J. Edward. "The Influence of Dugald Stewart and Richard Price on Emerson's Concept of Reason: A Reassessment." *ESQ* 18 (1972): 179–83.

Schelling, Friedrich Wilhelm Joseph. *Werke.* Edited by Manfred Schröter. 12 vols. Munich: C. H. Beck'sche Verlagsbuchhandlung, 1927–1959.

Schiller, Friedrich. *Werke.* Edited by Herbert Kraft et al. 4 vols. Frankfurt am Main: Insel Verlag, 1966.

Scholem, Gershom. *Kabbalah.* 1974. Reprint, New York: New American Library, 1978.

Selinger, Eric Murphy. " 'Too Pathetic, Too Pitiable': Emerson's Lessons in Love's Philosophy." *ESQ* 40 (1994): 139–82.

Smith, Norman Kemp. *A Commentary to Kant's "Critique of Pure Reason."* 2d ed. 1923. Reprint, Atlantic Highlands, N.J.: Humanities Press International, 1992.

Spinoza, Baruch. *Opera.* Edited by Carl Gebhardt. 4 vols. Heidelberg: Carl Winters Universitaetsbuchhandlung, 1925.

Stewart, Dugald. *The Collected Works.* Edited by Sir William Hamilton. 11 vols. Edinburgh: Thomas Constable and Co., 1854–1860.

Sullivan, Roger J. *Immanuel Kant's Moral Theory.* Cambridge: Cambridge University Press, 1989.

Taylor, A. E. *Plato: The Man and His Work.* London: Methuen and Co., 1960.

Taylor, Charles. *The Ethics of Authenticity.* Cambridge, Mass.: Harvard University Press, 1991.

————. *Sources of the Self: The Making of the Modern Identity.* Cambridge, Mass.: Harvard University Press, 1989.

Thurin, Erik Ingvar. *Emerson as Priest of Pan: A Study in the Metaphysics of Sex.* Lawrence: Regents Press of Kansas, 1981.

Toulmin, Stephen. *The Return to Cosmology: Postmodern Science and the Theology of Nature.* Berkeley: University of California Press, 1982.

Van Cromphout, Gustaaf. "Areteic Ethics: Emerson and Nietzsche on Pity, Friendship, and Love." *ESQ* 43 (1997): 95–112.

———. *Emerson's Modernity and the Example of Goethe.* Columbia: University of Missouri Press, 1990.

Van Leer, David. *Emerson's Epistemology: The Argument of the Essays.* Cambridge: Cambridge University Press, 1986.

Vlastos, Gregory. *Platonic Studies.* Princeton: Princeton University Press, 1981.

Weber, Max. *Gesammelte Aufsätze zur Wissenschaftslehre.* Tübingen: Verlag von J. C. B. Mohr (Paul Siebeck), 1922.

Weinrich, Harald. *Linguistik der Lüge.* Heidelberg: Verlag Lambert Schneider, 1970.

Wellek, René. *Confrontations: Studies in the Intellectual and Literary Relations between Germany, England, and the United States during the Nineteenth Century.* Princeton: Princeton University Press, 1965.

West, Cornel. *The American Evasion of Philosophy: A Genealogy of Pragmatism.* Madison: University of Wisconsin Press, 1989.

Whicher, Stephen E. *Freedom and Fate: An Inner Life of Ralph Waldo Emerson.* 1953. Reprint, New York: A. S. Barnes and Co., 1961.

Whitehead, Alfred North. *Science and the Modern World.* 1925. Reprint, New York: Free Press, 1967.

Willey, Basil. *The Eighteenth Century Background: Studies on the Idea of Nature in the Thought of the Period.* 1940. Reprint, Boston: Beacon Press, 1961.

Williams, Bernard. *Ethics and the Limits of Philosophy.* Cambridge, Mass.: Harvard University Press, 1985.

Wills, Garry. *Inventing America: Jefferson's Declaration of Independence.* 1978. Reprint, New York: Vintage Books, 1979.

Wimmer, Reiner. *Universalisierung in der Ethik.* Frankfurt am Main: Suhrkamp Verlag, 1980.

Windelband, Wilhelm. *A History of Philosophy.* Translated by James H. Tufts. 1901. 2 vols. Reprint, New York: Harper and Row, 1958.

Wittgenstein, Ludwig. *Philosophische Untersuchungen / Philosophical Investigations.* Translated by G. E. M. Anscombe. New York: Macmillan Co., 1953.

———. *Tractatus Logico-Philosophicus.* Translated by C. K. Ogden. London: Routledge and Kegan Paul, 1981.

Wood, Allen W. *Hegel's Ethical Thought.* Cambridge: Cambridge University Press, 1990.

Woodbury, Charles J. *Talks with Ralph Waldo Emerson.* New York: Baker and Taylor Co., 1890.

Zoja, Luigi. *Crescita e colpa: Psicologia e limiti dello sviluppo.* Milan: Edizioni Anabasi, 1993.

Index

Abrams, M. H., 124, 136–37, 139*n12*, 147
Abyss, 71, 72*n17*
Action: and conscience, 67–68; and character, 75–78; and self-culture, 81–84
Adam Kadmon, 139
Alcmaeon, 71
Alcott, Bronson, 157–58, 163
Alienation: and nature, 133, 136, 138–39, 142, 146; and literature, 163–64
Ambrose, Saint, 144
Anselm of Canterbury, Saint, 51
Aquinas, Saint Thomas, 58
Aristotle: on prudence, 8; on *akrasia*, 8*n2*; and the passions, 9; on moderation, 10; and law of nature, 11; and theoretical vs. practical reason, 11–12, 45; and casuistry, 12; and intellectual elitism, 24; and "first philosophy," 54; and politics, 90; on friendship, 110, 111; influence on Emerson, 111; defines the good life, 115; and empiricism, 132; mentioned, 15, 44, 57, 58
Arnold, Matthew, 158
Augustine, Saint: and will, 8, 37; on evil, 37; on time, 53; and subjectivity, 70; and language, 150

Babbitt, Irving, 127
Bacon, Francis, 15, 54*n44*, 157
Baker, Herschel, 24, 70
Barish, Evelyn, 7, 35

Basil the Great, Saint, 144
Bate, Walter Jackson, 43, 44
Beck, Lewis White, 61–62
Benevolence: and "inward turn" of ethics, 16–17; and Being, 37–38; vs. beneficence, 68; and other-regarding ethics, 95–101
Bentham, Jeremy, 19
Berkeley, George, 134
Bernard of Clairvaux, Saint, 32
Blake, William, 65*n10*, 161
Böhme, Jakob, 62*n8*, 71
Brown, Lee Rust, 139
Browne, Sir Thomas, 31–32
Bryant, William Cullen, 158
Buell, Lawrence, 141, 158
Burke, Edmund, 105
Burkholder, Robert E., 1
Bush, Douglas, 15
Butler, Joseph, 14, 31

Calvin, John, 32*n8*
Cambridge Platonists, 17, 18. *See also* Cudworth
Carlyle, Thomas: as interpreter of Kant, 43, 62; and Goethe, 80; on custom, 119; on creative literature, 158; as "prophet," 161; mentioned, 113
Cassirer, Ernst, 8, 121, 135
Cavell, Stanley, 43*n26*, 61, 91, 91*n3*, 98*n10*, 129, 130, 133, 150*n4*
Cayton, Mary Kupiec, 102
Channing, William Ellery, 79
Cicero, Marcus Tullius, 8, 162
Clarke, Samuel, 14, 18

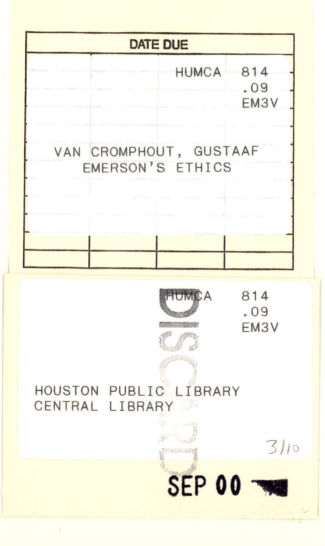